Lifting
Depression

Also by Kelly Lambert, Ph.D.
Clinical Neuroscience (with Craig Howard Kinsley)

Lifting Depression

A NEUROSCIENTIST'S HANDS-ON APPROACH TO ACTIVATING YOUR BRAIN'S HEALING POWER

Kelly Lambert, Ph.D.

BASIC
BOOKS

A Member of the Perseus Books Group
New York

Published by Basic Books,
A Member of the Perseus Books Group

Books published by Basic Books are available at special discounts for bulk purchases in the United States by corporations, institutions, and other organizations. For more information, please contact the Special Markets Department at the Perseus Books Group, 2300 Chestnut Street, Suite 200, Philadelphia, PA 19103, or call (800) 255–1514, or e-mail special.markets@perseusbooks.com.

Designed by Pauline Brown
Set in 11.5 point Fairfield LH by Wordstop Technologies ℗ Ltd.

Library of Congress Cataloging-in-Publication Data
Lambert, Kelly.

Lifting depression : a neuroscientist's hands-on approach to activating your brain's healing power / Kelly G. Lambert.
p. cm.
Includes bibliographical references and index.

ISBN–13: 978-0-465-03772-8 (alk. paper)
ISBN–10: 0-465-03772-0 (alk. paper)

1. Depression, Mental—Popular works. 2. Reward (Psychology)—Popular works. I. Title.

RC537.L338 2008
616.85'27—dc22

2007043409

10 9 8 7 6 5 4 3 2 1

To Gary and his enduring love and support—the perfect emotional elixir for my mental health.

Happiness, then, is something final and self-sufficient, and is the end of action.

—Aristotle, *Nichomachean Ethics,* 350 B.C.

Contents

1

Depression
Strikes Deep

A LL MY TRAINING as a neuroscientist couldn't protect me from the feeling that my brain was being turned inside out on that hot Alabama morning in 1996. The night before, after a two-year battle with non-Hodgkin's lymphoma, my fifty-three-year-old mother had been rushed to the hospital. I arrived from my home in Virginia just in time to climb into the ambulance before it sped away.

As I held my mother in my arms, I knew my world was falling apart. But my only concern was making her last moments as comfortable as possible. In the calmest voice I could muster, I whispered the names of people and places that had brought her the most joy during her life. "Think of the beach," I said softly, reminding her of our favorite vacation spot on the Gulf Shores of Alabama. "Think of your Jay, the love of your life" (Jay was my stepfather). I talked about my daughter, Lara, who was my mother's only grandchild. They adored each other. I also spoke about my brother—she'd always been so proud that he's a

1

physician. I mentioned her parents, her loving sister, her many friends, the little boutique she had built into a successful business. Maybe my strategy worked because she appeared peaceful as she closed her eyes for the final time.

During this devastating experience, my attention was focused solely on my mother's well-being. Instinctively, I put my own needs and feelings aside. But just a few hours later, as I drove from the hospital in Birmingham to my hometown, I was flooded with grief. My overwhelming sadness was, of course, an appropriate response to losing a beloved parent, but knowing this didn't make me feel any better.

I'd driven this same stretch of Interstate 20 twice a day when I commuted to college in the early '80s. In those years, as I began my intellectual journey into the brain's architecture, I'd use my driving time to think about new ideas, class assignments, upcoming tests. I'd also ponder relationships and plan my future. Now, it was as if hope, joy, and optimism had somehow been deleted from my brain and I was observing the Interstate with a new set of eyes. Why did people go to all the trouble of constructing elaborate buildings or putting up tacky billboards on the side of the road? Why waste so much effort when we were going to die so soon anyway?

Just thirty-two years old, I had never had thoughts like this. Through all my ups and downs, never before had I felt that life was so futile. These depressive thoughts persisted for weeks. For the first time, I even found myself questioning the job I loved. At the time, I was a psychology professor at a small liberal arts college, Randolph-Macon College, in Ashland, Virginia. Today, after nearly twenty years at Randolph-Macon, I enjoy serving as the department chair. When I am not in the classroom, I'm in the laboratory working with my students to learn more about how behavior and environment influence the brain.

But now I couldn't remember why I ever thought that any of this was so important. Would I ever be able to return to my classroom and deliver enthusiastic lectures on the movements of ions across the tiny membranes of our brain cells? Weren't there more useful ways to spend my time?

I had a few weeks before classes began, a time usually spent furiously writing syllabi and updating my lectures after a busy summer in the laboratory, all of it done with my usual workaholic fervor. In the weeks after my mother died, however, I couldn't find a good reason to go to the office. At night I managed to find the energy to talk with my husband, Gary, during dinner and to put on my mommy face for my precious two-year-old, but I desperately needed to be alone during the day. I sat. I paced. I spent hours looking out the window. I still could not feel even a hint of happiness, or take pleasure in things I'd always enjoyed.

This was the context of my first and only personal experience with depressive symptoms. I had plenty of professional experience with depression's impact, since I regularly lectured my students on its history, symptoms, and likely causes. What I was feeling certainly met the criteria. According to the fourth edition of the *Diagnostic and Statistical Manual* (DSM IV), published by the American Psychiatric Association, to be diagnosed with depression you must experience a depressed mood or loss of interest or pleasure, as well as at least four other of the following symptoms: significant change in body weight, sleep alterations, slowed motor abilities, fatigue, feelings of worthlessness, difficulty concentrating, and recurrent thoughts of death. The symptoms must persist for at least two weeks (typically longer in bereavement cases) and not be the result of an underlying medical condition.

The dark reality of depression is, of course, much less clinical. "You are falling away from the sunlight toward a place where the shadows are black," wrote Andrew Solomon in *The Noonday Demon,* his widely acclaimed book about the emotional impact of depression. "Inside it, you cannot see, and the dangers are everywhere (it's neither soft-bottomed nor soft-sided, the abyss). While you're falling, you don't know how deep you can go or whether you can in any way stop yourself." Intellectually, I knew my feelings of depression would likely pass with time, but emotionally, as Solomon describes, the pain was overwhelming and seemed inescapable.

As a psychologist, I was well aware of the treatment options for depression, but none of them seemed right for me. Though I felt as if an old, itchy, wet emotional blanket had been dropped on my brain, I was too stubborn to try any of the therapies I had so vigorously questioned in my own lectures. Talk therapies? Intellectualizing my loss seemed unappealing to me. No, talking to a therapist felt as if it would require analytical skills beyond my mental grasp at that moment.

What about drugs? They seem like such an easy solution. Just about any general practitioner can write prescriptions for antidepressants like Zoloft or Prozac, a class of drugs known as SSRIs, or selective serotonin reuptake inhibitors. In fact, my brother kept suggesting that I start taking one. But with so many questions about their effectiveness and side effects, I never felt they were an option for me.

In fact, whenever I outline my concerns about these medications during my class lectures, it makes a lot of students, many of whom are on antidepressants themselves, uncomfortable.

SSRIs have become as much a part of their culture as Diet Coke and iPods. They actually enjoy reading about how the Zoloft dot character, found in so many magazine and TV ads, feels so much better after taking the drug. There's even a cartoon strip depicting how Zoloft makes their little dot lives more fulfilling.

Thanks to the relentless beat of drug marketing, many of us are confident that depression has been figured out. We "know" that the cause is a chemical imbalance and that the most effective treatment is antidepressants. Since the introduction of SSRIs, which increase the levels of serotonin between brain cells, most scientific research has focused on how these drugs, and others like them, influence depression. In fact, the depression "story" has been dominated by the role of serotonin and the theory that low levels of this neurochemical affect our moods in negative ways.

But I haven't been able to buy into it. If these drugs are such an effective treatment for depression, why, despite millions of patients in the United States receiving prescriptions for SSRIs each year, are depression rates higher than ever? The World Health Organization estimates that depressive and anxiety disorders lead the list of mental illnesses across the globe—with 121 million people currently suffering from these conditions. They're responsible for approximately one quarter of all visits to health care centers worldwide. In the United States, where SSRIs, are readily available (about 189 million prescriptions were written for antidepressants for approximately 15 million Americans in 2005 alone!), the *Washington Post* recently reported that the percentage of adults using SSRIs between 1994 and 2002 had tripled. But despite the astounding number of people on these medications, depression rates continue to rise.

Clearly, this is a problem that still needs to be solved. In fact, for years now, there's been a growing consensus in the scientific community that serotonin isn't the central piece of the depression story. The search for what is at the heart of this devastating emotional disorder motivated me to reopen the case and reexamine this mystery called depression.

Investigating the mysteries of the brain is nothing new for me. A significant portion of my research in the lab has focused on the effects of chronic stress and anxiety on the mammalian brain. Using animal models of anxiety and depression, I have searched for consistent patterns of coping and resilience. Over the past two decades, my students and I have been fortunate to have the opportunity to present approximately one hundred research studies to colleagues at national and international professional meetings and receive valuable feedback about our work. In accordance with the scientific process, we've gone on to publish many of these studies in peer-reviewed scientific journals, an endeavor that allows for further development and dissemination of scientific ideas. You won't find these journals, such as *Behavioral Neuroscience* or *Hormones and Behavior*, in the checkout line at your local supermarket, but they are filled with all the latest information about maintaining healthy brains.

After years of investigating interactions between brain functions and depressive responses in rats, as well as reviewing the reams of fascinating research conducted around the world by neuroscience colleagues, I have identified important clues in the ongoing investigation of depression. What I've discovered is that there's a critical link between the symptoms of depression and key areas of the brain involved with motivation, pleasure, movement, and thought. Because these brain areas regularly communicate back and forth, they are considered a circuit, one of many in our brains. (In electronics, a circuit is defined as a complete path through which an electric current can flow, and the process is somewhat similar in the brain.) In fact, the rich interactions along this particular brain circuit, which I call the *effort-driven rewards circuit,* provide us with surprising insights into how depression is both activated and alleviated.

Keeping the effort-driven rewards circuit well engaged helps you interact effectively and efficiently with challenges in the environment around you or in your emotional life. What revs up the crucial effort-driven rewards circuit—the fuel, if you will—is generated by doing certain types of physical activities, especially ones that involve your hands. It's important that these actions produce a result you can see, feel, and touch, such as knitting a sweater or tending a garden. Such actions and their associated thoughts, plans, and ultimate results change the physiology and chemical makeup of the effort-driven rewards circuit, activating it in an energized way. I call the emotional sense of well-being that results *effort-driven rewards.*

My research shows that in our drive to do less physical work to acquire what we want and need, we've lost something vital to our mental well-being—an innate resistance to depression. In fact, as I will demonstrate in the pages that follow, there are many ways in which our contemporary lifestyle may actually promote depression and aggravate the tangled web of emotions once it sets in.

In upcoming chapters, I will describe how effort-driven rewards may help to build resilience against the onset of depression. Taking an antidepressant medication changes your brain's chemistry, but it has no meaningful relation to anything that's currently going on in your life. Effort-driven rewards and other real-world interactive experiences generate much more intense and pervasive reactions in your brain than the neurochemical alterations produced by a single pill.

The result? You begin to feel more control over your environment and more connected to the world around you. This reduces stress and anxiety and, most important, builds resilience against the onset of depression.

MY NOVEL APPROACH TO TREATMENT

Of course, in the first days after my mother's death, I was not remotely concerned with neuroscience theories or conjectures. I was simply overwhelmed by pain and sadness from my loss. Needless to say, I didn't expect to find a successful treatment at a flea market, but I did. After my mother's funeral, my husband and I drove to Georgia to pick up our daughter, who was staying with my in-laws. To lift my spirits, Gary suggested that we get out of the house, so I let him drag me to the liveliest place in town on that Sunday afternoon—the infamous Trade Day in Collinsville, just over the Alabama state line. Walking through row after row of trucks, campers, and makeshift booths, I saw knockoff designer purses and jeans, prized "collector" Beanie Babies still in their original containers, even pot-bellied pigs.

Then something caught my eye. In one aisle, a young man was selling refurbished vacuum cleaners, including the Rainbow. Recently, my neighbors had raved about this vacuum's virtues. Instead of sucking dirt into a dry bag, this state-of-the-art cleaning machine captures dust and hair in a pan of water, making it difficult for the grime to escape. Noticing that I showed modest signs of life whenever we passed these vacuums, Gary bought a refurbished one, which we loaded into the minivan and brought home.

A few days later, despite feeling deeply despondent and lethargic, I pulled out the Rainbow to test it out. I vacuumed all the rooms on the first floor, and then emptied the water container, filled with pet hair, dust, and dirt, in the woods at the edge of our yard. Next, I vacuumed the upstairs, again emptying the container on the pile. Every day for the next few weeks, I found some new nook or cranny in the house to vacuum—the drapes, the molding, every closet floor, under every bed. I had always hated vacuuming, yet now it seemed to be the only activity I could find the energy to do.

After so many weeks of feeling that none of my efforts made any difference in the world—as hard as I'd tried, I hadn't been able to save my mother—I was slowly gaining a sense of control over my environment. Each time I saw tangible evidence of the dirt and grime I'd physically removed from my house, I felt my efforts were valuable. By removing potentially dangerous germs from my home, I was protecting my family. As the pile behind our house got larger, I began to feel that perhaps my efforts in the rest of my world weren't so futile after all. At the time I realized that this was a novel approach to treating depression, but I didn't try to understand what was happening. I simply kept doing what made me feel better—I just kept vacuuming.

I'm happy to report that my emotional wet blanket soon lifted. My passion for teaching and enthusiasm for research slowly returned as the semester progressed. Once again, I could describe to my students the most intricate details of how the brain works. Doing research in my laboratory again felt like riding a roller coaster at an amusement park—a rush of excitement and adrenaline. Even so, given the impact my mother's death had had on me, I found myself reflecting more and more on the debilitating experience of depression. What abrupt changes had occurred in my brain minutes after my mother died that so powerfully altered my emotional world? What is the most effective way to treat depression?

A year later, I began writing a textbook about the science of mental illness, collaborating with my longtime friend and colleague Craig Kinsley, who is a neuroscientist at the University of Richmond. I spent the next six years learning everything I could about mental health and mental illness. As we immersed ourselves in the literature, it became clear to us that to gain a thorough understanding of any mental disorder, it was important to look through multiple windows. To get the most comprehensive view, we need to consider the anatomy, physiology, and chemical structure of the brain, as well as environmental, behavioral, developmental, and evolutionary factors.

Unfortunately, when it comes to depression, most of us—laypeople and professionals alike—are looking through only one window: the neurochemical one. And, frankly, the view from that window is anything but clear. You'd never buy a house based on what you could see looking through only one window. Likewise, we should never settle on a therapeutic strategy based on a single view of such a complex condition. Imagine how uninformed a diabetic patient would be if a doctor merely prescribed insulin, without talking about the importance of a modified diet and lifestyle.

As I studied the scientific literature across many disciplines, I began to develop the effort-driven rewards theory, an alternative, more action-oriented approach to depression. Effort-driven rewards showed me why, when my emotional world was falling apart, a refurbished vacuum cleaner helped my brain understand that my efforts could again lead to desirable consequences. It was not just the physical work of performing simple household tasks that made the difference. It was also the sense that my actions were meaningful because I was protecting my family. These behavioral baby steps were critical in lifting my depression.

But can physical responses actually alter the structure of our brains? Is physical movement a legitimate window that will offer insight into the inner workings of our emotional lives? As we will learn later, scientific research confirms that physical activities such as running and manipulating our environments with our hands result in dramatic changes in our brain's landscape. Thus, just as taking a pill alters the brain's functions, physical actions such as effort-driven rewards have a significant impact on our brains.

Of course, I'm not suggesting that people who are depressed can relieve their symptoms simply by cleaning their houses. If that were true, there would be a huge run on household appliances. Anyone who feels the sustained lowered energy and mood characteristics of depression, and certainly anyone who meets the full DSM IV criteria for this disorder, should work with a mental health professional to find the most effective treatment strategy. But what I experienced in the aftermath of my mother's death may provide critical clues to unraveling the depression story and point the way toward new treatment strategies.

Before I begin to describe how effort-driven rewards (a more technical name than "the vacuuming theory") work, it's worth examining why so many of us are still peering through that one dingy window in an effort to combat depression.

THE HISTORY OF DEPRESSION 101

Historically, the treatment of depression has been a series of unfortunate missteps mixed with a few bright, hopeful moments.

For centuries, people with mental illness were lumped into a single category and routinely warehoused, often in shackles, in what looked like animal cages. This evolved into what were believed to be more "enlightened" treatments, which included spinning chairs, bloodletting, and induced blisters. Eventually, these approaches were also dismissed as both cruel and lacking supporting scientific evidence.

In 1813, Quakers in Philadelphia opened the first of many asylums emphasizing what was known in America as the "moral" treatment of the mentally ill. Founded by Thomas Scattergood, this hospital was fashioned after the mental "retreat" built by the businessman William Tuke in York, England. Several of these privately funded asylums had the same blueprint—aesthetically pleasing facilities built on beautiful grounds graced by lawns and flowerbeds. Each day, there were planned activities, including gardening, reading, playing games, and attending educational lectures and seminars.

The most successful example of the moral treatment model was created by the Quaker physician Thomas Kirkbride, who supervised the Pennsylvania Hospital for the Insane for forty years, until the 1880s. As described in Robert Whitaker's *Madness in America,* this asylum contained a room for playing games, a bowling alley, greenhouse, museum, and intricate gardens. Patients got up early and exercised. There was an emphasis on personal grooming. Then they spent their days reading, sewing, or engaging in structured activities. Evenings were filled with theatrical performances and guest lectures. Kirkbride encouraged patients to spend less time blaming others for their situation and more time rethinking their own behavior, establishing social ties, and learning that they possessed the ability to live fuller, more productive lives.

This integrative, proactive type of therapy was an early version of cognitive behavioral and interpersonal therapies, which show patients how to use scientifically based strategies to influence their behavior and improve their mood. Kirkbride's success rate was impressive. Approximately 50 to 60 percent of patients were noted as cured and released from the asylum. From a scientific standpoint, it's difficult to assess whether it was the social, cognitive, or active part of this holistic approach that was the most beneficial. But the hospital administration did keep track of the many patients who were released and who subsequently led productive lives.

In the middle of the nineteenth century, the mental health reformer Dorothea Dix attempted to provide easier access to this healing environment for all those suffering from mental illness. Ironically, her efforts were instead largely responsible for the downfall of Kirkbride's innovative treatment strategy. As these institutions grew to accommodate more and more patients, the comfortable, homelike atmosphere—the hallmark of the initial Quaker asylums—was abandoned. Beds had to be filled, so those with other conditions, including syphilis, alcoholism, and age-related dementia, were housed side by side with the mentally ill. As states provided larger facilities in response to Dix's successful lobbying, the number of patients in the asylums increased dramatically over the next fifty years, from twenty-five hundred to seventy-five thousand patients. Warehousing was back with a vengeance.

Around the turn of the last century, talk therapy entered the treatment arena. In Vienna, Sigmund Freud introduced psychoanalysis, an innovative theory and treatment approach for mental illness. The "talking cure" was embraced by American psychiatrists, in part because it provided a way for doctors to get out of the insane asylums and into private practices. Psychoanalysis soon became the exclusive domain of psychiatry, although there was no valid reason why psychologists or social workers couldn't practice it as well.

Although Freud began his career studying neurons, the tiny cells in our nervous system, he soon began to focus on unconscious motives and urges, mostly related to sexual and aggressive conflicts stemming from childhood events. His work has been described as fitting more into the humanities than the biomedical sciences. In fact, Freud himself admitted that he was not a scientist. In a letter to his friend Wilhelm Fliess in 1900, he wrote, "I am actually not at all a man of science, not an observer, not an experimenter, not a thinker. I am by temperament nothing but a conquistador—an adventurer, if you want it translated—with all the curiosity, daring, and tenacity characteristic of a man of this sort."

Still, even today, most people think of Freud when asked to name a psychologist or psychiatrist. Nearly every situation comedy featuring a psychiatrist makes him a Freudian psychoanalyst. It's as if a century's worth of research into the brain, human behavior, and mental health conducted by thousands of other scientists doesn't exist. Sadly, Freud's primary influence on the study of depression amounted to distracting people from the promising biomedical and scientific psychological approaches also being studied at the time.

In 1921, the German psychiatrist Emil Kraepelin began classifying mental illnesses. To study the biological origin of mental illness and develop a clinical neuroscientific approach, he assembled an impressive group of scientists, including Alois Alzheimer, who later identified the disease that would bear his name. Kraepelin set depression and mood disorders apart from other mental illnesses. He observed that people with depression usually entered a recovery phase after about four months, even without treatment, while those with continuous, progressively worsening disorders such as schizophrenia did not. Although today we tend to think that people have a biological predisposition toward depression and remain vulnerable for their entire lifetimes, it's interesting to note that it was once viewed as a more transient condition.

Despite Kraepelin's promising scientific approach, treatments for depression during the first half of the twentieth century were mostly random stabs in the dark. How else can you describe such "therapies" as freezing baths, rib-breaking electroconvulsive shock therapy, treatment-induced malaria, and barbaric surgical treatments? None of these "therapies" had valid theoretical underpinnings, and they generated less than impressive results.

RELIEF IN A PILL

By the 1950s, the notion that depression could be cured merely by taking a pill was welcomed by psychiatrists and patients alike. If depression was indeed a disease of the brain—a brain swimming in neurochemicals—a medication that altered the mix in specific ways could be just what the doctor ordered. As researchers uncovered new ways to study the brain, the field of psychopharmacology, which focuses on the relation between drugs and mental processes, grew exponentially.

Physicians were tipped off to the potential effectiveness of drugs for depression after they noticed that certain medications developed for other ailments affected patients' moods. One promising early candidate, Iproniazid (known as a monoamine oxidase inhibitor, or MAO), was first used as an antibacterial agent. When doctors observed that it improved the moods of tuberculosis patients, neuroscientists tried to determine how and why it worked. Iproniazid and other drugs that had mood-altering qualities affected three related neurochemicals—serotonin, noradrenaline (also known as norepinephrine), and dopamine. In the mid-1960s, the Harvard psychiatrist Joseph Schildkraut declared that an insufficient amount of norepinephrine—known for its involvement in arousal and focused attention—was the key contributor to depression.

More tests and drug research ultimately narrowed the focus to serotonin, a neurotransmitter located in several areas throughout the brain that influences important physiological functions such as our sleep/wake cycles, temperature regulation, and general aspects of mood regulation.

Indeed, the introduction of fluoxetine in the 1970s by the pharmaceutical company Eli Lilly changed the course of the treatment for depression. More commonly known by its brand name, Prozac, this drug increases the amount of serotonin in the synaptic gaps between nerve cells by interrupting an important step in the recyling of our brain's neurochemicals, a process known as reuptake. After a certain amount of time, a nerve cell initiates signals for a neurochemical to be taken back up into the releasing nerve cell so that it can be repackaged and used again. Because antidepressants, such as Prozac, inhibit the reuptake/recyling process of serotonin, drugs of this type became known as selective serotonin reuptake inhibitors, or SSRIs. In 1987, Eli Lilly was licensed to sell its drug in the United States. Similar drugs followed.

As I mentioned earlier, the premise of SSRIs is that depressive symptoms are associated with low levels of serotonin. Obviously, in order to confirm the viability of this theory, researchers needed to establish that depressed people actually *had* low levels. This presented a methodological challenge right from the start because there is currently no direct way to measure serotonin levels in the brains of living human beings.

One way to test this hypothesis is to approach it from the opposite angle. We've known for a long time that tryptophan, a common protein in our diets, is converted into serotonin. Foods such as bananas, turkey, and milk all have high levels of tryptophan and likely produce increased levels of serotonin in our brains. Because of the neurotransmitter's involvement in the sleep/wake cycle, this probably explains why you may get sleepy after Thanksgiving dinner. Consequently, depriving people of this dietary protein would theoretically deplete serotonin levels in the brain.

Pedro Delgado at the University of Arizona conducted a fascinating study to test this idea. He found that a tryptophan-free diet (and presumably lower brain serotonin levels) had virtually no effect on healthy people without a family history of depression. But for those who had a genetic predisposition or were currently on antidepressants, the results got a lot more interesting. When deprived of tryptophan, approximately one-third of the healthy patients with a family history of depression exhibited depressive symptoms. And a whopping two-thirds of the patients who were being treated with antidepressants at the time of the experiment showed a relapse of depression after a mere five hours.

What do we take from this innovative research? In healthy people with little genetic predisposition to depression, serotonin levels do not seem to be related to the onset of depression. Some people with a genetic predisposition to depression may be sensitive to alterations of the serotonergic system, but 66 percent of even that group did not have this sensitivity. However, once the brain has been altered by the persistent use of antidepressants, it responds quickly to depleted levels of serotonin, confirming the pronounced effect that SSRIs have on a patient's neurochemistry once he or she starts taking them. Further research is needed before we can understand what these results mean outside of laboratory-induced conditions.

The serotonin hypothesis gets even fuzzier when you consider that tianeptine, a drug that results in decreased, rather than increased, serotonin levels, also results in a reduction of depression symptoms!

Another troublesome question: If serotonin levels are the key to depression, why does it take so long for SSRIs to have a therapeutic effect? The tryptophan-restricted diets had a negative effect after just a few hours on people taking SSRIs. Yet, when someone begins taking SSRIs, the effects are far from immediate. Although past research indicated that improvement typically took several weeks to months for most patients to notice a reduction in depressive symptoms, more current meta-analyses of previously conducted research indicate an initial effect after a week that continues over the next couple of months. As I'll discuss later, these drugs may trigger intermediate effects in the physiology of our brains that eventually result in lifting the severity of the depression symptoms. But there are likely other pathways with more direct effects that can provide more efficient and effective ways to treat the problem.

Given the fact that millions of prescriptions are written each year for SSRIs, how effective are they in relieving depressive symptoms? Well, that gets interesting, too. Recently, researchers combed through the majority of studies designed to measure the success rates of antidepressants and reported that antidepressant medications do indeed work. But there were some pesky problems. First, it was difficult to find studies that used appropriate methodological protocols, so many of them had to be excluded from the analysis. Second, the response rates to antidepressants were actually not as impressive as early research had indicated: they ranged from 56 to 60 percent.

On the surface, this appears close to the success rate of Thomas Kirkbride's integrative therapy in the nineteenth century, which was also 50 to 60 percent. It's important to emphasize, however, that his numbers represented actual cure rates, whereas the antidepressant numbers reflect only an initial response (these patients were followed for only about eight weeks). Further, the response rates to taking a placebo, such as an inactive sugar pill, ranged from 42 to 47 percent in the antidepressant trials. Thus, a differential of about 10 percent separates the reactions to the medication and to a placebo.

In another study, the success or efficacy rates of antidepressants were compared to those of cognitive behavioral therapy, interpersonal therapy, psychodynamic therapy (which, à la Freud, searches for unconscious, hidden motives and mechanisms related to depression), and the power of the good old sugar pill: the placebo.

Cognitive behavioral therapy draws from rich scientific explorations into how emotions, actions, and thought patterns interact. Therapists work with clients to develop thought processes and behavioral strategies that influence their emotions in healthier ways. Interpersonal talk therapy, which zeroes in on relationship issues, was initially designed to be used in conjunction with antidepressant medication, but it actually proved to be as effective as the medication alone.

This latest research suggests that cognitive behavioral and interpersonal therapies, which, unlike medications, have no lingering side effects, are just as effective in alleviating depressive symptoms as SSRIs. Antidepressant use, on the other hand, may result in sexual dysfunction, blunted emotions, and even elevated rates of suicide. (Psychoanalysis proved no more effective than a placebo; it has not fared well in previous attempts to show its efficacy in treating depression.)

Still, in order for SSRIs to be approved by the Food and Drug Administration (FDA) for use by the public, they were subjected to clinical trials. Obviously, because these drugs are on the market, a sufficient number of trials reported higher efficacy rates than doing nothing (i.e., taking a sugar pill), and these successful studies are readily available in the scientific literature.

There may be more to this story, however. David Healy, a psychopharmacologist at the University of Wales, explains in his book *Let Them Eat Prozac* that several of the initial efficacy trials failed to show that the drug was better than the placebo. In clinical research, it's considered acceptable to exclude failed trials (that is, trials in which SSRIs did not improve depressive symptoms more effectively than the placebo) from the final analysis, so it's difficult to know how consistently SSRIs fared across all these studies. We'd get a more complete picture by looking at all clinical trials submitted to the FDA.

In 2005, a *Scientific American* article titled "Antidepressants: Good Drugs or Good Marketing?" expressed similar reservations. "Pharmaceutical companies have cherry-picked data for decades; only 50 percent of all drug trials over the past half a century were reported or published. This means that the 56–60 percent overall response rate hailed by the recent report represented only half the studies that were conducted. One has to wonder what the response rates were in the studies that the pharmaceutical companies elected not to publish after spending so much money to conduct the research."

Thanks to research by Irving Kirsch and Thomas Moore, from the University of Connecticut and George Washington University, respectively, we now know. Using the Freedom of Information Act, they obtained all the efficacy data that were submitted to the FDA for approval for six of the most popular SSRIs. These researchers found that an astonishing 80 percent of the patients' response to these drugs was duplicated in the placebo group. When people in each group took a depression inventory following treatment, the scores once again differed by a mere 10 percent. After a close analysis of these SSRI studies, Kirsch and his colleagues reported that close to 60 percent of the SSRI trials failed to show that these drugs worked better than sugar pills!

These discrepancies regarding SSRIs are unsettling. There seems to be very little research supporting their therapeutic potential. In fact, there is growing evidence indicating that other neurochemicals, stress hormones, and brain growth factors may be more relevant to the depression story. So why do we continue to hear so much about SSRIs? Is there something I'm missing? Many other professionals in the field have expressed similar concerns.

"Although it is often stated with great confidence that depressed people have a serotonin or norepinephrine deficiency, the evidence actually contradicts these claims," wrote Elliott Valenstein, a behavioral neuroscientist, in *Blaming the Brain*.

"I wrote that Prozac was no more, and perhaps less, effective in treating major depression than prior medications. . . . I argued that the theories of brain functioning that led to the development of Prozac must be wrong or incomplete," declared Peter Kramer, a psychiatrist and the author of the book that first popularized Prozac, *Listening to Prozac*.

And David Burns, a psychiatrist at Stanford and author of the influential book *Feeling Good*, which supports behavioral approaches to treating emotional disorders, weighs in: "I spent the first several years of my career doing full-time research on brain serotonin metabolism, but I never saw any convincing evidence that any psychiatric disorder, including depression, results from a deficiency of brain serotonin. . . . Some neuroscientists would question whether the theory is even viable, since the brain does not function in this way, as a hydraulic system."

In fact, it's been nearly forty years since the discovery of SSRIs, and we still don't understand the exact mechanism that results in the eventual relief of depressive symptoms for some patients. It would be surprising to learn that serotonin, as pervasive as it is, plays no role at all, but it is probably not a critical factor in relieving depression. At best, it's likely that it plays only an indirect role. If so, a better way to treat depression would be to initiate a more direct attack against its symptoms: a form of mental protection that is not predicated on taking neurochemical-altering medications.

So if SSRIs remain so problematic, where's the oversight that protects the American public from false or misleading advertising? You may think that the FDA takes care of this for us. But the agency does not require preapproval of drug advertisements; they monitor ads only once they're released. Although warning letters have been sent to manufacturers of antidepressants, the FDA has yet to cite a single pharmaceutical company for misleading advertisements. Thus, millions of potential users are exposed to these marketing campaigns every day through magazine, Internet, and TV ads.

Again, think about understanding depression through multiple windows. There is a classic analogy of a drunk who has lost his keys and keeps looking under one street lamp. When asked by a police officer why he was limiting his search of the entire parking lot to the small area around the lamp, the drunk replied that he was looking where the light was better.

It seems that we have spent too much time looking for answers to the mysteries of depression by searching around the serotonin lamppost. It is now time to spread out over the entire neural parking lot and consider other factors in the depression story. In the pages that follow, we'll examine the role certain areas of our brain play in depression. We'll also get out our neurobiological flashlights and consider how our culture, lifestyle, environments, and behaviors influence this mood disorder and associated brain processes. And we'll come closer to understanding why that Rainbow vacuum cleaner became my antidepressant of choice.

2

Why *Are* We So Depressed?
The Lifestyle Paradox

FOR SEVERAL DECADES, the multibillion-dollar antidepressant industry has pointed to imbalances in the neurochemical serotonin as the cause of depression. But research has yet to find convincing evidence to support this claim, and despite the unprecedented number of pharmacological treatment options available today, depression rates are higher than ever.

If Big Pharma doesn't have a cure for depression, shouldn't we pursue a fresh approach to this vexing problem? Could there be a nonpharmacological treatment strategy that would bring relief to the increasing number of people struggling with this mood disorder? What do we know about how to maintain good mental health? Is it possible to maintain a sense of control over our increasingly stressful daily lives, so that we can refocus our attention on more meaningful psychological endeavors, such as the challenging issues of problem solving and planning for our futures?

To build a new, more integrated theory of depression, I've searched the literature for possible evolutionary triggers of emotional responses, reevaluated what we know about how the brain functions in both healthy and unhealthy ways, and identified pivotal lifestyle factors that might be affecting our society adversely. Is there something about how we live today that's actually toxic to our mental health? Were earlier generations somehow less susceptible to depressive symptoms? If so, what can we learn from how they lived that will help us rebuild our resilience and emotional well-being?

I began thinking about the impact our contemporary lifestyle has on our mental health more than ten years ago after attending a lecture by Martin Seligman, a psychologist and the pioneering creator of the Positive Psychology movement, who was then president of the American Psychological Association. Seligman described two studies conducted in the 1970s in which people in different age groups were questioned about bouts of depression they had experienced during their lifetimes. The researchers then compared the responses of different generations.

This is a no-brainer, I thought at the time. Of course older people would report more bouts of depression. After all, they had lived through the Great Depression and two world wars, and suffered far more hardships and loss just by virtue of having lived longer. How could their mental anguish compare to the shorter, easier, and much less traumatic lives of a younger generation?

To my surprise, the exact opposite was true. Seligman reported that younger people were much more likely to have experienced depression. In fact, one study found that those born in the middle third of the twentieth century were ten times more likely to suffer major depression than those born in the first third of the century. These findings were later corroborated in a second study.

What's behind this startling disparity? Well, for one thing, earlier generations did far more physical work than we do today. I was reminded of just how much our daily lives have changed six years ago while reading a bedtime story to my younger daughter, who was three at the time. Skylar had chosen *Little House on the Prairie* for that evening's reading—one of my childhood favorites.

Over the years, as I've read to my daughters, I've often used the time to think through my to-do list for the next day. This bit of cognitive multitasking was a piece of cake with books such as *Goodnight Moon,* which I'd read countless times when my girls were younger. Goodnight room. . . . *I need to update that section in Wednesday's lecture.* Goodnight moon. . . . *and remember to take the chicken breasts out of the freezer.* Goodnight cow jumping over the moon. . . . *I have to finish those analyses of the rat brains in the lab tomorrow.* Goodnight light. . . . *I need to sign that permission slip for Lara's field trip.*

But that night, even as distracted as I was, the story about life on the prairie somehow drew me in. I found the demanding lives of Ma and Pa Ingalls so compelling that I actually had to pay attention to this one! Laura Ingalls Wilder, their daughter, described in detail how the family planted, harvested, and hunted down all their food throughout the year. That made my trips to the supermarket and merely reading the heating instructions for much of the food I "prepared" seem, well, lame.

I always complained about doing laundry, but my efforts paled in comparison to those of Ma Ingalls. She had to scrub every garment on a washboard and then hang the clothes out to dry. And this was only after she had made all the garments with her own hands! Bathing my daughters didn't require collecting rainwater or drawing water from a well; I merely had to turn on a faucet. The Ingalls had to make most of the things I simply purchased at the local mall, including toys, candles, soap, honey, and butter.

Little House crashed this working mom's pity party that evening. My life is a walk in the park compared to the lifestyles of a mere century earlier. I've never seen unloading my dishwasher in quite the same way since rereading those Laura Ingalls Wilder stories to my daughter.

Clearly, I'm not suggesting that we go back to churning butter and tanning hides. But I do think we have to examine whether our cushy, digitally driven contemporary lifestyles—replete with SUVs, DVDs, laptops, cell phones, and, yes, microwave ovens—may be at the root of the soaring rates of depression in people born in the latter part of the twentieth century. After all, the profound lifestyle changes that have accompanied all this dazzling new technology have coincided with the dramatic increases in depression rates in our society. Did we lose something vital to our mental health when we started pushing buttons instead of plowing fields? From a neuroanatomical point of view, I believe the answer is an emphatic yes.

The Work/Pleasure Connection

Our brains are programmed to derive a deep sense of satisfaction and pleasure when our physical effort produces something tangible, visible, and—this is extremely important—meaningful in gaining the resources necessary for survival. In fact, our brains have been hardwired for this type of meaningful action since our ancestors were dressed in pelts. After all, nature needed a way to keep the earliest humans from becoming "cave potatoes." Hanging out all day didn't put freshly caught game on the campfire or help maintain a safe place to live.

As I mentioned earlier, I call this emotional payoff effort-driven rewards. There are other important benefits to this type of effort beyond a greater sense of psychological well-being. We also experience an increased perception of control over our environment, more positive emotions, and, perhaps most important, enhanced resilience against mental illnesses such as depression.

Think about effort-driven rewards as a clever evolutionary tool, a way to motivate early humans to maintain the level of physical activity needed to obtain the resources to live—to find food, protect themselves from the elements, and procreate to continue the species. Anthropological evidence suggests, for example, that our ancestors expended tremendous physical effort to obtain their food. Their skeletal remains indicate the presence of considerably more muscular tissue than we find in our bodies today. According to S. Boyd Eaton at Emory University, an expert on Paleolithic diets, "Life during the agricultural period was . . . strenuous, but industrialization has progressively reduced obligatory physical exertion."

Effort-driven rewards don't come just from physical effort, however. They also involve complex movement coupled with intricate thought processes. Imagine thousands of years ago, when our ancestors were tracking a pack of wild boars through a forest or across a plain. Because these animals are such vicious fighters, a successful strategy typically involved the coordinated efforts of a few hunters, requiring effective social communication and support. They needed to be wily as they chased their game or lured their prey into a trap that they'd built. All their efforts were fueled by anticipation. In fact, anticipating something pleasurable creates more activity in the pleasure center of the brain than actually achieving the goal. Once they caught their prey, our hunters were suffused with a sense of accomplishment and satisfaction as they skinned the animal before dinner.

Our hands play a crucial role when it comes to effort-driven rewards. From an evolutionary perspective, it's easy to see why they have always been so critical to our survival: they allow us to gain control of our environment. In fact, an essential premise of my proposed effort-driven rewards theory is that movement—and especially hand movements that lead to meaningful outcomes—plays a key role in both preventing the onset of and building resilience against depression and other emotional disorders. Furthermore, we are predisposed to hand movements that our ancestors needed for survival—those necessary for nurturing, cleaning, cooking, grooming, building shelter, and farming.

But we shop at Whole Foods and drive Hummers. What does all this have to do with our modern lives and depression? Our brains are generally the same size and have all the same parts and chemical composition as those of the earliest humans. This doesn't mean that we are stuck in an evolutionary time warp—human brains continue to evolve and change in subtle ways—but there's no evidence that we have any new neuro-transmitters or have developed brain areas that our ancestors didn't have. So even though our lifestyles have changed radically, it's reasonable to assume that we have retained the innate need for effort-driven rewards.

No matter how enriching or pleasurable we find surfing the Web, e-mailing, listening to our iPods, reading a novel, or watching *American Idol,* our brains *still* crave the feelings associated with the survival-based outcomes that were so important in its own evolution. We're programmed to experience satisfaction and a sense of well-being after we exert meaningful effort and use our hands in ways that ensure our survival. So how adaptive is our Westernized lifestyle with all its built-in conveniences, diversions at the flip of a switch, and effortless satisfactions?

Is it okay that we have systematically removed physical effort—and all the complexity of movement and thought processes that it implies—from effort-driven rewards? Is contemporary society actually robbing us of certain forms of pleasure so fundamental to our mental health?

How Our Brains Reward Effort

As I looked for the possible evolutionary triggers of depression, I also began to reexamine the primary symptoms. Over the past few decades, researchers have identified certain areas of the brain associated with some of these symptoms. But could I match every single one—including loss of pleasure, feelings of worthlessness, slowed motor abilities, and difficulty concentrating—to a specific part of the brain? And, significantly, were those different brain areas interconnected or linked in some clearly identifiable way?

A natural place to start was the nucleus accumbens. This peanut-size structure is known as the pleasure—or reward—center of the brain and seems to have evolved to keep us engaged in behaviors that are important to our survival, including eating and sex. It plays a crucial role in how the brain functions, as it determines how to respond to environmental stimuli such as a piece of chocolate cake or that handsome guy at the bar.

An integrating center of the brain, it receives inputs and outputs from many neural areas. But for our purposes, I'm focusing on its intimate connection to three other primary areas. The accumbens is positioned between the brain's motor system, or striatum, which controls our movements, and the limbic system, a collection of structures involved in emotion and learning. Essentially, the accumbens is a critical interface between our emotions and our actions. The closely linked motor and emotional systems also extend to the prefrontal cortex, which controls our thought processes, including problem solving, planning, and decision making.

It is this accumbens-striatal-cortical network—the crucial system that connects movement, emotion, and thinking—that I call the effort-driven rewards circuit. It's the neuroanatomical network underlying the symptoms associated with depression. In fact, it's possible to correlate every symptom of depression with a brain part on this circuit. Loss of pleasure? The nucleus accumbens. Sluggishness and slow motor responses? The striatum. Negative feelings? The limbic system. Poor concentration? The prefrontal cortex. (I talk more about this fascinating integrative brain system in chapter 3.)

As if to impart renewed energy to our behavior, the motor structures that control our movements are intimately connected to the reward center—where we register pleasure—and the cortical area of our brain that controls higher thought processes. Because of the interconnectivity of the brain areas that control movement, emotion, and thinking, doing activities that involve a number of these components fully engages the effort-driven rewards circuit. So we get a deep sense of emotional satisfaction and well-being when we do something that requires some physical effort, including coordination and especially movement of the hands, and which also involves our problem-solving and reasoning abilities.

In fact, the more the effort-driven rewards circuit is kept activated and humming, the greater the sense of psychological well-being that results. It's as if an electrical current is coursing through the network. When it's buzzing at top capacity—when, for example, installing that new light fixture requires both hands—the cells in those areas of the brain are turned on and secreting neurochemicals, such as dopamine and serotonin, which are involved in generating positive emotions. Neural connections are strengthened and reinforced. Perhaps most important, this kind of meaningful action—that is, effort-driven rewards—likely stimulates neurogenesis, the production of new brain cells. Neurogenesis, which I'll explain in more detail later, is believed to be an important factor in recovering from depression.

Our hands play a crucial role in this circuit. They occupy most of the real estate of the motor cortex, located in the higher cortex. In fact, our hands are so important that moving them activates larger areas of the brain's complex cortex than moving much larger parts of our bodies, such as our backs or even our legs.

As I continued to delve into the scientific research on depression, I found myself thinking more and more about the role of hands-on work and effort-driven rewards in our mental lives. Could adding simple tasks to our daily repertoire of activities help maintain emotional resilience? For the answer, there was just one place to go—back to the laboratory.

THE TRUST FUND RATS

Because the rat brain has all the same parts as the human brain (it is just smaller and less complex), rodent models are a great starting place for mental health research. Could the rats tell me if there was anything to the connection between depression and physical effort?

Two undergraduate students, Kelly Tu and Ashley Everette, helped me design a study to test my theory. We put four mounds of cage bedding in the testing apparatus and buried a Froot Loop—a culinary favorite among my laboratory rodents—in each mound. We trained the rats to search the mounds for the treat, and each day we changed the positions of the mounds in a random pattern. The animals soon learned that each new mound had a Froot Loop, so once they retrieved one prize, they moved on to the next mound. I designed this to mimic the task of "harvesting"—picking fruit, vegetables, or, in this case, Froot Loops from the "fields."

Within a few days, the rats immediately approached the mounds and started digging for their prized cereal pieces. We trained these rats every day for five weeks so they would have ample opportunities to make associations between their physical effort and desired rewards.

Our control group consisted of rats that we also placed in this novel environment every day. But regardless of the physical effort they exerted, they received their Froot Loop rewards in a lump sum in the corner of the apparatus. My students enjoyed calling these rats the *trust fund rats* and the digging rats the *working rats*.

In the next phase of the experiment, we developed a puzzle that the rats had to learn to solve. This would allow us to assess whether the worker rats or the trust fund rats were more persistent in problem solving. We put a Froot Loop in a plastic cat toy ball, a novel toy stimulus that would be mildly threatening to the animals because it had a bell in it. We made certain that the coveted cereal piece would not fit through the openings. That meant that no matter how clever or bold the rat was, it would not be able to retrieve the reward in the test's three-minute time frame. Of course, the rats wouldn't know this, so we could assess the amount of time they spent trying to get the treat. The task involved boldness and persistence—characteristics that serve us all well during challenging times.

To make this task official, Craig Kinsley, my colleague from the University of Richmond who collaborated on this project, suggested we call it the "novel manipulandum task." This sounded much more impressive than the "cat toy test."

What did we find? Although we made sure that both groups had equivalent levels of "emotionality" or anxiety before training began, we observed remarkable differences in how the animals approached the challenge task. The worker rats picked up the ball in their mouths and slung their heads from side to side, tossing the ball across the cage. They also tried to stick their tiny paws through the openings to obtain the reward. While the trust funders were just as motivated to retrieve the Froot Loop (both had the same food restriction regime) and used similar strategies, they were not nearly as persistent.

In fact, the worker rats spent approximately 60 percent more time trying to obtain the Froot Loop reward and made 30 percent more attempts to do so than the control group. In their own way, the worker rats were telling us that their prior training sessions had made them more confident that they could overcome the challenge and retrieve the reward.

As I considered these findings, I was reminded of the widely reported study conducted several decades ago by Martin Seligman and his colleague Steven Maier. In this famous experiment, dogs gave up responding and problem solving after they realized they couldn't escape from cages in which they received mild shocks. The researchers referred to this effort-consequence disconnect as *learned helplessness.* Could our findings, then, be called *learned persistence?*

Clearly, we had empirical evidence of the adaptive value of effort-based rewards. The simple behavior of digging in mounds of bedding for cereal rewards had given the rats the motivation and confidence to persevere on a completely different challenging task.

Just as a gymnast needs to complete simple muscle repetitions before she can learn complex routines, we need ongoing, positive experience with simple effort-driven rewards to execute the complex mental gymnastics that comprise our enriched mental lives. Anything that lets us see a clear connection between effort and consequence—and that helps us feel in control of a challenging situation—is a kind of mental vitamin that helps build resilience and provides a buffer against depression.

THE LINK BETWEEN LIFESTYLE AND DEPRESSION

Even though our nervous systems have the same anatomical makeup and chemical composition, we are clearly using our brains and our hands differently than our ancestors—or even people who lived a mere century ago. In his book *When Culture and Biology Collide,* E. O. Smith, an anthropologist at Emory University, noted the dramatic changes that humans have experienced during the last few thousand years. According to Smith, "the rate of biological evolution approximates the speed of a glacier in comparison to the rate of change in our culture." He expressed concern that the discordance between our contemporary environment and the behavior our brains evolved to execute sets contemporary humans up for substantial conflict between the dictates of our modern culture and our evolved psychological predispositions.

We have long since left our nomadic and agricultural roots behind. Today, many more of us are knowledge workers than physical laborers. In fact, the percentage of farmers in the workforce was 38 percent at the turn of the twentieth century but only 3 percent at its end. There have been vast increases in service-related jobs, from 31 percent of the workforce in 1900 to 78 percent of all workers in 1999.

Doing the sorts of cognitive tasks that use our higher, more executive functions can be rewarding. But as the majority of us spend most of our days focused nearly exclusively on higher-level functioning—writing a book, for instance—we have, in effect, left our bodies behind. We are no longer engaging all the essential elements of the effort-driven rewards circuit in our day-to-day lives, especially the brain areas controlling our hands.

No, moving a mouse or joystick and typing on your laptop don't count! These movements are mostly repetitive and reflexive, not as complex as, say, doing carpentry. The cognitive, emotional, and physical effort that goes into hunting for one's dinner significantly outweighs the brain's effort required to e-mail a friend about dinner plans.

Of course, you may feel a sense of accomplishment when you zip through your cognitive to-do list. The pleasure derived from just intellectualizing a problem is rewarding because it activates the prefrontal cortex. But effort-driven rewards activate the problem-solving prefrontal cortex plus the movement-controlling striatum and the reward/motivation center known as the accumbens, leaving you with a fuller brain experience that prepares you for life's next challenge. The decreased brain activation associated with increasingly effortless-driven rewards may, over time, diminish your perception of control over your environment and increase your vulnerability to mental illnesses such as depression.

As I've mentioned, our brains evolved to acknowledge and reward the fruits of our ancestors' labors. Given the amount of physical effort they had to exert simply to survive, the enormous sense of satisfaction and control they derived encouraged them to maintain that level of labor. Are our perceived rewards as meaningful when we fax a document or close a business deal? As we'll see in the next chapter, new research suggests that our brains register more "reward" when more effort is expended to obtain it.

HUNGRY? JUST PUSH A BUTTON

This decline in physical effort and visible, meaningful results—which my research indicates is an essential contributor to the overall rise in depression—does not stop at the office. As refrigerators, dishwashers, vacuum cleaners, and clothes washers and dryers entered our homes, we needed less physical exertion to maintain our households. This technology freed up time so that homemakers, once tied to the home to produce the products necessary for the well-being of their families, were able to shift their efforts and seek paid jobs outside of the home.

The introduction of packaged food, frozen dinners, and, eventually, the onslaught of convenient fast food also had a significant impact on our lifestyles. Forty years ago, Americans spent 19 percent of their food budget on food prepared in restaurants. Today we spend more than twice that amount eating out—and those numbers are rising. Growing, harvesting, hunting, and preparing food have been replaced by driving through pickup windows, sitting down in restaurants, and "nuking" prepared meals.

You don't have to go back a century to understand how much effort it once took to feed a family. I can go back a mere two generations.

On top of a career managing women in a textile plant, my maternal grandmother, who lived in Talladega, Alabama, spent the spring months preparing her garden and planting all our favorites—okra, tomatoes, potatoes, squash, cucumbers, green beans, butter beans, black-eyed peas, corn, onions, lettuce, and peppers. She spent many hours tending and nurturing her garden—weeding daily, and staking the tomatoes as they started growing tall.

Once the vegetables started to ripen in midsummer, the work got more intense. After harvesting a little each day, my grandmother used the vegetables for dinners and Sunday lunches throughout the summer. The intense physical exertion, complex hand movements, and cognitive skills necessary for successful gardening—efforts that always seemed to give my grandmother so much satisfaction and pride—eventually produced tangible outcomes in the form of food for her family—a perfect example of effort-driven rewards.

Although my grandmother gave some of her garden's bounty to neighbors not fortunate enough to grow their own gardens, she also spent long hours preserving, canning, or freezing much of the extra food. That meant that she spent many evenings on the front porch shelling and peeling, followed by entire days over boiling pots of water cooking vegetables and making jellies, jams, and pickles.

My grandmother always had plenty of canned stewed tomatoes, vegetable soup, green beans, pickles, and much more to
supplement family meals throughout the fall and winter. Each
meal provided strong and delicious reminders of the consequences of her past efforts. The following spring, she started
the process over again. Sure, she could have purchased these
items at the grocery store, but for her, that would not have compared to growing and preparing these foods herself, something
she enjoyed year after year.

Of course, as a child I took everything she did for granted.
But today, as I reflect back, I am in awe of the tireless energy
she expended in feeding her family. Even in her early eighties,
she got up at five o'clock on Sunday mornings to prepare a special lunch for her children and grandchildren.

And, by the way, my grandmother was one of the most
cheerful and upbeat people I've ever met. I have vivid memories
of her smile as she cooked those huge meals or learned the
latest accomplishments of one of her six grandchildren. In
fact, I still laugh when I think of one of her Christmas Eve dinners about twelve years ago, when she'd cooked so much food
that the entire kitchen table collapsed under the weight. Even
when she was in her seventies, she had boundless motivation
and energy.

Barbara Kingsolver's book *Animal, Vegetable, Miracle* provides a more contemporary example of the mental benefits of
directing both cognitive and physical energy toward food preparation. After being raised in a household where all the meals
were made from scratch, Kingsolver's daughter, Camille, writes
that it was very different when she became a college student at
Duke University:

I missed picking fresh greens from the garden, or taking a jar of dried tomatoes from the pantry, as the starting point of a meal. It's obviously convenient to grab a salad or package of sushi from the dining hall between classes, but eating on the fly seems like cheating to me. Maybe I feel this way because my make-it-yourself upbringing drummed into me the ethic of working for the things I want. I've been involved in growing and cooking the food that feeds me since I was a little kid, and it has definitely given me a certain confidence about relying on myself. . . . If everything my heart desired was handed to me on a plate, I'd probably just want something else.

Were Earlier Generations Really Less Depressed?

Can we say with any degree of certainty that the work my grandmother did in her garden made her less susceptible to depressive symptoms? Or that Camille's upbringing on a farm will provide a buffer against potential mental illness in the future? Did the more physical, agrarian lifestyles of earlier generations actually bolster their mental health and resilience?

We don't have definitive data on depression in earlier generations. In fact, depression was identified and characterized as a mental illness only in the 1920s. So the only way we can frame this argument is to look at depression levels in present-day, less industrialized cultures. In these societies, people tend to exert far more physical effort (and all that implies) during the course of their daily lives than we typically do. If their rates of depression are lower, could that be a consequence of effort-driven rewards?

The people in the Old Order Amish community live much as their nineteenth-century forebears did: They do not use electricity or telephones, and they travel by horse and buggy rather than by motorized vehicles. Their children generally do not go to school beyond the eighth grade and are trained in mostly vocational work such as homemaking for girls and farming for boys. Their simple way of life provides a window into the lives of earlier Americans, allowing us to compare our contemporary lifestyles with those of several generations ago.

Research shows that the Amish spend about ten hours a week in vigorous physical activity and approximately forty-three hours a week in moderately intense activity; in fact, they spend approximately six times more time on purposeful physical activity than the typical American today. With their efforts so directly connected to their physical needs and resources, the *accumbens-striatal-cortical circuit* is continually active and has little "downtime."

According to the U.S. Public Health Service, the Old Order Amish have somewhere between one-fifth to one-tenth the rates of depression of the general public. Seligman points out that the current depression rate in the Amish is about the same rate observed in our culture two generations ago. Their religious practices and their close communal lifestyle may also contribute to their mental health. But the degree of control they have over their low-tech environment may also be the significant difference between their culture and ours.

Further support for the connection between physical effort and depression can be found halfway around the world in China. Of course, different cultures have different definitions and diagnostic criteria for depression, and the diagnosis is viewed with varying levels of understanding and acceptance.

Both affluence and poverty—important contributors to mental health and illness—vary dramatically across cultures. But in some cases, it is appropriate to accept the methodological risks in order to acquire even a glimpse into these cultural windows.

In one 1999 study, teams of psychiatrists and psychologists assessed nearly twenty thousand people over the age of fifteen in different areas of China. They reported that only sixteen people met the criteria for lifetime affective disorders such as depression. According to these findings, the prevalence rate of depression in China is eight-hundredths of a percent, a rate hundreds of times lower than that reported in the United States. Although some researchers have attributed those lower rates to cultural differences (e.g., a tendency to deny depression or express it somatically), it is difficult to imagine that these skilled clinicians completely missed evidence associated with depression in their diagnostic interviews.

While most Americans live in urban settings, two-thirds of the Chinese population still live in rural areas. Their agrarian lifestyle is characterized by independence and self-sufficiency. Farming and attachment to the land are fundamental cultural threads woven through the various populations in China. Even as people have moved into urban settings, many have maintained the ideals associated with that agrarian lifestyle. As China becomes increasingly industrialized, it will be interesting to see if increases in overall rates of depression emerge.

The striking difference in rates of depression between the sexes suggests another gauge of the impact of modern society on our mental health. In highly industrialized, Westernized societies, women are twice as likely to experience depression as their male counterparts. Throughout the world, regardless of the overall rate of depression, women's rates are consistently twice that of men. Reproductive hormones and brain differences may contribute to this disparity, along with some of women's cognitive habits that can put them at risk for developing depression or for coping poorly with it. But, interestingly, when we look at the role of effort-driven rewards, those disparities all but disappear. Susan Nolen-Hoeksema, a psychologist at Yale University, reported no difference in depression rates in cultures where women's physical efforts produce meaningful outcomes. For example, in Nigeria and rural Iran, women play a significant role in society and are expected to contribute to the economic resources of the family and community. Nigerian women engage in farming, fishing, and craft work alongside Nigerian men.

The same holds true for Old Order Amish women here in the United States. Like women at the turn of the last century, today's Amish women are expected to produce their families' food and clothing. Not surprisingly, studies report no significantly higher rates of depression in Amish women than in men.

As we move to research on more typical contemporary American women, the picture becomes less clear. Working mothers who have husbands who contribute to household chores and have no difficulties arranging child care have lower levels of depression than working women with less consistent child care and less help at home. Working mothers who report being responsible for too much outside of their control—not having a backup baby-sitter for a sick child, for instance, faced with repairs around the house that they don't know how to make, or having to drop everything for important meetings at work—report high rates of depression.

Moreover, homemakers who have more control over their efforts but who perceive themselves engaging in repetitive actions that lack meaningful outcomes also report high rates of depression. So it appears that women are less vulnerable to depression if they feel that their efforts help give them a sense of control and meaning whether they are homemakers or work outside the home.

It's becoming increasingly evident that maintaining balance in our emotional lives is critical to sustaining mental health. When something minor happens—you spill your coffee on your pants, or a driver double-parks and blocks you from pulling out—most of us are able to regroup quickly and keep on going. We find a way to cope. But when the stress and pain begin to mount—you experience a series of unsettling slights in a disintegrating relationship with your boss, or someone you love receives a devastating diagnosis—then the attack on the body's internal balancing act eventually reduces your resiliency levels. At this point, the symptoms of depression may begin to emerge. So when the chips are down, we need to be able to maintain our stability through those inevitable emotional challenges. What can we do to protect ourselves against the onset or tenacious persistence of depression?

Remember how vacuuming every nook and cranny of my house after losing my mother helped me regain my mental equilibrium? The physical effort that is related to desirable and tangible outcomes—in that case, clearing my house of dust and grime to protect my family—helped reactivate my effort-driven rewards circuit and restore my sense of control over my environment. There are many other ways to get that critical circuit humming again. Poring over a scrapbook project or knitting a sweater may distract you from the stress in your life and engage your brain in intense ways that are beneficial to your mental health. Going out to the park or gym to exercise, especially if you perceive the activity as meaningful, can also boost important, emotionally relevant neurochemicals such as serotonin and endorphins. Such activities may alter the brain in more meaningful ways than any dose of a single drug could accomplish. Why? Because they are performed within the context of your life. When you are faced with a challenge and embark on the dynamic process of deciding on an effective strategy, implementing the plan, and observing the final desirable outcome, your brain takes note of these situations so that it can access similar response strategies in the future.

Changing the brain's neurochemistry with a drug does not require taking the emotional and behavioral contexts of your life into account. Consequently, this form of therapy does not help your brain register important consequences of effort-driven rewards to ward off future symptoms of depression. It does, however, train the brain to continue to take the medication to avoid negative emotions in the future.

Now that we've begun to explore the effort-driven rewards theory and I've outlined the behavioral data from the trust fund rats to support the operating principle behind it, we need to consider the role of the brain in these responses. Understanding more about the neuroanatomy of the effort-driven rewards circuit is critical to understanding how our responses can lead to depression.

3

Building the Effort-Driven
Rewards Brain Circuit:
Use It or Lose It

I LOVE COLLECTING old, rare psychology and neuroscience books. At a conference six years ago, I bought John Fulton's *Frontal Lobotomy and Affective Behavior,* published in 1951, to use as background for a chapter I was writing on the history of neuroscience. I was surprised to see inside a handwritten inscription—a Tennyson quote and a note wishing the recipient, a psychiatrist in New York, a Merry Christmas. It was signed by Paul MacLean on December 25, 1951.

When I saw the signature, I was starstruck. Paul MacLean was one of the giants of neuroscience in the last century. His novel and innovative research on the evolution of the brain has long been admired by scientists in psychiatry, psychology, neurology, and neuroscience. In the early 1950s, MacLean first identified and described the brain's circuit for the expression of emotions. He called this emotional circuit the limbic system, after the Latin word *limbus,* meaning edge or border, because this circular system forms a border around the central part of the brain. Fully engaged in our emotional responses throughout our lives, the limbic system encompasses brain areas involved in basic reflexive responses, as well as more advanced social and cognitive functions.

MacLean demonstrated that our emotional behavior is influenced by primitive parts of the brain. We have an ancient reptilian brain component that contains hardwired neurological programs for very basic, specific behaviors, such as those involved in aggression and sexual behavior. Thus, our brains are an interesting combination of the reptilian brain, the more recently evolved mammalian brain (bringing onboard more complex responses such as parental behavior, play, and rudimentary communication), and the even more advanced cerebral cortex (enabling more advanced cognitive functions such as solving a crossword puzzle, talking to a friend, or reading this book).

I was thrilled to learn that MacLean lived a mere ninety miles north of my home in Richmond. After a few phone conversations, he invited me to visit. While we talked, he seemed to travel back in time as he described the neuroanatomical adventures that led to his seminal writings about the brain's emotional circuit. Looking in a microscope, he said, was like "walking through a cathedral."

To convey how powerful his theory is to this day, I showed him a book I was reading titled *The Amygdala*—nearly seven hundred pages devoted to just one component of the complex limbic system. This almond-shaped structure is known primarily for its involvement in the emotional response of fear. When I said I could spend the rest of my career simply researching only one part of this circuit, MacLean laughed.

I was horrified! What had I said?

"Kelly, if you spent the rest of your career researching just one component of a larger complex circuit, you wouldn't accomplish very much," he said. "Brain areas are located in proximity for a reason. It's not a random organization. You shouldn't waste your time researching such a limited area." When scientists focus on isolating the tiniest physiological common denominator, he added, they risk not seeing the neuroanatomical forest for the cellular trees. It was ridiculous to think that our amazingly complex emotions and behaviors could be controlled by a single brain structure or a single neurotransmitter functioning in isolation and not connected to other relevant areas and circuits.

Today we understand that the brain is as an amalgamation of separate yet integrated areas that work in concert to enable us to carry out even the most basic behaviors, such as picking an apple from a tree. An area of the brain that has a specific set of functions is known as a "nucleus"—that is, a cluster of similar types of neurons located in proximity to one another with a common function. The amygdala and nucleus accumbens are nuclei. The individual neurons making up these larger nuclei branch out, sending extensions to other areas of the brain. Neural processes come into these brain areas as well, so a brain area receives feedback from several brain destinations, creating a considerable amount of input and output flowing among a certain cluster of brain areas. Neurochemicals are the fuel of these neuron connections, allowing the extensions to stimulate or "talk" to the other brain areas by emitting a particular neurotransmitter.

Let me explain how neurotransmitters work. We have about a hundred billion neurons in our nervous system, which includes the brain, the spinal cord, ganglia, and nerves throughout the body. And we have well over one hundred different neurotransmitters helping neurons communicate with one another. Neurons have long hairlike projections that connect to other cells. If the cell receives the appropriate amount of stimulation, an electrical charge (known as the nerve impulse or action potential) travels down one of the hairlike projections, prompting the release of little "sacks" of neurochemicals or neurotransmitters that travel across the tiny little gap, known as a synapse, so they can stimulate the next neuron.

Essentially, neurochemicals provide another means of cross talk besides physical connections. A brain area may have specific receptors to receive neurotransmitter molecules from a completely different circuit, so there is no physical connection, only a chemical connection. In a sense, the brain is one big gossip party—each brain area wants to know what the others are up to!

The most complex behavior is maintained by clusters of brain areas that are activated at the same time and that have some common communication or feedback. We call these clusters brain circuits. Certain neurotransmitters are associated with particular brain circuits—and there are neurotransmitter circuits as well. For instance, dopamine is important in experiencing reward, noradrenaline is involved in arousal, and serotonin is critical in the sleep/wake cycles and other functions.

As connections are developed among neurons, a neural network forms. For example, now that I've been working on this book for a while, I would guess that several connections have been made among the prefrontal cortex (thinking, reasoning, planning), the amygdala (fear of trying to figure out the publishing world and getting the project completed), and the nucleus accumbens (good feelings/excitement/anticipation about working on the book). When I think of any one component of the book project, I experience a sea of responses due to the reverberating activity (action potentials followed by neurotransmitter release) of the entire circuit.

As I drove home from my meeting with MacLean, I knew that my understanding of the brain had changed forever. At a time when neuroscientists are being trained to look for the most reductionist mechanisms (the specific neurochemical receptors, specific genes), MacLean had forced me to think about brain circuits and evolutionary predispositions and to view the brain and its functions from a more global perspective. My behavioral training took me a step further and made me consider context, that is, the specific environmental situations prompting our behavior and mental processes. I wondered what MacLean would think about the idea that the diverse collection of symptoms we call depression could be explained by a single neurotransmitter—and could be corrected by consuming pills. I was certain he would think that we could do better.

A Composite Sketch of the Depression Circuit

Just as police detectives develop a composite sketch of a suspect's face, I set out to develop a composite picture of the areas of the brain involved in the constellation of symptoms associated with depression. Was there one brain circuit, similar to Paul MacLean's limbic system, that connected depression's diverse array of behaviors—a depressed mood, changing sleeping habits, slowed movement, recurring thoughts of death, absence of pleasure, difficulty concentrating?

I focused immediately on the brain's pleasure center—the nucleus accumbens, that small structure located in the lower part of the forebrain. When you put a piece of chocolate cake in your mouth, this area brims with activity. In the days when resources were limited, activation of this pleasure center increased the chances that our ancestors would engage in survival behaviors such as eating and sex. Skipping a meal would have been a bad idea when there was no guarantee of another in the near future. We still feel the evolutionary pressure of the nucleus accumbens today when we find it difficult to drive past a favorite fast-food restaurant. Most of us are confident that we'll eat tomorrow, so avoiding these temptations isn't really going to hurt us. Still, it's difficult to resist. That warm, pleasurable feeling you get as you savor those burgers, shakes, and fries is the accumbens doing its job well.

Mostly known for its role in rewards, the accumbens also influences many basic functions in our lives, such as integrating emotional and motor functions. It's strategically positioned between the brain's motor system (striatum) and emotional circuit (limbic system). The core of the accumbens, which is believed to be involved in voluntary movement, extends to the striatum. Its shell, which is linked to our motivational/emotional systems, extends to the limbic emotional circuit. Both these systems also connect to the cortex, which governs our thought processes.

Think of the accumbens and its inputs and outputs as a motive circuit, a motivation executive center of sorts, which decides how to respond to relevant stimuli (or environmental cues) such as desirable foods or the awesome shoes in the department store window. When you stumble upon a snake, the limbic system structures respond immediately to this stimulus by assessing the emotional relevance of stimuli. Then it sends the information to the higher centers of the brain, the prefrontal cortex, for more sophisticated assessment and evaluation, before communicating with the nucleus accumbens, which makes the ultimate decision about how to respond to the snake. Only then does the brain's pleasure/motive center trigger the appropriate motor circuits for running, if the snake is an unwelcome guest—or picking up the snake, if it's the family pet.

As I thought about Paul MacLean's advice, I began to understand the futility of focusing on just one element of this fascinating, integrative system. Clearly the interactions among the accumbens, the striatum's motor units, and the higher executive center of the prefrontal cortex were important in determining whether we would respond or just sit passively in any given situation.

So my composite sketch pointed to the accumbens-striatal-cortical circuit as a prime suspect for the neuroanatomical circuit underlying the symptoms associated with depression. Until now, no such circuit for depression had ever been considered. The bulk of attention had been focused on the individual neurobiological components, mostly neurochemicals like serotonin. Yet, as I systematically reviewed the cluster of depression symptoms, I was able to correlate each one to part of the effort-driven rewards circuit.

- Diminished pleasure and reward, or a depressed mood, could certainly be caused by alterations of the accumbens.

- Slowness of responses and fatigue could be influenced by the striatal components of the circuit, because they are so closely involved in movement.

- Decreased motivation could be a result of some alteration in the integrated motor and reward components of the accumbens as well as altered limbic functions.

- Diminished cognitive abilities, such as difficulty with concentrating and problem solving, as well as repeated thoughts of death, could be influenced by the brain's more executive prefrontal cortex, as well as the circuit's cross talk with specific areas of the emotional limbic system.

I quickly realized that more research was needed to determine how alterations in this circuit generate the symptoms of depression in the context of real-life conditions. How was this circuit affected by effort-driven rewards?

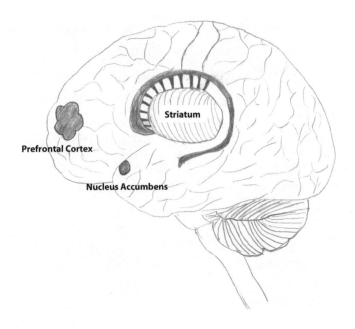

Effort-driven rewards circuit. Multiple direct and indirect connections exist among the components of the effort-driven rewards brain circuit. Executive functions such as planning and decision making are facilitated by the prefrontal cortex, whereas our pleasure and commitment to certain ideas or challenges emerge from the nucleus accumbens. The striatum facilitates the implementation of our planning and passions by executing the necessary movements to realize our goals.

MOTIVATION IN ACTION

I turned to rodent research to help me get a better sense of how physical changes in the accumbens-striatal-cortical system can influence motivation. Several studies suggest that disruptions of the accumbens pleasure center altered both the type of reward preferred by an animal and how much effort it was willing to exert for the treat, thus causing a rat to experience a lack of motivation similar to what a depressed person might feel. After researchers destroyed parts of this brain area, animals that would ordinarily have been willing to work for a larger, delayed reward preferred tasks that required less effort and yielded more immediate, although smaller, rewards.

The same response occurred when the medial prefrontal cortex, the "thinking" component of the effort-driven rewards circuit, was damaged. This area of the brain is involved in many of the cognitive functions that tend to be altered in depression, such as focused attention, decision making, goal-directed behavior, and working memory. (When you keep repeating a phone number to remember it, that information is in the working memory phase. If you commit the number to memory and are able to dial it two weeks later, that information has moved to more long-term memory storage.) In one study, animals were tested to see if they preferred to cross a large barrier in a maze to obtain a large reward or cross a small barrier to receive a smaller treat. At first, animals opted to work harder for the larger prize. However, after they underwent a surgical procedure that damaged part of the medial prefrontal cortex, rats preferred the smaller barrier and the smaller reward.

After carefully ruling out the possibilities of reduced spatial memory or a reduced sensitivity to rewards, the researchers suggested that this area of the cortex was essential in determining whether an animal chose to exert more physical effort to obtain larger rewards. It appears that this and other closely related areas in the cortex are important in making informed decisions about which responses will lead to the most meaningful outcomes. The impaired decision-making ability and lack of motivation to work for greater rewards are reminiscent of the symptoms observed in depression.

Do our brain's pleasure center and its communication with the higher cortical areas determine whether we'll spend hours preparing an elaborate dinner or settle for takeout? The tendency in our society to do less and less physical work suggests that it may be more "rewarding" to obtain a treat without exerting the effort. Why else would we be so eager to pay others to do our own chores each day?

A fascinating study utilizing fMRI (functional magnetic resonance imaging, a type of brain scan that provides images of brain activity) conducted in the laboratory of Gregory Berns, a psychiatrist at Emory University, suggests that we may be paying others to do the tasks that could actually bring our brains some degree of pleasure. While in the scanner, research participants in one group observed a computer "game" in which money was randomly dropped into "their" money bags. They played only a passive role. People in a second group could manipulate the software so that they were able to move the money and "work" toward maximizing the amount of money in the bag. Both groups were told they would receive the actual amount of money put in their bags.

Berns and his team found that the active group showed greater activity in certain aspects of the right and left portion of the striatum (the motor component of the effort-driven rewards brain circuit) and the right nucleus accumbens. In other words, the reward circuit of the brain exhibited more activity when the subjects expended a little effort to obtain the reward. Perhaps we should think twice before hiring the kid next door to mow our lawn. We may be depriving our accumbens-striatal pleasure circuit the activation it so rightly deserves!

In the quest to add detail to my composite sketch of the brain's effort-driven rewards circuit, I next investigated which neurochemicals played a role in the depression circuit. Or put another way, could the neurochemicals known to be involved in the symptoms of depression be traced to the effort-driven rewards "scene of the crime"?

Dopamine, the primary neurotransmitter found in the nucleus accumbens, is known for its involvement in both movement and rewards. Research suggests that reductions in dopamine prompt animals to shift to response strategies that require less physical effort, resulting in smaller rewards. It's as if we need certain levels of dopamine to sustain the memory and motivation necessary to keep us working hard at a task that does not immediately produce a reward.

The used-car salesman who continues to approach customers after fifteen rejections in a day must have a good dose of dopamine running through his brain's reward system. Otherwise, how can he persist in thinking that the next customer may buy a car and produce a payoff? Animal studies suggest that if someone were deficient in this neurochemical, those fifteen failures would instead dominate the salesman's thoughts, making it very difficult to persist in such a frustrating career.

In a rodent version of an unpredictable sales career, when rats were shifted from a training program in which they received a reward after every response to one in which they were only rewarded after making several responses, researchers found increased dopamine activity in the prefrontal cortex. This may indicate that the increased opportunities for anticipating the reward, as opposed to actually consuming the treat, represent a healthy exercise for our brains.

But what about serotonin, the neurochemical darling of the depression industry? Stephen Maier and his colleagues at the University of Colorado recently conducted a study that suggests that serotonin does play at least an indirect role in the effort-driven rewards circuit. The researchers were studying the role of the more executive medial prefrontal cortex in two different situations. In the first, known as the escapable stress condition, rats received a mild shock to their tails but were able to turn off the shock by turning a wheel in the cage. The rats in the inescapable stress group had no control over the delivery of the shock. When Maier looked at the area of the brain stem known as the *dorsal raphe nucleus*—the major source of serotonin-producing cells in the brain—he found that the medial prefrontal cortex activated the serotonin-producing raphe nucleus, which prompted the body and brain's stress response to handle the impending threat.

Here's where it gets really interesting: In the group that perceived more control because they could exert physical effort to turn off the shock (that is, effort-driven rewards), activation of the raphe nucleus was inhibited. Their brains sent messages to halt the firing of serotonin neurons. It was as if the medial prefrontal cortex were conveying to this more primitive brain stem area that it had everything under control. Maier's work suggests that enhanced activation of the neurons secreting serotonin leads to increased anxiety, as observed in the inescapable shock condition. This observation seems at odds with the notion that taking SSRIs to increase levels of serotonin decreases anxiety and the symptoms of depression. Still, this research confirms that dopamine and serotonin do play significant roles in the accumbens-striatal-cortical circuit underlying effort-driven rewards, even though we don't exactly know how.

Now that I'd established the connection between the neurochemicals involved in motivation, reward, and the effort-driven rewards circuit, I began to search for neurochemicals that could potentially mitigate the cognitive factors—such as difficulty in focusing attention on a task, or the lack of goal-directed behavior—that are so prevalent in depression.

In an actual laboratory reenactment of *Who Moved My Cheese?* (a book by Spencer Johnson, M.D.), the neuroscientists Martin Sarter, John Bruno, and their colleagues, who were all at Ohio State University at the time, conducted research in which they trained rats to lick a citric acid solution in order to "earn" a cheese reward. They found that successful performance, or engagement in the task, resulted in an increase in acetylcholine, a neurotransmitter known for its involvement in attention and cognitive tasks in the medial prefrontal cortex. This increase, to the tune of approximately 200 percent, accompanied a more predictable increase in dopamine release in the nucleus accumbens. Thus, engaging in work for the cheese resulted in enhanced activity of the neurochemical known for its involvement in learning and memory.

There was now enough evidence to build a case supporting the influential roles of the effort-driven rewards circuit and several related neurochemicals in the emergence of the symptoms associated with depression. But was the accumbens striatal cortical circuit of an actual depressed person altered in some significant way? A thorough review of the animal neuroscience literature had provided strong support for an underlying circuit contributing to the emergence of depression, but evidence from depressed human patients was critical before the value of the circuit could be determined.

THE MOMENT OF TRUTH

I soon learned that a Toronto-based team had conducted fMRI scans of unmedicated depressed and nondepressed people. *This was it,* I thought. If there were no alterations in the areas I'd identified in the effort-driven rewards brain circuit, then my theory about depression would not hold up. With the same kind of anticipation a lottery player has waiting for the winning numbers, I nervously read the report published in the *Archives of General Psychiatry.* Would my theoretical predictions be accurate?

The authors conveyed their interest in how the brain's reward system may be involved in the maintenance of depressive symptoms. They were thinking along the same lines I was—so far, so good. To test their hypothesis, they recruited twelve patients who met the criteria for depression and twelve patients who were not depressed and gave each a dose of an amphetamine known as dextroamphetamine sulfate. This is a stimulant similar to cocaine that is sometimes prescribed for depression or narcolepsy.

Why use a stimulant? The researchers wanted to observe the brain's response to dopamine, the fuel of the brain's reward system, as it reacted to the stimulant. Each person received a brain scan before getting the drug and another during the peak drug effect, which occurred about ninety minutes after the injection.

The fMRI study showed modifications in all three components of the proposed accumbens-striatal-cortical circuit. The nondepressed subjects had considerably more activation in these components than the depressed subjects, so the brains of the depressed subjects were responding differently to a hit of "rewards fuel." In addition to having lower levels of brain activity in the prefrontal cortex and striatal areas (caudate and putamen), there were interesting differences in the participants' reward center.

This nucleus accumbens is a small structure, which makes it difficult to assess accurately using fMRIs. To gauge the sensitivity of the rewarding effects of the drug, the researchers gave the subjects a paper-and-pencil test. They offered items such as: *I feel now as I have felt after a very exciting experience; I feel so good I know people can tell it.* Compared to the nondepressed subjects, the depressed patients had a hypersensitive response to the stimulant. In other words, the test indicated that the brain's reward system had been significantly altered in the depressed subjects. The researchers concluded that the brain's reward system is more critical to the symptoms of depression than previously thought, prompting them to suggest that it was probably misguided to focus on just a single neurotransmitter system when trying to understand depression.

But why hypersensitive? Doesn't that suggest that the depressed patients' brain reward system was working just fine—better than fine, perhaps?

It could, but a more plausible explanation is that this system doesn't get enough dopaminergic "action" during the course of a depressed person's day-to-day life. In an attempt to compensate for the lack of pleasurable responses, the nerve cells in this area became supersensitive, perhaps sprouting new receptors or more sensitive receptors, in order to maximize the response to any circulating reward chemicals that might pass the nucleus accumbens' way. In other words, the system's response to a sudden flood of amphetamine would be pronounced—a real brain reward party!

There was another significant finding. Before administering the stimulant, the researchers noted that the *cingulate cortex,* a component of the limbic system that has direct connections to the prefrontal cortex, was more active in the depressed patients than the nondepressed group. This communication area, which is involved in processing emotionally relevant stimuli and is an obvious "player" in the accumbens-striatal-cortical circuit, may be in overdrive in the depressed patients, leading to excessive worry.

Other research, conducted by Michael Platt, a neurobiology professor at Duke University Medical Center, suggests that neurons in the cingulate cortex also play an important role in risky decisions. Monkeys were trained to shift their gaze to a visual stimulus to obtain a fruit juice reward. Because this brain area fired, or lit up, twice during the testing sessions—when making the visual response and upon receiving the reward—it was concluded that the cingulate cortex processes "reward-prediction" errors. That is, this area could alter our ability to make rational predictions regarding whether our actions will produce desirable results.

The importance of the cingulate cortex in emotional responses was also recently reported in the prestigious journal *Nature.* Researchers at New York University and University College London explored brain activation in subjects instructed to consider positive emotional events such as winning an award and compared the brain activation profiles to subjects experiencing more pessimistic thoughts. The subjects self-reporting more optimistic responses exhibited a pattern of increased activity in two key areas of the limbic system, the amygdala (generally known as the brain's fear circuit) and the cingulate cortex. When interviewed about this study, the researcher Elizabeth Phelps conveyed that the more optimistic responses enable people to take control of their lives, whereas depression does just the opposite. "The problem with depression," she commented, "is that people are so pessimistic that they don't engage in actions that could make their lives better."

If your efforts fail to produce the expected rewards (three months of job searching but no job offer), the cingulate cortex may be altered. Due to its rich interactions with the effort-driven rewards brain circuit, this brain area could be responsible for maintaining some depressive symptoms, such as heightened anxiety, incessant worry, and a lack of motivation—all of which would compromise your ability to work hard to attain the goals you've set for yourself.

For example, if you're overly worried and anxious, you become less motivated to take chances and push forward. A student with this altered cingulate activity may study diligently for an exam, but based on a warped sense of reality due to overwhelming anxiety, she may decide she is going to fail the test anyway and so she doesn't even show up. The reality is that studying was the correct response to earn a decent grade, but her clouded judgment caused her to make the maladaptive choice of skipping the exam and most certainly failing.

Another brain imaging technique, known as positron emission tomograpy (PET), has been used to assess brain functions by measuring how radioactive-labeled glucose is consumed by certain areas of the brain. A recent PET study may shed some light on the gender differences in depression.

Earlier research had shown that men and women respond differently to scary movies. Armed with that information, Larry

Cahill, at the University of California at Irvine, used a special adaptation of the PET scan to assess blood flow in specific brain areas, especially the amygdala, during times when no scary stimulus was being presented. Cahill and his colleagues asked thirty-six men and thirty-six women to close their eyes and relax. When the researchers looked at the normal ebb and flow of blood in this area, they found that increased blood flow to the amygdala in men's brains activates areas involved in interacting with the external world such as motor and visual centers. On the other hand, increased amygdala blood flow in women results in increased activation in brain areas that drive the body's stress response. In other words, men's brains responded to the increased blood flow by preparing to take action, but women's brains responded with the anxiety associated with stress.

When the brain's fear center works in concert with more "active" coping brain areas, it may help reduce the prevalence of depression in men. But for a woman, the amygdala's immediate activation of the stress response may further exacerbate anxiety and reduce the likelihood that she will actively respond to her fears. Women also showed more activation in the left amygdala. (We all have one in each hemisphere of the brain.) Since the left hemisphere is our language center, the fact that women showed this bias may contribute to increased rates of talking about the stress in their lives. This activational pattern also makes it more likely that women engage in cognitive rumination (persistently revisiting troubling thoughts throughout the day), which is associated with increased rates of depression in women.

For me, reading the results of these fascinating brain imaging studies were the equivalent of winning the lottery. This research showed that the tide may be turning toward a more global theory of depression that embraces the role of the brain reward system in the genesis of its symptoms. The massive communication that takes place between our brain's reward system and its emotional, cognitive, and motor systems points to a critical and defining role in the constellation of symptoms known as depression. Communication disruptions anywhere along the critical areas of the effort-driven rewards circuit could result in the suppressed motivation, increased anxiety, and disruptive thoughts characteristic of depression. There are indeed many windows through which we can gain access to the brain's depression circuit. As you'll see in the next section, we also gain valuable perspectives from many different sources—including popular culture and hibernating bears.

LESSONS FROM *CALVIN AND HOBBES*

Bill Watterson, the creator of the cartoon strip *Calvin and Hobbes,* has shown himself to be one of society's great neurophilosophers. He named Calvin, the boy in the strip, after the sixteenth-century theologian who advocated the idea of predestination, and Hobbes, the talking stuffed cat, after Thomas Hobbes, the seventeenth-century philosopher known for his dim view of human nature. Together, they present a witty and acerbic running commentary on the human condition.

I was particularly intrigued by a strip that Watterson titled "the late-twentieth-century drug of choice"—in which he explores what happens when, in effect, we don't flex the accumbens-striatal-cortical brain circuit. Calvin sings the praises of TV, thanking the electronic box for "elevating emotion, reducing thought and stifling imagination." In the last panel of the strip, Calvin notes that watching TV is a *complete forfeiture of experience,* not requiring the use of *any muscles at all.* He then happily extends the passivity to his entire being, stating, *I wallow in my lack of participation and response,* concluding his commentary with the statement *I can almost feel my neural transmitters shutting down.*

Calvin has plenty of company. The average American spends three to four hours a day watching TV, which means that in a sixty-five-year life span, a person will spend nine years in front of the tube. Could such passive recreation actually compromise the effort-driven rewards brain circuit, which is fueled by effort as opposed to passivity? Are our neurotransmitters indeed shutting down? The research reviewed in this chapter supports Calvin's claims, especially those indicating that dopamine is affected in such passive experiences. Other neurochemicals, such as serotonin, acetylcholine, stress hormones, and brain growth factors, may be influenced in some way by extreme passivity as well. Our overly passive contemporary lives may also alter the neurobiological systems that enhance vulnerability to depression via other physiological pathways.

Hibernating bears provide valuable insights here. John Tsiouris, a researcher at the New York State Institute for Basic Research in Developmental Disabilities, recently theorized that there are distinct similarities between hibernation in bears and major depression in humans, including withdrawal from one's environment, metabolic changes, lack of energy, sleep alterations, and increased stress hormones.

Interestingly, while hibernation is triggered by deep hypothermia in most mammals, bears hibernate in response to only mild hypothermia. If Tsiouris's hypothesis is correct, could it be that, in addition to hibernation triggers such as temperature levels, the brain may respond to an animal's activity levels as a sign that there are fewer resources available, resulting in the activation of a human version of a hibernation system?

In other words, as our activity levels have diminished in Westernized culture, the symptoms of depression may result from reduced activation of the effort-driven rewards brain circuit. This may in turn activate the additional brain circuits needed to trigger the process of conserving energy in order to deal with what the brain perceives as the impending prospect of "harsh times," which results in modifying metabolic, neurochemical, and sleep processes. The cyclical nature of this mood disorder (considering that it typically gets better after some time, only to reoccur later), as well as the presence of specialized versions of depression such as seasonal affective disorder, provides further and striking similarities to the rhythmic hibernation response.

Calvin's blissful passivity while watching his favorite TV shows is a double-edged sword—one that weakens the brain circuit sustaining our effort-driven rewards. According to Peter Whybrow and Robert Bahr's book *The Hibernation Response*, humans have become "walking hibernators." Indeed, the way our brain "conserves" cognitive responses in those suffering from depression (the lack of drive and problem-solving skills) suggests that this condition may be viewed as a "mental hibernation" of sorts—with the promise of restored function when the mental coast is perceived to be clear. As we'll see in the next chapter, the brain's elegant control of our hands when we interact with the world around us may be the perfect strategy for restoring function to those people who consider hibernation and passivity the best responses to a threatening world.

4

Giving the Brain a Hand

W E USUALLY SEE our hands as simply an extension of our body and a means to manipulate our physical environment. But it has become increasingly apparent that the movement of our hands is also intimately associated with the mental manipulation of our world and the quality of our social interactions. Our hands' ability to carry out the intentions generated by the effort-driven rewards circuit is what makes their role so critical to our mental health. In fact, the hands' direct route to our motivation, positive emotions, and cognitive abilities confirms their importance in our mental as well as physical lives.

Both the evolution and neuroanatomy of hand movement in humans suggest that the manual exploration of our physical world is integral to the accumbens-striatal-cortical circuit that regulates effort-driven rewards. As using our hands enhanced our ability to manipulate resources for food, clothing, and shelter, we also gained the luxury to build the kind of rich mental world in which ever more sophisticated manipulations could take shape. These experiences led to a greater sense of control—

a hallmark of emotional well-being that builds resilience against the emergence of depression. Thus, important clues to motivation and depression may have been in our hands all along—or for at least a million years or so!

Our hands' integral relation to the effort-driven rewards circuit has led to the amazing resilience and productivity of our species. But what happens when we rely less and less on our hands for productive activities? Today, instead of using them in engaging and elaborate ways, we rely on more simple manual skills such as pressing buttons and navigating a pointer across a screen with a computer mouse. As I've been suggesting, these more limited interactions with our physical world dampen our motivation to interact further with our environment. And, most significant, this diminished physical activity can lead to depressed thoughts and emotions.

MARIA MONTESSORI'S HANDS-ON LEARNING METHOD

When my older daughter, Lara, turned three, I decided that she should attend preschool part-time to have a more structured learning and social environment. Settling on a preschool that used the Montessori method of teaching, I made an unexpected discovery that reinforced just how critical a child's hands are to the development of her mind.

Maria Montessori, born in 1870 in Chiaravalle, Italy, was the first woman to obtain a medical degree in Italy. She began working with underprivileged children and soon became interested in the science of education. After reading the works of the founding fathers of psychology such as Wilhelm Wundt, who emphasized the importance of sensory experience in the functions of the mind, she incorporated these ideas into her own teaching methods. She believed that in addition to sensory experiences, motor responses—especially movement of the hands—were critical to learning.

Montessori was eager to apply the exciting new science of psychology to the education process. She designed ingenious activities for students that were self-paced and self-regulated and that involved mostly natural materials such as wood, water, and sand.

Certain activities were designated as "work" to be performed during a quiet time that was to be respected by all. She observed that as children performed these tasks, they not only refined their physical movements, they concentrated for extended periods of time. To Montessori's surprise, there seemed to be an emotional payoff, too. Once a child focused on finishing the task at hand, such as stacking blocks of different sizes so that each block was smaller than the last, he seemed to become an active worker, feeling calm and full of joy. In one case, a child concentrated so deeply that she repeated a task forty-two times. Even when her chair was picked up and moved in an attempt to distract her, she kept working.

Unaware of the brain circuits that she was activating in these children, Montessori wondered why the work appeared to be so rewarding. Why, after focusing so hard and long on a task, did the children seem so rested and content with themselves? She noted that the youngsters often ignored enticements such as special treats or gave them away in order to continue what they were doing. She was obviously tapping into a deep reward system that could not be rivaled by more superficial distractions.

One challenging aspect of my daughter's school was that parents were required to work one or two days a month in the classroom, mostly wiping noses and settling disputes during free playtime. I must confess that I was reluctant to rearrange my busy work schedule to do this, but that was before learning what a true delight this "job" would turn out to be.

From the first day, I was completely captivated by what I saw in the work area. Each child quietly chose an activity from a shelf and, without being told to do so, began focusing on it. The tasks varied—odors to be matched with actual objects such as flowers or cinnamon sticks, colors to be arranged in order from lightest to darkest, and the alphabet to be learned by tracing sandpaper letters with their fingers. There was no talking, no running around the room, no annoying kids' music or distracting videos. Once a child felt he'd worked long enough at a certain activity, he arranged the puzzles or blocks the way he'd found them and put them neatly back on the shelf. The teacher quietly assured the students that they were doing good work, but she never interrupted or corrected them.

I felt as if I had arrived in an exotic land populated by a newly discovered species of human preschoolers. I wanted to run to my lab to get a clipboard and video camera so that I could document this bizarre behavior.

More than a century ago, Maria Montessori developed the quintessential method to fully activate the brain areas underlying the effort-driven rewards circuit. She offered tasks so appealing to the children's senses that they stimulated their pleasure center (accumbens), which directed them to their activity of choice; extensive involvement of their hands, which activated the striatum as the kids picked items up, measured, and stacked them; thought processes required to compare, contrast, and categorize, which were provided by the prefrontal cortex. The extended time devoted to each task solidified the intricate connections among the brain components of the effort-driven rewards circuit, which in turn further increased the child's attention span and the amount of time he or she stayed "on task."

Assessing educational programs is difficult because there are few constants in children's lives. The little research done on Montessori-educated children has not shown that they earn significantly higher academic scores. Instead, the payoff seems to be in emotional well-being. In one study of middle school students, the researchers found that Montessori-trained children were more energetic, had higher levels of intrinsic—or internal—motivation, and showed more ability to concentrate while doing school activities. Traditionally educated students saw the academic work as important but had low intrinsic motivation while they were engaged in activities inside the classroom.

Mihaly Csikszentmihalyi, one of the authors of this study, is known for his research into emotionally satisfying work. Currently a professor at Claremont Graduate University in California, Csikszentmihalyi introduced the term *flow* into the literature years ago. After interviewing hundred of athletes, artists, surgeons, musicians, and chess masters, he discovered that those people who spent considerable time engaged in their preferred activities experienced an optimal mental state described as being "carried away by a current, effortlessly, like in a flow."

These experts claimed that nothing else seemed to matter when they were engaged in their favorite activities. The actual experience—not the salary or the acclaim it produced—was enjoyable. In his many books and articles on the subject, Csikszentmihalyi suggests that we are at our happiest when we are in a state of oneness with an activity. As we engage in our favorite tasks, we get "in the zone"—that is, in a state of flow—and become unaware of the passage of time.

Csikszentmihalyi hasn't explored the brain circuits underlying "flow," but the effort-driven rewards circuit would certainly explain the pleasure associated with meaningful work. We're more likely to become lost in thought and time when our thoughts are supported by actions directed by our accumbens-striatial-cortical circuit. When the circuit is in full gear, we enjoy a "hit" of the accumbens dopamine, capped off by the tranquility and synergy of having our motivation, reward, and movement activated simultaneously. We may experience this gratifying feeling while doing all sorts of activities—gardening, woodworking, knitting, playing with our children.

The jump-start that the Montessori program likely gives children could be very important to their developing brains. It may set the stage for a more responsive and rewarding mental life in the child's future. As our nervous system matures and we become better able to focus attention on tasks, our mental lives become less dependent on intense hand interactions with our environment. After all, as adults we frequently get lost in activities that don't involve our hands—listening to music, reading (or writing!) a book, or watching a movie. Still, continuing to use our hands in productive, active ways remains important. Just as muscles need repetitive boosts to maintain the agility and strength of our movements, our effort-driven rewards circuit is more fully engaged when tasks requiring actual handiwork are occasionally interspersed with our daily or weekly activities.

Periodically doing crafts or other forms of work with your hands may help recharge your emotionally drained brain batteries. If your emotional or cognitive life becomes compromised, a hefty dose of Montessori-style activities may reactivate a sleepy effort-driven rewards circuit, leading to your having more focused attention and robust memory circuits. In fact, researchers are experimenting with a therapeutic form of Montessori intervention for Alzheimer's patients in an attempt to build new brain connections to compensate for the neuron damage caused by this devastating disease.

I'm sure that Maria Montessori would not have been surprised to learn that the worklike, purposeful activities she designed for preschoolers engaged so much of the brain in such relevant ways. Her pioneering thinking about the need to activate both the sensory and manual neurobiological systems of children should have earned her a far more prominent place in the history of psychology.

HAND GESTURES PROVIDE GLIMPSES INTO THE BRAIN'S FUNCTIONS

When our hands aren't busy working to produce resources, they play a crucial role in another endeavor important to our mental health—communicating with others. Healthy social communications lead to healthy emotional lives. When we speak with our colleagues and friends, we often highlight important points with our hands. We gesture effortlessly, often without conscious awareness, to punctuate the meaning of our words.

David McNeill, a psycholinguist at the University of Chicago, is trying to determine how attuned our brains are to the movement of our hands. He's convinced that hand gestures are "windows into our thought processes." Indeed, they seem to be as prominently involved in our conversations as the words themselves. The palm turns up, then flips down; fingers point. Sometimes there's even double hand action to emphasize an important idea. Occasionally, when my students get anxious in the midst of giving oral presentations, they overcompensate with so much hand movement that I'm afraid they'll take flight!

To demonstrate the close ties between your hands and your thoughts, the next time you share a story with a friend or family member, make a concerted effort not to use your hands. That's right—no gestures, no pointing, no clapping. I was forced to do this myself during a recent interview when the cameraperson told me to keep very still while I answered questions. When I watched the interview later, I was amazed at the lack of flow and continuity in my responses. I attributed my less than impressive performance to the fact that I had literally "sat on my hands," which also severely restricted my ability to communicate effectively.

Research conducted by Spencer Kelly at Colgate University has found that the brain emits a type of wave known as N400 when we encounter something unexpected in our environment. For example, if his study subjects heard the sentence, "He spread his toast with socks," Kelly saw N400 waves when he recorded their brain activity. The brain's surveillance also extended to hand gestures. When subjects watched a video in which the hand gestures contradicted the language—such as verbally describing a very tall glass while making the gesture that indicates a very short one—the N400 waves emerged as well. In other words, hand gestures are so important to our communication processes that our brain sends out its own version of an alarm signal if there's a discrepancy between a person's gestures and words.

The close relation between the movements of our hands, language, and thought processes can also be seen in the ways our hands develop over time. For the first nine months or so of an infant's life, he reaches for the objects he wants with an open hand—with all his fingers extended, much like a chimpanzee. About the time the baby attempts to form words, such as *da* or *wawa,* the open-hand gesture evolves into a single finger directed at the desired object. As the language center matures, the areas of the brain controlling hand gestures mature as well and become more refined for facilitating communication—a very important cognitive staple if we are to function successfully in this highly social world.

THE EVOLVING USE OF OUR HANDS

It is likely that when our primate ancestors descended from the trees about two and a half million years ago our hands became more prominent players in our cognitive and emotional worlds. We no longer needed long, curved fingers and short thumbs to swing from limb to limb, so shorter, straighter fingers and longer thumbs evolved. As our hands and wrists morphed into their current structure and form, they allowed us to perform the fine-tuned motor skills necessary for sophisticated tool use.

But then our progress stalled. *Homo habilis,* who came on the scene two million years ago, is believed to be the first species of the genus *Homo.* They were the first toolmakers, earning the nickname "handy man" from the famed paleontologist Louis Leakey. For about one and a half million years, our ancestors used the same generic type of hand ax. During this time, the development of the prefrontal cortex, along with the ability to manipulate the environment, was extremely limited. In short, the effort-driven rewards circuit that might have led to the kind of sustained attentional processes, motivation, and creativity needed to create more advanced tools was not apparent.

There are many theories regarding the events that eventually propelled our ancestors out of their evolutionary rut. John Shea, an anthropologist at Stony Brook University, suggests that modern humans' ability to create a more sophisticated dagger, made from antelope horn, was a defining moment. These refined manual efforts gave the ancestors of modern humans a distinct advantage over the brawnier Neanderthals, who kept producing less effective stone tools. The larger and more awkward Neanderthal dagger could be thrown only about twenty-three meters (sixty-plus feet), but the sleeker dagger could be catapulted a distance of about forty-two meters (about one hundred twenty-plus feet).

How does Shea know such specific information about these prehistoric tools? He and his students actually reproduced them in order to gain firsthand experience by putting the tools to a throwing test. These demonstrations suggest that the Neanderthals were required to get much closer to their prey, so close that they probably placed themselves in danger of becoming dinner themselves. Modern humans' ancestors most likely hunted from safer distances and surroundings—and the result, as they say, is history.

Stanley Ambrose, a paleoanthropologist at the University of Illinois at Urbana-Champaign, provides further insight into the critical events that transformed early humans into a species capable of thriving in the technologically advanced information age. Ambrose hypothesizes that some cataclysmic natural disaster (for example, drought, volcanic ash, or a severe climate change) forced a group of early humans to migrate from Africa to unknown, unpredictable environments. Once our ancestors embarked on this journey (a prehistoric version of the popular TV reality series *Survivor*), the need to create more effective tools to respond to novel challenges was probably a driving force in the evolution of the modern human brain and mind. Here again, it's our hands that stand out as a crucial contributing factor that led to the enhancement of our rich emotional and cognitive lives.

Ambrose also notes that speech and tool use, both related to the function of the hands, are controlled by areas in the brain that are in close proximity. Examinations of cranial endocasts (fossilized casts reflecting the shape of the brain that filled the skull) of *Homo habilis,* the first human, indicate an impression of Broca's area, which is known for its involvement in the fine-motor control of language, in the left hemisphere. Broca's area is adjacent to the motor cortex and is thought to be derived from the part of the motor cortex that controls precise hand movement.

Thus, higher-order areas of the human brain likely evolved to accommodate the increasingly sophisticated hand movements necessary for effective tool use. Producing and using tools required more sophisticated planning and complex problem solving, which appears to have forged the neuroanatomical bonds between our hands and the higher executive functioning areas of our brains.

As humans continued to evolve, other handiwork requiring complex brain circuitry was produced. Steven Kuhn, an anthropologist, and his colleagues at the University of Arizona found ornamental beads, some of the earliest forms of "art" created by humans, along the northern Levantine coast in Turkey's Ucagizli. Cave and at Ksar Akil, Lebanon. The beads were made out of marine shells and created with early stone tools. Radiocarbon-dating technology suggests that these tooth-shaped beads were crafted about forty-one thousand years ago.

Here is a novel and creative use of the hands that reflects emerging cognitive abilities. The beads may have been used to facilitate communication about personal identity (I'm a woman, a mother, a hunter). Or they may have represented a more complex type of social interaction, such as a "payment" for safely entering a new territory. The anthropological significance of these beads provides scientific support for the comment made by the character Clairee Belcher, portrayed by the actress Olympia Dukakis, in the movie *Steel Magnolias,* written by Robert Harling: "The only thing that separates us from the animals is our ability to accessorize."

In addition to their integral roles in tool use and ornamentation, the use of our hands to produce food was undeniably pivotal in the lives of early humans. Andrew Sherratt, an Oxford University archaeologist known as an Old World prehistorian, provides evidence that our ancestors' skill in acquiring food played an important role in the evolution of the modern human brain. "A propensity to interfere with the environment in unexpected ways seems to have been an inherent characteristic of modern humans. . . . [B]ehaviorally modern people like to mess around with plants," he wrote.

Thomas Wynn and Frederick Coolidge, of the Departments of Anthropology and Psychology, respectively, at the University of Colorado, have suggested that the use of "managed foraging" to obtain food from plants and animals required an enhanced working memory, contingency planning, and an optimism about the future—skills that would serve any CEO well even today. Thus, as modern humans fine-tuned the use of their hands, they could further manipulate their environment by locating and generating more reliable sources of food (hunting, farming) necessary for survival. Clearly, the cognitive abilities sharpened by the practice of managed foraging such as problem solving and optimism are also important in maintaining mental health and building a buffer against depression.

The earliest settlers in the Americas were undoubtedly dependent on their hands when it came to acquiring the food necessary for their survival. The recent anthropological discovery of the Kennewick man, a nearly complete skeleton found along the banks of the Columbia River near Kennewick, Washington, provides some exciting insights into how a man of that era lived. Detective work by Douglas Owsley, a forensic anthropologist at the Smithsonian Institution, indicated that the Kennewick man lived more than nine thousand years ago—making his one of the most complete and oldest skeletons ever found in the Americas. His bones reveal that he stood five feet nine inches tall and was very muscular. The bones of the right arm were considerably larger than the left (indicating right-hand dominance). In fact, they were so robust that the bones were bent, suggesting that the Kennewick man had built up an impressive amount of arm musculature from a lifetime of hunting and spear fishing.

The role that hands played in the evolution of the modern human mind drove the ongoing development of tool use, ornamental arts, and foraging systems. Clearly, the use of our hands to manipulate our environment, especially to produce tangible rewards that we can see, is consistent with our brain's evolutionary trajectory and even today helps us sustain active, well-functioning lifestyles. Still, the scientific support for the effort-driven rewards theory does not stop with this anthropological research. Compelling evidence for the importance of the hands can be found in neuroanatomy, too, especially when we consider a strange little man known as the *homunculus*.

THE HOMUNCULUS WITHIN

Early Western writings indicate that the brain was thought to be involved in the body's execution of movement. But while doctors observed the motor dysfunctions that followed head injuries, the specific details of our bodies' ability to plan and execute movements remained a mystery for centuries. Important clues were not discovered until the nineteenth century, when Gustav Fritsch and Eduard Hitzig began to unlock the mysteries.

Fritsch was a surgeon on the battlefields of the Franco-Prussian War. As he dressed a soldier's open head wound, he noticed that the body seemed to twitch on the side opposite the head wound, which would later be known as the brain's *contralateral* control of the body. He also observed that the outside covering, or cortex, of the brain played an important role in behavior, which was a novel idea at the time. Indeed, the cortex, literally meaning *rind*, was considered to be a mere outer shell covering the more important internal brain. Today, we know that just the opposite is true.

Fritsch continued exploring the cortical influence on movement by teaming up with Eduard Hitzig, a psychiatrist who had discovered that electrical stimulation of the head provoked eye movements in patients. In 1870, the researchers applied electrodes directly on the cerebral cortex of a dog. They recorded various forms of *Zuckungen*, or muscle twitches, that resulted from the specific placement of the electrodes. Their work suggested that it was possible to create a topographical map of body movements in the brain's cortex, which was truly groundbreaking in brain research at that time.

In the midtwentieth century, Wilder Penfield, a Canadian neurosurgeon, also became interested in the specificity of the cortical control of movement. While conducting brain surgery on epileptic patients, he electrically stimulated various areas of their exposed brain tissue. (As there are no pain receptors in brain tissue, this caused them no discomfort.) His research confirmed that certain areas along a specific strip of brain tissue—now known as the primary motor cortex—controlled the movement of particular muscle groups. Using diagrams based on the motor cortex of monkeys, Penfield mapped the topographic organization of the human motor cortex, one of several "motor/movement" zones in the brain, each with different functions. This higher cortical area makes sure the right muscles—in the hands, feet, and shoulder—are doing the moving.

He made two critical observations about the motor cortex. The areas devoted to the movements of muscle groups were neither equal in size nor proportional to the size of the muscle groups they controlled. Instead, the amount of cortical real estate allocated was directly proportional to the sensitivity and complexity of movement of a particular area. For example, back muscles are large but don't take up much cortical space. However, the hands and mouth take up oversized amounts because of the elaborate movements possible in these muscle groups and their extreme sensitivity to touch.

The second important observation was that the organization of the muscle groups on the cortical strip was not grouped in a head-to-toe fashion. Instead, the feet are controlled by the top areas of the cortex, and the mouth and tongue muscles are controlled by the lower areas. The area that directs the hands is located in the middle.

To understand the significance of this, we have to go back to the homunculus, our funny-looking man. What would a human look like if each body part were proportional to the area of the primary motor cortex devoted to its movement? The motor homunculus, literally *little man*, gives us the answer. His hands are overwhelmingly large, grossly overshadowing larger body parts such as the legs, stomach, and chest. This neuroanatomical map is a compelling representation of the importance of hands in humans' lives. Seeing him, it's easy to imagine why greatly diminishing the activity of these brain-rich hand movements would have dire consequences, including decreased motivation, reduced pleasure associated with our efforts, and less effective problem-solving abilities—all symptoms of depression.

Today, we understand the extensive amount of brainpower needed to do even simple tasks, such as cutting food with a knife and fork. The effort-driven rewards circuit plays a significant role in moving food from the plate to our mouths, from initiating the response to activating the area of the motor cortex that controls arms, wrists, and hands. The actions leading to rewards—in this case, savoring the piece of meat in our mouths—are closely monitored by the motor component of the effort-driven rewards circuit. The accumbens reward center is involved in our anticipation of tasting the food that we are aiming to put in our mouths, while our cognitive prefrontal cortex is making decisions about positioning the food and which cutting strategies might yield the tastiest pieces. It also determines whether we should feel guilty because we're eating too much of that tantalizing entrée. Then, the appropriate nerves emerging from the motor cortex engage the actual muscles required to cut up and chew that steak. Thus, using our hands to carry out such tasks activates the brain areas that we previously identified as important in maintaining mental health and avoiding depression.

Of course, other brain areas and circuits are also involved in almost every seemingly routine hand movement. What's surprising is how many parts of the brain are engaged and how they interact. Leah Krubitzer, a neurobiologist in the Department of Evolutionary Neurobiology at the University of California at Davis, has explored the dedication of large parts of the brain to the manipulation of our hands. Her neuroimaging studies indicate that the bilateral coordination necessary to perform tasks using two hands activates additional cortical areas such as the somatosensory and parietal cortical areas, known for their involvement in the perception of touch, and the control and position of our body parts. Activities involving both hands initiate extensive processing in the hemisphere controlling one hand before that information is projected to the other hemisphere, activating extensive circuits throughout the brain.

Although many scientists propose that language is the quintessential characteristic of the human brain, Krubitzer argues that the extensive brain area devoted to the sensory processing and movement of our hands makes hand movement an equally important characteristic. She makes the case that our hands generate a sense of self by providing information about where our bodies end and the rest of the world begins. As our ancestors used their hands to explore and survive their world, the constant need to change and adapt pushed the modern human brain to emerge.

The motor homunculus. *The body proportions of this strange character represent the amount of brain real estate (in the motor cortex) devoted to the movement of various areas of the body. It is easy to see that the human brain has a substantial investment in the movement of our hands.*

EMOTIONAL HANDOUTS FROM THE BRAIN

Given the growing evidence of the brain's special relationship with the hands and the extensive neurocircuitry controlling them, it seems logical that using our hands more in our daily lives will enhance our sense of well-being. Anthropological and neurobiological research suggests that we can all benefit from manual work, which reignites the effort-driven rewards circuit that was so important in shaping the modern human brain. It's likely that maximizing the use of the hands (that is, movement of arms/forelimbs, wrists, and fingers) may be the most effective way to kick the circuit into gear. Although many of us work more than forty hours a week, our work typically involves pushing buttons, typing, sitting, and talking—none of which activates our brains the way more manual tasks do.

"The types of jobs where people actually make something are disappearing," Harrison Higgins, a woodworker in Richmond, Virginia, recently wrote. "But it is a fundamental part of who we are as human beings, physically, mentally, aesthetically, and it gives a tremendous amount of satisfaction to the maker and recipient."

It seems clear that tasks involving the hands—cooking, gardening, crafts—have a therapeutic effect on many people, but interestingly, these observations haven't been discussed much in the scientific or popular literature. That may be why such hands-on therapeutic approaches are rare. Certainly, they're not considered on a par with the more popular psychotherapeutic and pharmaceutical approaches to treating mental illness. But there's good reason to think they should be.

Consider knitting. It requires both hands, comprises repetitive motion that likely results in the release of the neurotransmitter serotonin, and engages the effort-driven rewards circuit as the hands' efforts produce a sweater or scarf. Knitting has long been considered mentally therapeutic, even though it hasn't been studied scientifically. Indeed, one nineteenth-century author wrote that the needle arts "occupy a distinguished place, and are capable of being made not only sources of personal gratification, but of high moral benefit, and the means of developing in surpassing loveliness and grace, some of the highest and noblest feelings of the soul."

Of course, nineteenth-century physicians never mentioned effort-driven rewards brain circuitry in their writings, but they nonetheless seemed keenly aware of the associations between the manual efforts necessary for the craft and mental health. *Stitches*, a knitting magazine of that era, claimed that physicians recommended working on a simple piece of knitting, nothing too elaborate, to counteract restlessness and discontent. Anxiety-ridden women were told that the quick manual movements and the subtle clicks of the needles had a soothing effect.

More recently, Robert Reiner, a clinical psychologist and executive director of Behavioral Associates, a private psychotherapy institute in New York, supervised a preliminary study in which women with and without sewing experience were asked to carry out several leisure activities that required eye-hand coordination, including sewing, playing cards, painting, playing a video game, and reading a newspaper. After measuring heart rate, blood pressure, and perspiration, Reiner reported that sewing was the most relaxing activity. Playing cards and watching video games actually increased stress levels. In Nancy Molson's book *Craft to Heal*, she suggests that knitting relieves stress and anxiety through its repetitive, rhythmic movements. And the need to count stitches meticulously, she says, requires the knitter to focus concentration away from any troubling, stressful thoughts that may be on her mind.

Although the therapeutic effects of needle arts such as knitting require additional empirical study, we're seeing a dramatic increase in the number of people who knit for pleasure, which suggests that many more are discovering the calming effects of this hobby. A recent *New York Times* article states that knitting, once considered a pastime for our grandmothers, has recently become trendy for younger women. Hip New Yorkers are knitting in the subways, in cafés, and during lunch hours. Stories like this inspired me to buy a book titled *Chicks with Sticks: It's a Purl Thing* (written by Elizabeth Lenhard) for my preteen daughter. Even men are getting into the act.

Any activity that requires you to use your hands and that you enjoy, especially if it puts you into the flow zone, will energize your effort-driven rewards circuit. Take sculpture. The accumbens and prefrontal cortex are activated as you're pondering and planning what you will make. The striatum, as well as the motor cortex, directs the movement of the arms and hands and receives feedback from the prefrontal cortex as you plan each step and make judgments about the progress thus far. The real-time thoughts you need to guide this project require you to put worries aside momentarily, and the final result—the sculpture—reinforces the idea that you can use your hands to interact with the environment in purposeful, meaningful ways.

But something as mundane as housecleaning or chopping vegetables as you cook dinner can also activate the circuit. Even the most cerebral knowledge workers can benefit immensely from manual labor. Steven Knapp's academic pedigree is beyond impressive—undergraduate work at Yale, doctoral work at Cornell, a literary scholar and professor at the University of

California at Berkeley, dean and provost of Johns Hopkins University, and now president of George Washington University. Yet he enjoys balancing his cerebral life by doing manual labor on the sheep farm he and his wife own in Maryland. In fact, this college president was chosen the Maryland state champ at the state fair last year because of the quality of his sheep's fleece.

Knapp told the *Washington Post* that he does his strategic thinking at work and manual labor on the farm. As he described wrestling with a sheep to clean its hooves, he said, "It's nice to have a spread of activity. It keeps you healthy, I think. It gives you a balance on things." Manual labor appears to be an effective, adaptive tool for keeping the toxic stress at bay in his demanding career.

Being able to access positive emotions during troubled times is an effective buffer against the anxiety that, if allowed to go unchecked, can lead to depression. Taking a drug changes some functions of the brain, but it doesn't change the context of our lives the way a change in behavior can. In fact, the benefits that a little physical effort provides are an excellent antidote to heightened stress and frustration because they occur within the actual context of our lives. And, most often, this effort involves the recruitment of muscles directing our hands, although the exceptions to this—inspirational people such as Christopher Reeve, who maintained optimism in the midst of losing control of his entire body below the neck due to his paralysis—suggest the flexibility of this system.

Anthropological evidence points to the finely tuned actions directed by our hands as a gateway to modern human behavior. This indicates that a reduction of directed hand movements to obtain important resources may be especially damaging to the extensive brain circuitry sustaining manual sensitivity and movement.

The pleasure we get from our brain's acknowledgment that we have some control over our lives and our ever-changing environment remains an extremely valuable natural commodity—something only we can generate for ourselves. Periodically reminding the brain of its ability to gain that sense of control can inoculate us against the various types of chronic stress that I discuss in the next chapter.

Indeed, engaging the effort-driven rewards circuit appears to be the equivalent of taking a preventive dose of the most powerful antidepressants—and this therapeutic intervention is free! The neurochemical cocktail that accompanies the feeling that we have accomplished something with our very own hands cannot be reproduced with drugs, surgery, or other medicinal therapies—at least not yet. As the MasterCard commercials might tout: Taking antidepressants: *thousands of dollars a year.* Experiencing effort-driven rewards: *priceless.*

5

Coping Effectively with Stress

I LOVE READING THRILLERS, and I've noticed that the criminals in them often have an accomplice. After covering this "depression beat" for the past decade, I feel confident when I point an accusatory finger at stress. By far, it's the most frequent accomplice in depression—more of an instigator than a mere sidekick.

As I've shown in previous chapters, the effort-driven rewards circuit is the prime suspect in depression. Virtually all the symptoms—from apathy to anxiety—can be traced back to this important, integrative brain network. But what about stress? What is the role of this insidious accomplice? Before I answer that question in the context of effort-driven rewards, a little background is necessary. This briefing is not for the faint of heart. I've been following this suspect for my entire career and its character is dark, complicated, and frequently unpredictable.

After decades of close surveillance of the stress response, scientists have assembled overwhelming evidence that puts stress at the neurobiological scene of the depression crime. Robert Sapolsky, a neuroscientist at Stanford University and one of this country's most distinguished stress researchers, provides several scientific observations that link stress to depression: major stressors such as the loss of a loved one typically precede the onset of depression, high levels of stress hormones are associated with depression, and approximately half of depressed people have high blood levels of stress hormones. Those who are stressed have many common symptoms of depression, including compromised problem-solving ability, fatigue, and increased anxiety. And finally, clinical and animal trials with drugs that block the release of stress hormones—such as the corticotrophin-releasing hormone antagonist antalarmin—have antidepression effects.

BUILDING THE CASE FOR THE INVOLVEMENT OF STRESS IN DEPRESSION: THE INCRIMINATING EVIDENCE

Although most of us feel that the concept of stress has been around forever, this term has been used in medicine for only a little over a half century. In the 1920s, the Harvard physiologist Walter Cannon first used the word to refer to medical conditions, but it was the Canadian physician and researcher Hans Selye who popularized the term as we understand it today.

Engineers use the term *stress* to convey a point of vulnerability, or breaking point, in worn (or stressed) materials. Selye noticed that when rats were exposed to aggravating events such as loud noises and uncomfortable temperatures, they often reached a breaking point, just like the worn metals. The mammalian version was characterized by stress ulcers, shriveled-up immune organs, and swollen adrenal glands known to secrete stress hormones.

After publishing *Stress of Life* in 1956, Selye became known as the "father" of stress. He also developed the concept known as the *general adaptation syndrome,* which suggests that everyone experiences stress in a predictable pattern. He believed there were three phases—alarm, resistance, and exhaustion. He was captivated by the general nature of this phenomenon and argued that regardless of the specific stressful experience, we all experience the same series of neurobiological responses. No matter what method he used to stress his rats, they all ended up with similar sicknesses. This is the end result of activating the stress circuit of the brain, known as the hypothalamic adrenal pituitary (HPA) axis, and its release of the stress hormone corticosterone (or cortisol in humans). It takes a few minutes for the body to release this hormone, and then the axis helps redistribute the body's energy to combat the threatening situation.

A more "real-time" stress circuit also releases another stress neurochemical, adrenaline. Think about what happens when you just miss rear-ending the car in front of you. You feel the adrenaline (the chemical that controls your "fight or flight" stress response) racing through your body. Your heart feels as if it's about to explode. Today, most emergencies don't require us to fight for our lives or flee at top speed to avoid being eaten by predators, but our bodies still react as they did when our ancestors had to either fight or run.

Learning to get a handle on stress by being more mindful of our responses and coping strategies can help disrupt the stress-to-depression trajectory that seems so prevalent in our society. A team of German neuroscientists has provided compelling evidence that places both effort-driven rewards and stress at the scene when depression begins to take hold. In one of the team's studies, rats were subjected to chronic social stress by placing shy, submissive rats in little restraint holders and putting them in the cages of more aggressive, dominant rats daily for five weeks. This is the equivalent of your boss scolding you about your incompetence and questionable value to the company, and then forcing you to sit in a forlorn cubicle in his penthouse office every day for a month. Even if there were no more altercations, the mere sight of this domineering boss would likely trigger an unrelenting stress response each day.

In the rat study, this pure form of psychological stress—merely worrying about being attacked by the mean rat—did a number on the effort-driven rewards circuit. To determine whether the chronic stress in the rats' lives compromised their ability to experience pleasure and reward, the researchers gave the rats an opportunity to drink sugar water in addition to their plain water. The rats had two bottles in their cages at all times and could drink from either of them once they were returned to their home cages each day. Would stress make the rats drink less of the sucrose water or send them running to the bottle to make their emotional pain go away?

After about three weeks, the results were clear. The control rats, who'd experienced no social stress, maintained stable levels of sucrose consumption, but the stressed rats' consumption was drastically reduced. This pursuit of diminishing rewards was explained by a malfunctioning in the rats' brain reward system directed by the nucleus accumbens. The researchers found that physical exertion was compromised as well. The stressed rats proved less active in various tests.

Effort-driven rewards, in this case in the form of drinking sweet water, were reduced after facing weeks of unrelenting stress. Drinking the sugar water no longer seemed worth the effort. New situations that had once provoked lively curiosity all of a sudden seemed too risky to investigate. In other words, chronic stress was compromising the behavioral expression of effort-driven rewards, providing convincing evidence that chronic stress can lead to depression.

MOVE OVER, SELYE: THERE ARE NEW STRESS CONCEPTS IN TOWN!

Selye, who died in 1982, continues to be celebrated in biomedical texts for his pioneering contributions to the field of stress research. But my training as a psychologist and behavioral neuroscientist compels me to consider other ways of looking at the stress response. Contrary to Selye's fascination with general responses, I am more interested in individual differences among mammals of the same species because this strategy seems to point toward key factors that underlie different coping strategies.

In addition to being genetically similar, the rats in my lab have been exposed to the same or comparable environments for their entire lives. Despite these similarities, I'm always amazed at how varied their behavioral responses are to the challenges I throw their way. Several years ago, I asked one of my students, Tom Campbell, to expose three male rats in turn to a cotton ball soaked in fox urine, a natural predator odor for these rats even though they've never encountered a fox in their sheltered lives.

One rat started digging around the bedding of the cage, eventually covering up the cotton and its offensive odor. The second rat shredded the cotton ball and proceeded to stuff the remaining pieces in the top of the cage. And the last rat simply froze as if the fox were waiting to pounce on anything that moved. It's tempting to speculate about the advantages and disadvantages of each of these responses to this stressful situation, but to my mind, what was interesting was that the responses were all so different.

In humans, the response tends to be equally varied. On a trip to Whistler, British Columbia, my husband and I took our daughters zip-trekking, an extreme sport involving clamping yourself to a cable that runs between giant hemlock and Douglas fir trees. At two hundred feet above the beautiful landscape, you "zip" along at a speed of approximately thirty-five miles per hour. Although my children have somewhat similar genetic constitutions—they have the same parents and were raised in the same household—the variability in their responses was fascinating. Skylar, then eight, had a grin from ear to ear as she zipped along the course. Lara, twelve, was much more cautious and tentative about flinging her body off the stand to glide above the river—and for good reason!

One could certainly argue that my twelve-year-old's brain was more mature than my younger daughter's, and maturity could easily have played a role here. But I think there's more at work. As we described our adventures to adult friends upon our return, all with mature prefrontal cortices, some smiled and said they'd love to go themselves, while others declared, "You couldn't pay me enough money to do that!" This suggests that the stress response may be considerably less general than Selye originally proposed, because it indicates that mammals have some degree of flexibility in how they react to life's challenges. In addition to biological predispositions that lead to varying stress responses, the situations we find ourselves in also influence how we react.

Spit Happens!

Recently, I designed an activity for one of my freshman classes to explore the effects of stress in our lives. I took the students to an indoor rock-climbing facility so that they could climb a fifty-foot wall, stand on a very tiny platform, and then jump to a dangling horizontal trapeze bar. Although we were all equipped with the appropriate climbing gear and were being belayed from below, this activity, known as the "leap of faith," was terrifying. The small trapeze appeared so high and far away, it literally seemed as if you would plummet to the ground.

As I observed my students trying to complete this task, I once again saw dramatic evidence of variation in the stress response. Some students scampered up the walls, stood on the platform, and jumped to the bar without hesitation. Their stress response did not interfere with what they had to do. Some climbed up the wall but stood on the small platform for several minutes before mustering the courage to jump. Others climbed up onto the platform, then planted their derrieres on it until they were gently coaxed back down the wall. Talking them into jumping for the bar was impossible. Some students lost their nerve on the climb up and headed down before even attempting to reach the platform.

As each student returned to the ground, I asked him or her to chew on a sterile piece of dental rope for about a minute—enough time to generate a good bit of saliva—and then place it in a plastic tube. The idea was to measure their levels of the stress hormone cortisol. But even before I analyzed the saliva, I could see that they all experienced the "flight or fight" first response stress reaction: their hands were shaking so much that some of them had trouble putting the dental rope back in the tubes. I admit that my hands were just as shaky following my "leap of faith."

I compared the stress hormone levels after the leap-of-faith experience to saliva collected during a more relaxing moment in class. This allowed my students to observe firsthand how external environmental manipulations influence internal hormones. This class experiment provided strong evidence that even the perception of jumping to a certain death stimulated considerably more stress hormones than sitting quietly in class!

True to the complex nature of the stress response, there are exceptions to the stress hormone story. Some studies do *not* show a strong relation between cortisol levels and depression. And perhaps the biggest mystery involves post-traumatic stress disorder. Although it seems logical that the heightened anxiety following certain traumas would be accompanied by high levels of stress hormones, this does not appear to be the case. In fact, some studies have reported low levels of cortisol. As you'll see in the next section, neuroscientists are adopting novel ways of envisioning the stress response; perhaps these new strategies will illuminate important aspects of this response.

THE NEW NORMAL

Recently, a new concept, *allostasis*, has received much attention from several distinguished researchers. Allostasis is related to the more familiar term *homeostasis*, the tendency for biological systems to remain the same, or in balance, throughout our lives. When the balance in our physiological systems is disrupted, the result is stress to our body. According to earlier research, we relieve that stress by returning to balance.

The problem with this classic theory is that there aren't many physiological systems that have a single optimal level. There are a few—body temperature is one—but for the most part, variable responses are more desirable. Indeed, there appears to be an abundance of variation in important physiological systems throughout our body, and a more successful response is to allow our bodies to fluctuate in response to varying challenges.

Most likely, as you read this book, your heart does not need to be very active. But if all of a sudden you remember that you should have taken the muffins out of the oven ten minutes ago, you'll need a more active heart to pump increased blood and energy to your muscles so you can sprint into the kitchen to salvage your breakfast. It's your body's ability to change your heart rate to initiate and maintain the behavior you need the most at a given time that is at the essence of the term *allostasis*.

Allostasis refers to the body's ability to maintain stability through change and emphasizes the way ever-changing biological systems—rather than homeostatic systems—effectively respond to life's challenges. When you need to dash to scoop up your four-year-old before a swing hits him, your heart rate increases; when you walk slowly holding your sobbing child to console him, your heart rate decreases. The ease at which our heart rate, and the plethora of other physiological systems maintaining our bodies, can fluctuate from one level of response to another characterizes allostasis working at its best.

When our bodies are forced to work overtime in responding to many daily challenges, we experience *allostatic load*. If your heart rate takes several hours to calm down long after you know your child is safe, the added cardiac stress represents a hefty cost to your cardiovascular health. If two swimmers are treading water, the one exerting less energy will be able to survive much longer than the person who flails wildly underneath the water. On the surface, two people can look the same, but it's what's happening below the surface that determines the body's success at maintaining stability. Thus, avoiding allostatic load is key to adapting to stress and, ultimately, as I'll describe throughout the rest of the book, building resilience against depression.

Bruce McEwen of the Rockefeller Institute and other neuroscientists have written that allostasis clarifies some of the ambiguity inherent in the more traditional stress concept. Indeed, the concept of allostatic load means that it's possible to cope with life's stressors in adaptive ways. We can view the physical effort that leads to effort-driven rewards as a successful coping strategy because it has the potential to allow us to continue experiencing pleasure in the midst of stressful times. Research on different coping strategies—especially more active ones that allow us to interact effectively with the world around us—suggests that we may have some control over our stress trajectories. That means we may be able to remain in Selye's resistance phase rather than progressing to the less desirable exhaustion phase of the stress response.

Stress: The Brain's Kudzu

At the 1876 Centennial Exposition held in Philadelphia, onlookers were fascinated by the exotic Japanese garden on display, especially the large leaves and sweet-smelling blooms known as kudzu. Later, in the 1920s, this plant was touted for its potential to control soil erosion and as foraging material for animals. The radio host Channing Cope referred to kudzu as "the miracle vine" on his daily broadcast and in frequent articles in the *Atlanta Journal-Constitution*.

Kudzu's popularity declined in the 1950s for the simple reason that it just grew too well in the southeastern United States. Apparently, this geographical area provided a perfect climate, allowing the vine to grow as much as a foot per day in the summer. When the kudzu vines started growing over power lines and choking trees, it prompted James Miller, a research forest ecologist with the U.S. Department of Agriculture Forest Service on the campus of Auburn University, to look for herbicides to kill it. To his dismay, one herbicide only enhanced the growth rate while most others had little effect. It seemed virtually impossible to eradicate kudzu from the region. I remember as a child seeing mile after mile of this hearty vine, leaving no doubt that kudzu had become a permanent fixture of Alabama's landscape.

So what does this ubiquitous vine have to do with stress? Just as kudzu was an aesthetically pleasing plant that played an important role in its native Japan (where climate and predators could keep it at bay), acute or short-term stress in our lives is adaptive and allows us to recognize and respond to threats efficiently. An increase in your heart rate and level of stress hormones can even be enjoyable at times, enhancing certain events with adrenaline-laden excitement. How much fun would it be to win the lottery if your reaction were merely to accept the check and slowly walk away, showing absolutely no emotion?

Adrenaline-rich emotional reactions help emphasize the important events in our lives in our long-term memories, so we'll remember forever our first kiss, the conferring of that hard-earned degree, the wedding of our dreams, or the thrilling births of our children. Most would agree that stress is an important component of our emotional gardens, providing both protection and enjoyment at the appropriate times.

But if stress is so good for us, why do we keep hearing that it's toxic to our mental and physical health? The answer lies in the difference between acute (short-term) stress and chronic (long-term) stress. Robert Sapolsky, a biologist, eloquently described the distinction in his book *Why Zebras Don't Get Ulcers.* Zebras experience plenty of stress in their lives as they run across the African plains to avoid being eaten by lions. But, characteristic of acute stress, their stress response appears to end as soon as the threat has passed.

If a man were placed in the zebra's situation, however, he would probably exhibit chronic stress. Thanks to an advanced cerebral cortex, he'd constantly worry about where the lions were, when they were going to attack, and whether he was the weakest link in the herd. Of course, we don't need physical threats to feel stressed. Obsessing about an approaching deadline at work can activate the chronic stress switch. This "evolved" response comes with a hefty price tag for our brain and body.

Just like kudzu, stress can sometimes take root and grow heartily—too heartily—in our emotional lives. The important acute stress response that evolved in mammals to enhance survival found fertile ground in the human limbic and forebrain areas. As our species became more attuned to how changes in the environment affected our well-being, chronic stress in the form of toxic cognitive responses such as hypervigilance, worry, or dread took firm root in our emotional gardens. This was the chronic, long-term stress, due to artificial laboratory manipulations, that Selye observed in his rats—and it's the same in humans. If we continue to have high levels of anxiety for extended periods of time, we develop similar threats to our health and well-being. Allostatic load leads to the wear and tear on the brain and compromised delivery of valuable oxygen and glucose for the brain's functioning—all of which increases our vulnerability to depression.

Most research on the effects of chronic stress on the brain is focused on the hippocampus. This large structure is an essential part of the brain's emotional limbic circuit, but it also plays an important role in learning and memory. Like a meticulously planned garden with different rows of distinctly varying flora, the hippocampus contains rows of cells known as pyramidal cells (reflecting their pyramid shape) around its periphery and granule cells (more shrub-shaped) in its interior portion known as the dentate gyrus. Ever since the dentate gyrus was discovered to be a hotbed of the production of new cells throughout our lives, it's received celebrity status among neuroscientists. While it was once thought that all new cells were formed only in prenatal development, neuroscientists have now shown that thousands of new granule cells are produced in the hippocampus each day.

Just as trees covered by kudzu become unrecognizable and die after being deprived of the resources necessary for growth, chronic stress also changes the topography of the brain's hippocampus because it alters the arborization of the complex branches of the pyramidal cells. In the early 1990s, Bruce McEwen, a neuroscientist, working with Catherine Woolley and Elizabeth Gould, found that the rat stress hormone equivalent of cortisol, when injected over a twenty-one-day period, led to fewer and less elaborate branchings of the brain cells in the hippocampus. A similar finding was observed when rats were exposed to daily stress in the form of restraint, which rats resist. In fact, my students and I have shown that just five days of chronic stress in rats reduced the branching points of hippocampal neurons.

This restructuring has also been observed in people who have experienced chronic stress associated with depression. Brain imaging studies of previously depressed individuals reveal hippocampal shrinkage in the range of 8 to 19 percent. Similar findings have been observed in those suffering from post-traumatic stress disorder, as well as Cushing's disease, a condition that leads to the oversecretion of stress hormones.

Scientists have still not identified the exact cause of the stress-induced shrinkage of the hippocampus. Some believe it's due to the excessive excitation of the affected neurons, known as excitotoxicity. It has also been hypothesized that although stress hormones themselves are not toxic, they weaken the neurons so that they become more vulnerable to threats such as low levels of oxygen or glucose.

The hypothesis that's receiving the most attention, however, is that chronic stress and its associated hormones and neurochemicals that inhibit neurogenesis decrease the number of new neurons produced in the hippocampus. When Elizabeth Gould, a neuroscientist at Princeton University who was instrumental in demonstrating that neurogenesis occurs throughout our lifetime, examined the effects of chronic stress on the brain, she found that neurons cease investing in their production and growth. That is, neurogenesis comes to a screeching halt, which contributes to the demise of the hippocampus. In other words, chronic stress appears not only to suffocate existing neurons in the hippocampus, it decreases the rate at which new neurons in this area are produced.

Given the critical role this area of the brain plays in learning, memory, and emotional responses, plus the inputs and outputs it has leading to the effort-driven brain reward circuit, the hippocampus is undeniably a key player in the depression response.

The connection between neurogenesis and depression is still not fully understood. But the finding that antidepressant drugs raise the rate of new cell growth strengthens the idea that neurogenesis plays a role in depression. Thus, the time lag observed between taking an SSRI and evidence of improvement in depression symptoms suggests that the key mechanism of these drugs may be the more time-consuming, indirect effect of altered neurogenesis rates, rather than the more immediate effects antidepressants have on serotonin levels.

As I mentioned earlier, one other depression treatment has been shown to generate new cell growth. Electroconvulsant seizures in animals (serving as a model for electroconvulsive shock therapy sometimes used to treat depression) also leads to increased rates of neurogenesis in the hippocampus. But a few nagging details suggest that other factors may be involved. A promising new treatment for depression known as transcranial magnetic stimulation (TMS), which consists of placing a very strong magnet on the outside of the skull, has not produced altered rates of neurogenesis in rodent models of depression.

So what do we conclude from this sometimes confusing line of research? It is important to acknowledge that depression is probably a multifaceted condition influenced by several neurobiological variables. A good deal of current research supports the idea that stress-induced alterations in neurogenesis play a role in depressive symptoms. Whatever decreases the prevalence of chronic stress in our lives, such as gaining control of our environment through effort-driven rewards, provides protection against the onset of depression.

Further evidence of how significantly stress affects the health of our brains can be found in a study conducted by

Kristen Brunson and her colleagues at the University of California at Irvine. Trying to mimic the impoverished conditions some human children endure, researchers placed mother rats in substandard cages with only a paper towel, instead of traditional bedding, for one week following the arrival of their pups. This resulted in disrupted maternal care for the newborns, as the moms appeared distracted and failed to provide adequate grooming and nursing.

What effect did just one week of disrupted care have on the long-term mental health of these rodent offspring? It depended on their age. As adults (four to five months of age), the rats were subjected to a battery of learning and emotional tests, and the results were encouraging. No behavioral differences were observed between the postnatal stressed and control groups. But the animals were not home free. Another round of testing at one year of age, constituting middle age for a rat, revealed an entirely different story. At this stage, the previously impoverished rats showed severe deficits in their ability to learn new tasks. Researchers also found changes in the structure and function of the hippocampus. This was one of the first studies to provide evidence that even a short period of stress early in life may lead to delayed impairments of the hippocampus and result in an increased vulnerability to mental illness later in adulthood.

The long-term effects of early stress have been confirmed in humans. Research that focused on the stress response of women exposed to early childhood abuse, conducted by Christine Heim at Emory University, indicated that decades after the abuse, these women had exaggerated stress responses.

These findings have huge implications, emphasizing the importance of providing children with adequate care from day one. They also remind us that although it may appear that a child has beaten the odds if he or she appears symptom-free early on, the long-term effects of adverse experiences may become apparent later in life in the form of depression or other anxiety and/or learning disorders.

I mentioned earlier that stress is sometimes unpredictable. Karen Parker and her colleagues at Stanford University witnessed that unpredictable nature firsthand by documenting a positive outcome to short-term stress. To test whether a moderate dose of disruption diminished or exacerbated the stress response in squirrel monkeys, the researchers removed offspring from the mothers' care for a brief period. When rat pups are returned to their mothers after a separation, the moms immediately step up their grooming. But the squirrel monkey moms in this study did not increase their maternal attention toward their offspring following their return.

What became apparent was that the mild stress of being periodically separated from their mothers had more impact on the youngsters than whether they received more attention from mom. No doubt, maternal attention and nurturing are important, but the presence of an occasional manageable stressor early in a primate's life seems to serve as a "stress inoculation" of sorts, promoting stress resilience in the primate brain. When they were exposed to a novelty stress test, the previously stressed primates responded with lower stress hormones.

Later, we'll examine the idea that small doses of stress lead to subsequent stress resilience. But like kudzu in the southeastern United States, once chronic stress takes root in the brain, it's extremely difficult to eradicate the effects from its neuronal soil. The heartiness of the roots of stress deprives the brain's neurons of the sustenance they need to enable us to thrive in our constantly changing and demanding environments. So we need strategies that help us mitigate the ever-present stress response in order to maintain an emotionally healthy life.

In Search of the Best Coping Strategies

The idea of coping with stress became a popular concept in the 1960s when the cardiologists Meyer Friedman and Ray Rosenman categorized patients into Type A or Type B responders. Type As, with their competitive, high-achieving, time-conscious personalities, were more likely to develop cardiovascular disease than their relaxed Type B counterparts.

Subsequent studies by Redford B. Williams, professor of psychology and neuroscience at Duke University, challenged the Type A/B distinction as the crucial behavioral factor in heart disease. Instead, his research pointed to hostility—which often accompanies Type A behavior—as the most toxic coping strategy. Hostile people consistently respond to stressors with the intensity of running from a burning building: blood vessels become visible, the face becomes deep red, teeth are bared. When I viewed news clips of the famed basketball coach Bobby Knight slinging chairs across the gymnasium and screaming at a referee, I had little doubt that Knight consistently responded in a hostile manner, at least when he was coaching. This intense response may work when fighting off a dangerous assailant, but for the day-to-day aggravations in our lives, it's safe to say that reacting in this manner is over the top. If not squelched, it will likely lead to a toxic allostatic load because it takes longer than usual for the cardiovascular system to recover from such persistent emotional mayhem.

So how do we diffuse or slough off anxiety? Research with serotonin levels by Barry Jacobs, a professor of psychology at

Princeton University, suggests that movement may help reduce stress in more active animals. He found that cats that pace back and forth and engage in other forms of basic motor responses had more activity in the neurons that secrete serotonin, the neurotransmitter that has most often been implicated in the onset of depression. In fact, Jacobs has written that the primary function of serotonin neurons is to facilitate gross motor output, especially by stimulating movement and maintaining repetitive movement.

Farm animals that engage in repetitive movement (stereotypies) have been shown to develop fewer stress ulcers than more passive animals. The more active coping strategies in these animals apparently alter how the stress response affects the body.

Repetitive movements such as pacing back and forth while waiting for a friend to arrive, chewing gum, or swinging one's leg to and fro while taking an anxiety-producing final exam may be effective ways of calming our emotions during difficult moments. Because the effects of these repetitive movements are more immediate than taking SSRIs, there are likely different mechanisms accounting for their short-term calming effects. In fact, people with obsessive-compulsive disorder (OCD), who repeat movements over and over, may be engaging in a form of self-medication. Given the fact that the movement circuit is so closely integrated into the effort-driven rewards circuit, it's easy to imagine how the movement in OCD cases may reduce stress levels by both increasing serotonin and reducing stress hormones, as well as increasing one's sense of control over a situation.

When it comes to maintaining mental health, most researchers focus on coping strategies to handle traumatic events. But I prefer to focus on the day-to-day stressors in our lives. A groundbreaking study conducted by Sonja Cavigelli and Martha McClintock, both at the University of Chicago at the time, also opted for this approach. Rather than exposing rats to severe acute stress such as swimming or shock, these researchers merely exposed rats to novel stimuli—rocks and toys placed in their cages.

Their experiment involved giving brothers—who were the same age, very similar genetically, and living in the same environment—a coping test by simply assessing their behavioral response to a new object. The brothers that investigated the stimulus were assigned to the uninhibited/bold group and the ones that refrained from exploring the new stimulus were assigned to the inhibited/shy group. The researchers assessed their stress hormones during subsequent stress encounters and found that the bold rats' stress hormones returned to baseline much faster than the shy rats'.

This test was continued every six months for the duration of the rats' lives so that the consistency of the response, as well as the effect of the coping response on longevity, could be determined. The bold rats retained their bold responses throughout their lives, constantly investigating new objects in their environment, whereas the shy rats continued to keep their distance from these objects. Their stress hormone patterns also remained consistent, likely contributing to the amazing finding that the bold rats lived 27 percent longer than their shy brothers.

When I saw the results of this study presented at a conference several years ago, I was stopped in my tracks as I looked at a photo of a pair of rat brothers. The shy rat looked very old, with unkempt fur and weak-looking posture, while the same-aged bold brother looked like a young adult, about six months old. The differences in their health during old age were beyond dramatic.

These findings are profound. An animal's responses to little stressors it encounters every day are just as crucial to the mental health equation as its response to significant trauma. But it's also important to remind ourselves that this study assessed animals in the unnatural environment of the laboratory. In the "real" world, the bold rats may have been eaten by predators long before they benefited from their more efficient stress responses. If the rats had been humans, the bold ones would probably have died in motorcycle accidents before their shy counterparts died of anxiety-related disease. Still, all things being equal, this study eloquently shows us just how important stress hormones are throughout our lives.

As described later in this chapter and in chapter 7, this research prompted me to shift the focus in my laboratory to coping strategies in the midst of life's annoying little stressors—and the results have been very interesting. My students and I hope that these animal models of coping will stimulate more research in humans, identifying the most effective coping strategies and their underlying neurobiological mechanisms. The first step in reshaping our research toward coping strategies was influenced by some Danish piglets and several innovative researchers.

Willem Schouten and his colleagues at the University of Groningen, in Denmark, held young piglets on their backs, keeping them in a supine position for a mere minute to observe their responses. Piglets that resisted the restraint by fighting back and trying to escape were categorized as "active" or resistant copers, whereas those that didn't try to escape were classified as "passive" or nonresistant copers. Generally, the more active coping pigs were less inhibited and bolder than the passive ones when placed in novel environments. Additionally, the active copers had lower levels of baseline cortisol values.

Although evidence supports the notion that the more active copers gained more control over their environments, it troubled me that the intense reactions associated with this strategy could very likely lead to allostatic load down the line. Of course, more passive copers had their problems, too, considering their much higher stress hormones levels. Clearly, there are times we need to respond and other times when we need to hold back—meaning that both active and passive responders were losing out. Perhaps a more flexible coping response—one more in tune with the specific situation at hand—is the most effective one.

A dramatic example of the danger associated with having a coping strategy that's out of step with the extenuating circumstances can be found in an experiment assessing the temperament styles of guppies. They were categorized as timid (high anxiety), normal, and bold. Three days after being placed in a tank with a predator bass, 40 percent of the timid guppies remained compared to a dramatically lower 15 percent survival rate of the more active "normal" guppies. But not one of the bold guppies survived!

We can all appreciate the value of restraint during stressful situations. We bite our tongues to keep from verbally lashing out at an annoying colleague or refrain from using our car horns, hurling insults, or making certain hand gestures to convey our annoyance at a driver who won't let us merge from a quickly disappearing lane. Sometimes an active response is appropriate during stressful times, and sometimes, as demonstrated by the hapless guppies, it's much more effective to be passive.

In a recent theoretical article, Mechiel Korte and Jaap Koolhass, stress researchers from the Netherlands, joined John

Wingfield and Bruce McEwen, from the United States, to explore active and passive response styles to stress. They referred to the more active stress copers as *hawks* and the more passive ones as *doves*. Hawks are more likely to be aggressive, leading to impulse-control disorders. They are also more prone to hypertension, atypical depression, chronic fatigue states, inflammation, and sudden death. Doves, on the other hand, are more susceptible to metabolic syndromes, melancholic depression, anxiety disorders, psychosis, and infections.

I don't know about you, but neither the hawk nor the dove strategy sounds especially appealing. Is there a middle-of-the-road responder? I'm no ornithologist, so my knowledge here is limited, but the famous cartoon character Tweety Bird immediately comes to mind. He might be viewed as a passive, meek bird. But when the situation called for it, he always demonstrated creative responses to his dangerous predicaments, most often the threat of becoming dinner for the mischievous cat Sylvester. The more I thought about the disadvantages of the hawk and dove coping styles, the better the more flexible and effective coping model looked.

THE FLEXIBLE ADVANTAGE

Undergraduate students Kelly Tu and Darby Fleming spearheaded research in my laboratory indicating that neither active nor passive coping strategies are ideal. Like the pigs in the Dutch experiment, freshly weaned rat pups showed great variability in their responses to being gently restrained on their backs for one minute. Some vocalized and squirmed repeatedly, while others made no attempts to escape this stressful situation. Interestingly, when we repeated this exercise a week later, about 20 to 30 percent of the animals switched coping strategies. Some of the passive rats decided to fight and a few of the active ones seemed to accept the fact that they couldn't escape so they endured the minute of restraint with little movement. Thus, after the second test, we ended up with consistently passive and active subsets, as well as a flexible group. In other words, we had our hawks, doves, and Tweety Birds.

Our next step was to assess how responsive these coping strategies were. When the rats were exposed to a chronic stress situation known as activity-stress, we saw notable differences in how they coped. When we placed them on restrictive feeding schedules and housed them in activity wheels, the flexible and active rats ran more than the passives when responding to the stress, running several thousand revolutions each day. But the flexibles had drastically lower stress hormone levels—roughly 50 percent of either the consistently passive and active animals. Although both active and flexible copers ran excessively during this experiment, the active group's stress responsiveness was more intense and likely more toxic.

In another study, we exposed the rats to mild stressors, such as placing one of my daughter's tiny hair clips on their tails to simulate a bug bite. The flexible copers were the most vigorous in trying to remove the clip from their tails. Under other stressful conditions, however, we found the flexibles were not necessarily more active than the other coping groups. It all depended on the situation. Considering how toxic high stress hormone levels are to the brain's hippocampus and the effects on the effort-driven rewards circuit, we were intrigued by this finding.

We're currently looking at the effects of coping strategies on cardiovascular responses and brain activation, especially in the hippocampus. Our most recent results suggest that after being exposed to mild stressors in an unpredictable pattern for a few weeks (a less intense version of chronic stress), the flexible copers have lower systolic blood pressure measures, suggesting less allostatic load and stress-related toxicity than the others.

What's the take-home message? Our research suggests that as our environments have become increasingly complex, a "default" coping strategy of active or passive is probably not as adaptive as one that's more sensitive to the nuances of the situation. I'm still curious about the differences between the active and flexible copers. Since the behavioral responses were the same in these two groups, what defining variable led to lower stress hormones in the flexible group? Did they have stronger associations between effort (running in this case) and consequences, leading to a heightened sense of control? This is difficult to determine in the rats. However, an increased perception of control over the stressors in our lives seems to be linked to more effective coping strategies in humans.

Don't Let Stress Take Your Brain Hostage!

Just watching the news every night inundates us with stress. Each evening there's a new set of local, national, and international tragedies and threats. And in case we didn't absorb all the details of a stressful story the first time, we're bound to see the news clips over and over again. Although stress is pervasive in our lives, the most intense forms involve situations in which you lose all sense of control over your life.

When the journalist Terry Anderson was kidnapped by Shiite Hezbollah partisans during the Lebanese civil war in 1985, he began an intense, chronically stressful experience that would last a grueling seven years. In his memoir, *Den of Lions*,

Anderson describes his mental agony during his seemingly endless time as a hostage. Amazingly, since his release in 1991, he has written a best-selling book, taught journalism courses at the Columbia Graduate School of Journalism and at the E. W. Scripps School of Journalism at Ohio University, and been a frequent media guest, columnist, and advocate for political and charitable causes. He opened a blues bar, started training horses on his ranch, and even ran for the Ohio state senate in 2003. His behavior shows no sign of depression or residual mental illness, indicating an impressive recovery from his captivity.

It's likely that most of us would not have survived this stressful experience as well. Anderson spent most of his time as a hostage chained to a cot, yet he behaved as if he never lost his sense of control. He never stopped trying to communicate with the other hostages and even his captors, and he sought social contact from a mouse when no humans were around. He kept track of passing days, exercised by pacing back and forth in his tiny chamber and lifting water jugs, cleaned his body whenever he was around water, and engaged his mind by recalling Biblical scriptures and other material he had memorized throughout his life. He even kept his sense of humor, as he taught a guard to "speak English" by giving him the wrong words, such as saying the word "cup" each time he picked up the Bible. While others may have lost all sense of control and succumbed to stress-related physical and mental illnesses, Anderson responded with amazing resilience, probably enhanced by his effective coping strategies.

The importance of retaining one's sense of control during stressful situations is also apparent in the Italian movie *Life Is Beautiful* (*La Vita è bella*). In this film about the German occupation of Italy during World War II, Guido, a bookseller, falls in love with the beautiful Dora and they have a son, Joshua. Guido's exuberant life turns into a tragedy when the family is placed in a Nazi death camp. When the movie came out in 1998, it was considered controversial because of its somewhat whimsical portrayal of this nightmare. But the coping strategy Guido employed for the benefit of his son was extremely touching. To minimize his son's fear during this horrific time, Guido described the situation to the boy as a game in which they had all the control, and if they won the game they would get to ride in a tank. He explained three scenarios that would lead to losing the game, including if the child cried, asked to see his mama, and whined about being hungry.

This unique movie demonstrates the potent effect of gaining a sense of control even in the most stressful situations. Although Guido understood the likely consequences of their captivity in the concentration camp, his "game" provided Joshua with a priceless emotional gift that ultimately made the boy less afraid.

What most of us encounter on a daily basis is undoubtedly a more scaled-down, realistic version of stress. If we can gain a sense of control over our perceptions and responses, we are less likely to develop the illnesses associated with being either a hawk or a dove. Increasingly, it appears that a more informed response to stressful situations, rather than a merely reflexive one, makes the difference between mental health and mental illness. For one thing, it turns out that a little social support along the way can also drastically reduce the toxic stress response. In the next chapter, I'll talk more about the mental health benefits of positive social responses and their potential value for coping responses.

6

Our Social Brains

I'M NOT IN the movie industry, but if I'd received a film script describing the saga of a man stranded on an island who finds psychological strength through conversations with a confidant named Wilson, I'd probably be intrigued enough to keep reading. However, once I learned that the confidant was actually a Wilson volleyball that had washed ashore in a FedEx package, I probably would have laughed and tossed the script in the garbage.

Of course, I'd have passed up the chance to make the critically acclaimed movie *Cast Away*. Tom Hanks was nominated for an Oscar for his impressive performance as a castaway who survived his consuming loneliness by having philosophical conversations with a volleyball. Chuck, Hanks's character, did what any self-respecting human would do—he produced a friend via the power of his prefrontal cortex and proceeded to have meaningful social contact with this unique companion.

Our neurobiological wiring enabled us to accept this plot when it was played out on the big screen, even though at first glance the story line seems ridiculous. In fact, when I saw the movie, I never felt the dialogue was odd at all. When Chuck lost Wilson at sea as he was trying to get back to civilization, I felt as if he'd just lost his best friend, too. The reason this plot was so believable to moviegoers—beyond the deft acting of Hanks—goes back to our evolutionary roots.

Paul MacLean, who I described in chapter 3, has argued that the characteristics that separate mammals from reptiles are all social—including play, verbal and audio communications, and maternal behavior. Indeed, our brains are hardwired for social contact and communication. When we are deprived of this psychological sustenance, our stress gauges let us know that something is drastically wrong. Depression may soon follow.

We can use positive social contact throughout our lives to reduce the intensity of the stress responses that generate depression. In chapter 1, I described a study that showed that interpersonal therapy was just as effective as antidepressants in treating depression. This therapeutic approach focuses on strengthening relations with one's family and friends as well as showing patients how to maintain these relationships so that they have adequate social support.

Much of the research on the consequences of social isolation has been conducted on older populations. In a study conducted at the University of Porto in Portugal, about a thousand people sixty-five or older were assessed. Researchers reported that the feeling of loneliness was "the single most important predictor of psychological distress, and not knowing neighbors increases the probability of depression." A second study, conducted at the University College London, looked at twenty-six hundred able-bodied people sixty-five or older and found that more than 15 percent were at risk for social isolation. In further analyses, social isolation was associated with depressed mood as well as other problems related to poor health.

The brain areas involved in sustained social interactions overlap with the areas that comprise the effort-driven rewards circuit, thus tapping into the reward, movement, and thought centers of the brain. Our hands, which play such a significant role in maintaining so many critical interactions with our world, are also vital for social interactions. How we engage with others is the mainstay of our survival as a species in terms of reproduction and parental success.

The most valuable social currency we have is the natural touch dictated by our brains as they engage the effort-driven rewards circuit. We use touch to initiate, direct, and interpret meaningful encounters with friends, lovers, parents, children, pets, and the world around us. The mythological Greek figure Midas was admired because of his Midas Touch—everything he touched turned to gold. In many ways, human touch is even more vital to our well-being and happiness. Our contact and connection with others is the real Midas Touch. Without it, our physical and mental lives can fall apart.

CAN WE TALK?

Anthropologists continue to debate the driving forces that shaped the modern human species. In addition to walking upright and using tools, the emergence of language as a social vehicle is also considered one of the evolutionary events that contributed to our distinct humanness. As discussed in chapter 4, the brain's language center is located in proximity to the cortical areas controlling the hands, and consequently, some scientists believe our ability to use language may be intimately connected to conveying information about the intricate use of the hands to generate and use tools.

Still, no one knows definitively what the evolutionary purpose of language is. Robin Dunbar, an evolutionary biologist at the University of Liverpool, has conducted research suggesting that the contemporary human brain favors the use of language for social endeavors, not communicating technical information. His research strategy? He simply eavesdropped on everyday conversations. Einstein and Descartes may have used language to transmit technically complex information, but Dunbar found that the majority of participants in his studies talked about social relationships. In fact, two-thirds of the content of conversations he observed were dedicated to gossip!

Using our sophisticated language skills primarily to gossip may seem shallow. But in his book *Grooming, Gossip, and the Evolution of Language,* Dunbar describes the significant role gossiping may have played in obtaining and maintaining social status. As grooming, practiced extensively by our primate cousins, fell by the evolutionary wayside, gossip may have filled the niche. Most of us don't feel comfortable establishing social trust by picking dander off our friend's scalp, but we're perfectly at ease engaging in a conversation filled with gossipy tidbits that strengthen his social commitment to us by diminishing the status of someone else in our social group.

Though language has replaced earlier forms of social grooming, there's no denying that social touch remains a vital part of human social interaction. And once again, our hands play a pivotal role. The evidence lies in our anatomy. As I've noted, the largest component of our motor cortex, part of the highly evolved cortex associated with the movement of our bodies, is devoted to the movement of our hands. We use them to engage in the bulk of our social contact—shaking hands, running our fingers through a loved one's hair, or patting a friend on the back after a brief hug.

Touch is the first sensory system to develop in animals. The somatosensory cortex, a strip lying behind the motor cortex, is devoted to monitoring the sense of touch throughout the body's two square meters of skin. In addition to keeping our biological fluids contained inside our bodies—and keeping out threatening pathogens—this massive amount of skin also lets our brains know who or what may be in contact with our body. Similar to the layout of the motor cortex, the brain has devoted most of its somatosensory brain real estate to the interpretation of touch occurring on the hands, face, and mouth.

The evolutionary significance of touch and social contact can be seen when these important variables are taken away from us. Research conducted over the past decade by my colleague Susan Parker and her collaborators have monitored the growth and maturation of institutionalized children in Romania. The critical importance of social contact in terms of physical and mental health is painfully evident in boys and girls who are in their late teens but look no older than five or six. Although these children had adequate nutrition as they grew up, they lacked the social contact typical of most loving maternal-infant relationships. This psychosocial dwarfism leaves no doubt that nurturing forms of touch are just as important for the body and brain's proper growth as other nutrients.

A curious little rodent known as the prairie vole has also increased our understanding of social relationships. This animal has received a lot of attention by neuroscientists because of its love life. It practices monogamy for life. Meticulous research conducted by Thomas Insel, currently the director of the

National Institute of Mental Health, and Larry Young at Emory University and others has identified a few key neuropeptides— small chains of peptides in the brain, believed to be responsible for maintaining the strong social bonds in the prairie voles. Specifically, researchers looked at the areas of the brain that were responding to oxytocin, a neuropeptide mostly known for its role in birth and lactation, but which also plays critical roles in building social bonds and reducing the stress response. They found that the components of the effort-driven rewards circuit—the nucleus accumbens, striatum, and prefrontal cortex—lit up like a Christmas tree in these extremely social prairie voles, especially when they interacted and touched.

Sue Carter, a neurobiologist at the University of Illinois, Chicago, has also conducted extensive work with this interesting little rodent. She and her colleagues recently reported that isolating these highly social prairie voles by housing them individually rather than in social pairs resulted in a cluster of symptoms reminiscent of depression, including increased anxiety, diminished effort to receive rewards (in the form of sugar water), and more passive and cautious responses in various behavioral tasks. She has proposed that social isolation provides an adequate model of depression in these social animals.

Effort-driven rewards and social contact appear indeed to go hand in hand in the maintenance of mental health. But, of course, the way we maintain social connections in our technically advanced society has changed radically.

JUST A CALL AWAY

In the 1980s, the telecommunications giant AT&T hired the advertising firm N. W. Ayer to design a TV ad campaign that would motivate consumers to make long-distance calls. The "reach out and touch someone" commercials that Ayer produced were wildly successful. As viewers watched grandparents share milestones with their grandchildren—hearing a baby speak his first words or a middle schooler describe her first home run—they felt compelled to call their own family members to share highlights or just hear a supportive voice.

From an evolutionary point of view, this campaign was nothing short of genius. Just as ads that target our basic motivational drives such as sex and hunger tend to be influential, these commercials resonated with our predispositions for social contact, especially the nonthreatening warmth associated with loving familial relationships.

The irony is, of course, that by using the telephone, you no longer have to have visual or tactile contact to engage in a social interaction. Instead of walking to a neighbor's house to have tea or coffee, the "reach out" campaign reminded us that all you have to do to connect is pick up the receiver.

But in reality, that's simply not enough to ensure good mental health. As physical effort has diminished over the past century, our opportunities for social contact have also diminished. The result? A double whammy for our brains. Effort-driven rewards directed toward gaining control over our environments and enhancing social contact are no longer critical for securing the resources necessary for survival. Both the motor and somatosensory cortex areas of our brains have found themselves in a brave new world, with unexpected consequences.

Of course, telecommunications have changed even more with cell phones and PDAs, such as BlackBerrys, Palm Pilots, and Treos. Does the increased convenience of electronic communications ultimately make us more social, given the fact that we're making more calls than ever before? Or has it in fact made us less social by diminishing the face-to-face communications so vital to our species? And has this influenced our mental health in any way?

A recent study of high school students in South Korea investigated the relation between cell phone use and mental health. The researchers found that the heaviest users in the study used their phones every ten minutes. And the majority of that "use" did not even require listening or talking, since text messaging was the preferred form of communication. Thus, the once highly engaging experience of social contact (handshakes, hugs, and interpretation of facial gestures, words, and intonations) has been reduced to reading a few words on a cell phone screen.

Not surprisingly, the researchers found that the heaviest users struggled with self-esteem issues and were more anxious, possibly making them more vulnerable to developing depression in the future. Studies like this certainly suggest that such diminished social contact compromises our resilience to depression.

Elizabeth Gould, a professor of psychology at Princeton University, approached the issue in a different way. In a rodent version of the study described above, she housed rats, which tend to be very social animals, one to a cage. While the isolated rats could hear and smell their neighboring rats, their social contact was greatly reduced. She found that these rats did not benefit from the effects of running exercise, although their counterparts housed with other animals did. Running typically increases neurogenesis, the creation of new cells, which we've seen is important in building resilience against depression.

This study suggests that even though these animals were engaging in activities that are highly recommended for the maintenance of mental health, the social shortcuts (the muted sounds and smells received by the rats housed in isolation) were not enough to sustain those protective benefits. An optimal social and environmental context appears to be necessary in order for the therapeutic effects of running to work.

Could these same factors influence the effectiveness of antidepressants? Perhaps depressed people experience inconsistent response rates from taking SSRIs because of their real-life contexts. Social isolation or limited interactions with others may thwart the brain's ability to respond to the medication with therapeutic effects such as enhanced neurogenesis rates.

Next, let's consider another type of social contact—an even more primal one—and its impact on components of the effort-driven rewards circuit.

MATERNAL CONTACT AND EFFORT-DRIVEN REWARDS

Being a parent is one of nature's richest social contexts. If ever a study suggested that maternal contact is rewarding, it has to be the fascinating one conducted by Joan Morrell, a neurobiologist at Rutgers University, and her colleagues. When given the choice between entering a chamber equipped to give injections of cocaine or a chamber that could produce three pups at a time, rat moms make some interesting decisions.

Eight days following the birth of their pups, moms preferred the pup chamber to the cocaine chamber. A female chose her pups over one of the most addictive and rewarding drugs. A few days later, however, the moms opted for cocaine when their pups began gaining their independence as they approached their rat adolescence period, a phenomenon many moms of teenagers can probably relate to. Subsequent studies in Morrell's lab have suggested that two components of the effort-driven rewards circuit, the prefrontal cortex and the nucleus accumbens, were activated in these pup-preferring moms.

Are the prefrontal cortical and accumbens reward areas also activated in human mothers? Research conducted by Jeffrey P. Lorberbaum, assistant professor of psychiatry at Pennsylvania State University, confirms the involvement of these effort-driven rewards circuit areas in us as well. He conducted fMRI scans on mothers as they listened to audiotapes of their own babies crying. The prefrontal cortex lit up as the moms heard their infants cry. Researchers at University College London have found that the accumbens reward area became activated when mothers merely gazed at their own children.

Of course, the importance of the movement component of the effort-driven rewards circuit is also undeniable. Retrieving, nursing, cleaning, and soothing babies involve physical effort, primarily hand movement for humans and oral-facial movement for rodents.

Paul MacLean has argued that the human female's tendency to cradle her baby with her left arm and hand over her heart (the mom's heartbeat is thought to soothe the child) led to the reliance on the right hand to continue to interact with the environment. This maternal-induced hand preference may have contributed to the bias of right-hand preferences in humans (up to 90 percent of humans are right-handed), since the ability to manipulate the world with the right hand had the evolutionary advantage of being able to "work" effectively while holding an infant with the left hand.

In fact, the extensive activation of the right cortex that controls the left hand may have influenced the functional and anatomical expansion of the right hemisphere in women, leading to a more balanced brain. The right hemisphere, generally known for its involvement in emotional processing, is likely critical in the successful care and monitoring of offspring. If, indeed, the human female's right hemisphere is pumped up from its involvement in maternal care, this may contribute to women's cognitive ruminations—typically about social interactions—a tendency that contributes to increased depression.

Social contact in the form of parental interactions appears to contribute to mental health as well. Kerstin Uvnas Moberg, a researcher at the Karolinska Institute in Stockholm, showed that although both males and females secrete the social hormone oxytocin, it's particularly important in the birth process and lactation. The increased levels of the hormone coursing through a new mother's body lead to a laundry list of health benefits, including decreased anxiety, lowered blood pressure, increased social contact, more effective digestion, reduced muscle tension, and a more efficient immune system. There's more—increased boldness and curiosity, a diminished sense of pain, facilitated learning, and a sleep-inducing calming effect in large doses. No wonder lactation is generally viewed as a brain-healthy time.

This resonates with me as I think back on the calm emotional state I experienced when I rocked my daughters as infants. The oxytocin secreted during the skin-to-skin contact of nursing and cradling a baby calms anxieties and leads to healthy physiological responses. The repetitive motion of rocking my infants probably increased the secretion of serotonin. Not only did the repetitive movement of my vocal cords as I sang lullabies produce serotonin, but the rhythm also benefited my daughters. In fact, infants in neonatal intensive care units experienced more rapid growth and faster discharge when they were exposed to the Brahms Lullaby each day.

Gazing into my little girls' eyes or seeing them looking relaxed and healthy activated my brain's reward circuit. My prefrontal cortex became engaged as I mused about the future of
my beautiful daughters—would they be scientists, doctors, authors? The brain changes associated with being a mom also produced in me a sharper, more focused and optimistic mode of
thinking. Indeed, these sweet moments were the perfect culmi-
nation of neurobiological, environmental, and social responses—producing a well-oiled effort-driven rewards machine.
At that time, more than any other in my life, all was right with
my neurobiological world.

Along with my colleague Craig Kinsley, I've spent over a
decade exploring how maternal, and more recently paternal, interactions lead to a healthier brain. We've been amazed at the
far-reaching impact a single reproductive experience has on the
rodent brain and behavior. Moms have consistently demonstrated increased mental sharpness by being more efficient at
foraging tasks. Plus, rodent moms are emotionally bolder when
taking on such tasks as venturing out on an uncovered bridge
(something rats are very reluctant to do) or investigating a new
object in their cages.

Rodent moms have also demonstrated the ability to multitask.
We gave them a foraging task with a twist—competing with two
animals that they had never met. This required them to overcome
their social anxiety and focus on the food reward. The moms,
especially our second-time moms, were much more successful
than the virgins. Note, too, that this task also required cognitive
abilities such as focus, motivation, and concentration, all of which
are certainly compromised when someone is depressed.

Recently, my student Torrie Higgins designed a more sophisticated attention task requiring the maternal rats to ignore

certain cues that they learned were not likely to result in a reward and focus on the important cues. After the rats were taught to dig for Froot Loops in tiny flower pots, they had to learn to ignore the different fillings (paper confetti vs. yarn) and focus on the pot's odor. The one with the mango scent had the reward in it and the lavender and chamomile odors predicted no reward. The rats' ability to understand the rules of this task amazed me. Even though I am a two-time mom, I'm not sure I could successfully complete it!

The second-time moms solved these tasks much faster than both the first-time moms and the virgins. Generally, about 40 percent of the virgins figured out the task in the allotted number of trials compared to 80 percent of the first-time moms and 100 percent of the second-time moms. (We are currently examining the brains of these animals to learn more about how their earlier parental social interactions prepared their brains for this impressive performance, characterized by enhanced motivation and persistence.) Clearly, healthy social contact may prime the effort-driven rewards circuit in ways we don't currently understand.

And what about the dads? Their brains may provide even more interesting evidence about the importance of healthy familial social interactions. In my lab we like to work with the California deer mouse, which is practically the poster rodent for family values because the males care for their offspring, doing everything the mom does except give birth and lactate. Our experiments show that these dads are better foragers and exhibit bolder responses than the bachelors, just as we have seen in our maternal rats. Also, when presented with an unsolvable problem—such as how to get a mouse pup out of a little cage (we call it a pup tent)—we see more activation in their prefrontal cortex areas and other areas involved in learning (such as the hippocampus) than displayed by their nonpaternal counterparts.

Elizabeth Gould, the psychologist at Princeton who experimented with isolating rats from their neighbors, recently found that marmoset monkeys who are fathers have far more of another social neuropeptide, vasopressin, in the prefrontal cortex than males who were not dads. By showing this increased activity in the prefrontal cortex—the most highly evolved area of the brain—it seems that mental functions such as empathy and sympathy, characteristic of nurturing parental responses, have taken "higher ground" in the brain. This may explain why the higher cognitive functions so often associated with bringing a human child into the world—such as hope and optimism—are the mainstays of emotional resilience.

Research suggests that the mental health benefits work both ways. Michael J. Meaney, professor in the Departments of Psychiatry, and Neurology and Neurosurgery, at McGill University, has shown that rat pups who received more attention from their moms in the form of anal-genital licks (a unique form of social contact!) developed more resilience against anxiety later in life. When they reached old age, the pups from the doting moms had healthier stress responses and enhanced learning compared to the more neglected pups. All in all, research suggests that sustained nurturing care and attention through social contact helps produce healthier emotional lives for both parents and offspring.

In her book *Touch,* Tiffany Field, a psychologist and the director of the Touch Research Institute at the University of Miami School of Medicine, described studies that analyzed interactions between moms and their preschoolers at McDonald's restaurants in Paris and Miami. Overall, French mothers touched their preschoolers more than the American mothers, and, interestingly, the French children were less aggressive than their American counterparts.

Of course, new motherhood is not always so ideal. What about maternity blues and its most severe form, postpartum depression? How can a biological response designed to keep a mother interacting with her child in a passionate and efficient manner lead to a condition that generates all the symptoms of depression? It's difficult to know the exact cause and effect, but at least one study points to the importance of touch. Mothers were observed interacting with their infants the second day after delivery. The moms who were ultimately diagnosed with maternity blues (postpartum depression is typically diagnosed much later) touched their infants far less than moms who did not exhibit emotional vulnerabilities. Research also indicates that women who felt social isolation through their pregnancies were at risk for postpartum depression down the road.

While other factors, such as drastic changes in reproductive hormones, are important in the mental health of mothers, social support throughout the pregnancy and healthy social contact with the infant help protect the mother against the onset of depression. Ultimately, this enhanced social connection seems to provide relief for the mom—and steer the infant away from emotional and physical vulnerabilities as he or she develops.

HEALING WHAT AILS YOU

Social contact actually reduces stress, another important factor in building resilience against depression. A side effect of the stress response is suppressed immune functions. When the body has to worry about fighting or fleeing during a full-blown stress response, fighting off potential pathogens in the form of viruses or bacteria takes a backseat. So one way that the health value of social contact has been determined is by assessing the strength of the immune system during stressful, threatening times.

For example, the hormone oxytocin can help diminish the negative effects of exposure to stress. Research in my lab shows that highly monogamous and very social California deer mice heal more quickly when they have a roommate in their cage. For two weeks, my undergraduate student Helen Ashley exposed deer mice with a small skin wound to two different stressors— annoying things such as predator odors, novel stimuli, and strobe lights—each day in an unpredictable manner. Half were housed with their same-sex siblings and half in isolation. As predicted, social isolation outranked the presence of chronic stress in delaying the healing of the wounds.

How does this play out in humans? Enhanced social contact seems to improve immune functions. Ronald Glaser and Janice Kiecolt-Glaser, both at Ohio State University, have found that medical students stressed out by taking exams have a lower level of immune cell production if they report being lonely. A study focusing on cohabitating males and females found that warm contact (defined as holding hands, watching part of a romantic film, engaging in romantic conversation, and hugging for twenty seconds) enhanced the production of oxytocin, which helps mitigate the stress response. When social contact is negatively affected by marital arguments, for instance, wound healing is delayed, likely due to disruption of the oxytocin system.

Social contact and touch have been shown to reduce stress and anxiety and to allow the body to continue functioning in a healthy manner. In a study conducted at the Centre for Complementary Care in Eskdale, Cumbria, England, scientists assessed the effects of a therapeutic regimen consisting of holding a patient gently and systematically touching painful areas around the body. This therapy reduced stress, led to pain relief, and enhanced coping abilities in the patients.

Tiffany Field has also conducted a study in which her staff gave deep pressure massages to infants born nine weeks prematurely. The massage therapy sessions were distributed across three fifteen-minute sessions per day for ten days. Although these infants received the same amount and quality of food as the control infants who were not massaged, the group that received the therapy gained 46 percent more weight and were discharged six days earlier than the nonmassaged infants.

The beneficial effects of touch aren't restricted to interactions with the same species. Temple Grandin, professor of animal sciences at Colorado State University in Fort Collins, and her colleagues investigated the impact of social contact on dogs housed in animal shelters, a very stressful environment. Grandin found that when people groomed, petted, and played with the dogs for forty-five minutes each day, it lowered their stress hormone levels. Once again, the healing effects work both ways. In a recent study conducted in South Africa, people engaging in positive interactions with pets had decreased stress hormones and increased oxytocin levels, suggesting that interacting with pets has many health benefits, too, especially related to mental health.

THE JOYS OF GROOMING

When I take my animal behavior students to Monkey Jungle in Miami, we notice that monkeys spend nearly all their waking hours relaxing and grooming one another. At times, it looks as if the recipients are barely alive. The complete loss of muscle tone in their dangling arms and legs during these grooming sessions make me a little more motivated to get a massage when I return home!

In an experiment using cynomolgus monkeys, researchers at Merck Sharp and Dohme Research Laboratories in the UK decided to ease the stress of not having another monkey in the laboratory cage by introducing a synthetic fleece pad that the monkey could "groom." At first, the isolated monkeys showed signs of laboratory-induced anxiety in the form of cage stereotypies, including repetitive movements such as pacing and rocking. But after placing a fleece fabric–covered cushion into the cages for eight hours a day, the researchers found that the grooming therapy cut the stereotypies in half and significantly increased the time the animals spent resting, suggesting that they were less stressed and more relaxed.

Perhaps even more relevant to the concept of effort-driven rewards, the researchers later added a "work" component to the mix by placing food crumbs on the fleece pads. When the animals had both tactile/touch stimulation and actual rewards due to "work," the stereotypies decreased by another 20 percent.

Robert Sapolsky, who has studied the social and stress lives of olive baboons in the Serengeti, has observed that when these animals were placed in a protected environment where resources were plentiful and they had to work less to obtain them, the animals were quick to generate social stress with their free time.

Overall, research indicates that the healthiest, most resilient brain activates effort-driven rewards in the context of a socially rich environment. One of the most poignant stories of the healing value of social touch and grooming involves Cambodian women who suffered unspeakable atrocities at the hands of the Khmer Rouge during the mid- to late 1970s. In *The Noonday*

Demon, Andrew Solomon told the story of the Nobel Peace Prize nominee Phaly Nuon, who found the women completely traumatized by these experiences. They were unable to talk or take care of their children, and they were completely incapacitated by intense post-traumatic stress. In addition to introducing knitting to these women, which likely began to activate their effort-driven rewards circuit, Nuon attempted to reestablish their social relationships through the use of grooming behavior. Solomon quotes her:

> And then when they have mastered work, at last, I teach them to love. I built a sort of lean-to and made it a steam bath. . . . I take them there so that they can become clean, and I teach them how to give one another manicures and pedicures and how to take care of their fingernails, because doing that makes them feel beautiful, and they want so much to feel beautiful. It also puts them in contact with the bodies of other people and makes them give up their bodies to the care of others. It rescues them from physical isolation, which is a usual affliction for them, and that leads to the breakdown of the emotional isolation. While they are together washing and putting on nail polish, they begin to talk together, and bit by bit they learn to trust one another, and by the end of it all, they have learned how to make friends, so that they will never have to be so lonely and so alone again. Their stories, which they have told to no one but me—they begin to tell those stories to one another.

As important as effort-driven rewards and supportive social contact are separately, they are clearly even more potent when they exist together. The combination of carrying out tasks such as manicures and knitting used in conjunction with the supportive social contact in the "touch" therapy proved to be a powerful mix—one likely to be far more effective than just taking an SSRI, which is a temporary fix. Changing the brain through drug therapy without actually changing the environment and/or behavior in a corresponding way will not have lasting results. After pulling a muscle or breaking a bone, you can take a painkiller to inhibit the pain messages sent to the brain, which makes you feel better. But doing physical therapy to help build the strength of a muscle is the most logical therapeutic strategy.

THE PERSONAL TOUCH

There's another important type of "touch"—that is, touch directed toward our own bodies as opposed to someone else's. Whereas social touch is important for communication and gaining social support, self-directed touch is also necessary for the maintenance of physical and mental health. Personal touch in the form of grooming or cleaning our skin is critical to keep pathogens at bay. Scratching, peeling, picking, and rubbing can soothe our anxiety as well.

In the study in which monkeys received the fleecy grooming pad, the monkeys increased self-grooming by 45 percent in addition to exhibiting fewer stereotypies and getting more rest. This autogrooming likely represents their anticipation and excitement over the prospect of receiving the enriching fleecy pad, but this type of self-care also leads to enhanced physical health.

Self-grooming can be used as an index of mental and physical health, just as self-neglect can be a warning sign for mental illness. Depression is often associated with personal neglect; in fact, dentists have noted that depressed patients show poor oral hygiene—another form of neglected self-grooming.

Researchers in Denmark, in their work with white leghorn hens, found compelling evidence of the importance of auto-grooming to our mental lives. They chose this particular fowl because of the hens' affinity for dustbathing, a complex behavioral response involving sand to keep the feathers in good condition. When these birds were deprived of the opportunity to dustbathe for two and a half years, they exhibited atypical behaviors such as excessive wing and leg stretching and self-pecking.

When hens that were allowed to take dustbaths during this same period were suddenly deprived of sand, their stress hormones elevated dramatically, too. And when given the opportunity, the wire-cage birds embarked on the activity immediately. This suggests that dustbathing is extremely important to these hens' survival. The increased incidence of self-pecking in the stressed birds probably indicates that extreme forms of grooming behavior are signs of mental illness or distress. It may be similar to people suffering from obsessive-compulsive disorder who compulsively groom themselves. In moderation however, grooming appears to be good for our mental health.

Grooming behavior in rodents also diminishes as stress and anxiety increase. When mice were exposed to chronic unpredictable stress, researchers noticed increased aggression in the animals, as well as a reduction in grooming. In a rodent version of a hair salon consultation, the fur of the mice was assessed throughout the stress period and scored according to how smooth, shiny, and fluffy it was. The researchers reported that there was a significant deterioration of the fur in the chronically stressed mice over the four-week chronic stress paradigm, which was used to induce symptoms of depression in rodents.

Cashing In on the Dopamine Jackpot

Much of the research discussed here confirms the importance of social contact and self-grooming in maintaining our physical and mental health through the reduction of anxiety. Any behavior that reduces stress and anxiety may work as a weapon against depression. However, the effort-driven rewards path to resilience also emphasizes the role of rewards, more specifically, dopamine activity in the brain's reward center, the nucleus accumbens. We've already learned how maternal social responses lead to enhanced activation of this brain area. Grooming also affects the brain's reward center.

Researchers in Argentina found that enhanced dopamine activity in the nucleus accumbens coincided with increased incidences of grooming in rats. Other researchers focusing on social grooming found that lactating rats had higher levels of dopamine in the brain's reward center when they licked and groomed their pups.

Another technique that scientists use to determine the rewarding properties of a particular response is to see if it can be used as a reinforcer that increases a certain behavioral response. Children tell us by their responses which efforts are effective reinforcers. For example, one child may study harder to get a monetary reward for making good grades but may not increase her studying behavior in order to increase family trips to the local science museum. Another may respond more positively to the museum trips. By keeping a close eye on the behavior that results, it's easy to evaluate the effectiveness of the rewards we're dangling in front of our children.

In a creative study conducted on male rhesus monkeys, the experimenters set out to determine if they could guide monkeys' responses by grooming them. When a monkey made a correct response in a visual discrimination task, the experimenters celebrated the moment by grooming his face, head, and neck with their own hands. As seen with the more traditional food rewards in these behavioral learning tasks, the monkeys improved their correct responses in order to receive a grooming session. Conversely, chimpanzees also will work to have the opportunity to groom the arm of the experimenter, as opposed to being groomed themselves.

As we've seen, social contact and grooming tap into the effort-driven rewards circuit in a variety of ways, helping to decrease anxiety. These responses are powerful ammunition against the onset of anxiety disorders and depression. The mental protection that comes from reducing stress and enhancing social connections leads us to an exciting new area of mental health, which is the subject of the next chapter: the neurobiology of resilience.

7

The Building Blocks of
Resilience

S EVERAL YEARS AGO, I interviewed Katherine Sherwood, an
artist and professor at UC Berkeley, who suffered a stroke
in her early forties that changed her life forever. She not only
lost control of her right hand, which she had used for painting,
she had to relearn how to speak and walk. She faced these
challenges while raising her daughter, who was five at the time.

Katherine had every reason to be depressed, and she was
headed in that direction as she attempted to cope with her severely altered abilities. Then one day at a doctor's appointment,
she caught a glimpse of her angiogram. The enlarged image of
the blood vessels in her brain reminded Katherine of her favorite
Chinese landscape, a painting that was more than a thousand
years old. Suddenly she felt driven to paint again, determined to
use these images in her art.

She returned to her studio and taught herself to paint with
her left hand. Her work changed drastically because she used
broader strokes and larger canvases. It also became less analytical, since she was now engaging her more artsy right hemisphere

to guide her left hand. She incorporated both seventeenth-century mystical symbols of healing and modern images of her own brain angiograms into each new piece.

Amazingly, Katherine has received more rewards and recognition for the paintings she's made following her stroke than she had received before it. Her ability to bounce back and produce even better art after losing the use of her right hand is a wonderful example of our capacity to rebound from adversity.

Whether or not emotional or physical setbacks result in clinical depression depends on a host of factors ranging from biological predispositions to individual differences in coping styles. But these coping styles are not carved in neuronal stone. To some extent, they are malleable, meaning that as you beome more mindful of how you respond to stressful situations and the best strategies for dealing with them, you can immunize yourself against the development of depression in the future.

The ability to weather emotional storms without sustaining long-term emotional damage is known as resilience. When a resilient person experiences such difficulties as losing a loved one or a job, his or her coping skills help prevent the stress from taking a tailspin into chronic anxiety or depression. In fact, some people, like Katherine Sherwood, bounce back from challenges stronger than ever before. They even seem enriched by what they've endured.

Regardless of whether a person displays day-to-day and/or once-in-a-lifetime versions of resilience, being able to deflect the toxic emotional effects of stressful or painful situations is critical to maintaining mental health and avoiding depression. Picture a coil being stretched beyond its normal form. When it's released from the tension, it springs right back into shape; that's a good mental picture of resilience. Less resilient coils may stay in the stretched-out, twisted position, or, worse, break under the pressure.

Our culture often views resilience as a "superhuman" quality. Based on the number of Superman and Spiderman sequels lately, we seem to have an insatiable desire to watch these characters use their special powers to overcome life's threats. I especially like the character in the *Fantastic Four* movies known as Mr. Fantastic. His special ability is to stretch like a rubber band to squelch the impending doom, then, just like that healthy coil, he snaps right back into shape.

But resilience is not an otherworldly ability out of reach to us mere mortals. It's more like ordinary magic, according to the psychologist Ann Masten. "Resilience appears to be a common phenomenon that results in most cases from the operation of basic human adaptational systems," she writes. And for many if not most of us, those coping systems begin developing during childhood. That may be why most resilience research has been done on children. Still, we can glean a lot about optimal coping strategies for people of any age.

Research on children suggests that two factors are the most important when it comes to the development of resilient kids: intellectual capacity and effective parenting. Children facing adversity seem most able to adapt if they possess high intellectual capabilities (problem-solving skills, good memory, focused attention) and authoritative, monitoring, and support-ive parents.

So being resilient doesn't require genetic mutations, alien citizenship, or unique chemical reactions. On the contrary, people with normal, functioning brains born into families with at least one nurturing parent seem to have a decent shot at staying the mental course through life's turbulent waters.

Realizing that your brain is dynamic and has the capacity to build resilience as you mature can go a long way toward building confidence in your ability to cope. For example, the aspiring screenplay writer Joe Dee has suffered from obsessive-compulsive disorder since childhood, he explained to me during an interview. The day he learned more about how his brain functioned he felt as if a huge mental weight had been lifted from his shoulders. Realizing that he had the ability to alter those functions had real therapeutic value for Joe, he said. In fact, after learning that his caudate nucleus (part of the striatum) was overactive during his obsessions, he decided to keep a piece of paper with "caudate nucleus" written on it, which he pulls out of his pocket whenever the anxiety becomes excessive. This therapeutic cheat sheet serves as a reminder that it's the overactivity of his brain, not a looming threat, that is causing his anxiety.

When I give lectures on neuroanatomy, I enjoy telling my groaning students that their new knowledge of brain structures and functions may have real therapeutic advantages throughout their lives—and that I won't even charge them extra for this added benefit of the class! By learning more about how your brain works, you—and it—can make more informed decisions about avoiding anxiety and maintaining mental health. So, far from being a mystical power, resilience can be the result of good old-fashioned information.

ENHANCING RESILIENCE WITH MENTAL VACCINATIONS

Many anxious parents who send their beloved progeny to college become "helicopter moms" (or dads), excessively hovering over their children to protect them from emotional turbulence.

Unable to cut the emotional umbilical cord, they continue to micromanage every detail of their kids' lives. These students don't know how to respond to challenges and make their own decisions; many can't even decide which classes to take without whipping out a cell phone to ask for a parent's advice.

In the 1960s, the popular "self-esteem movement" professed that we should all feel good about ourselves regardless of our accomplishments. This cultural attitude, which persists to this day, essentially replaces effort-driven rewards with noncontingent emotional rewards. Remember the trust fund rats that received coveted Froot Loops regardless of their efforts? Those treats were noncontingent rewards; the rats exerted no effort to receive them, and they gave up trying to complete a task much sooner than the working rats.

Noncontingent rewards are disturbingly common today— from the classroom to the playing field. Scores are no longer kept at youth soccer games so that all the kids can be winners and feel good about themselves. A parent comforts a child who did badly on an exam by telling him that the test wasn't fair. I've lost count of the number of times students who have failed an exam informed me promptly that the problem was the nature of the test, not their poor preparation. Without any sense of connection between achievement and rewards, these students are going to have a difficult time not just in college, but out in the real world.

The coping responses so critical to creating and maintaining resilience are compromised when parents won't let their kids make mistakes so that they can experience disappointment and failure. These children often find it difficult to persist when they encounter the kinds of obstacles life throws at us each day. Overcoming setbacks helps youngsters calibrate their emotional coping barometers as they develop into adults.

Researchers in the Department of Psychology at Queen's University in Kingston, Ontario, have shown that independence from parents and a sense of self-efficacy help facilitate a student's adjustment to college. *Self-efficacy*, a term related to effort-driven rewards, was introduced by the well-known Stanford University psychologist Albert Bandura. It refers to a person's perception that he or she possesses the ability to respond successfully to challenges. In short, how you view your competency in various situations has been associated with enhanced mental resilience. The importance of resilience has long been recognized. The seventeenth-century philosopher and physician John Locke believed that humans were born as a *tabula rasa* (blank slate) and had to acquire experiences to develop their minds. In a series of letters to his cousin, Locke recommended that she put holes in her children's socks and shoes during the winter to let them experience uncomfortable elements such as rain and cold. He assured her that exposing children to small doses of hardship would produce strong, healthy adults. In one letter, he wrote:

> How necessary health is to our business and happiness, and how necessary a strong constitution, able to endure hardships and fatigue, is to one that will make any figure be anything considerable in the world, is too obvious to need any proof.

Centuries later, Jonas Salk was also concerned about the importance of fostering resilience. After developing the vaccine for polio in the 1950s, he continued to think about the health of children, especially their mental health. In a conversation with the psychologist Martin Seligman, Salk said that if he had the opportunity to choose his career path again, he would focus on immunizing kids *psychologically* so they would be better at combating mental and physical illness.

These enlightened thinkers clearly understood the need to "vaccinate" children against the inevitable emotional challenges in their future. Just as a chicken pox vaccine exposes children to a small amount of the virus so that the body can build immunity against the perpetrator, allowing children to experience small doses of failure under our nurturing supervision helps build mental immunity against depression or other mental illnesses down the line.

As a parent, I appreciate that it's easier to write about building children's resilience than actually doing it. Last year, my then twelve-year-old came into my bedroom one evening extremely upset. Lara is typically very organized, but on this particular day she'd forgotten her math problems, which were due the next morning. I commiserated with her for a few minutes and then suggested that she go to school early and do the homework before class started.

Minutes later she was back, this time with crocodile tears streaming down her cheeks. She also had a small role in a classroom play the next day. When she looked for the pages with her lines in her book bag, they weren't there. Her anxiety escalated into panic as she described how she was going to fail her math assignment and also make a fool of herself in front of her class, not to mention letting down the other actor in the scene.

My first instinct was to suggest that she just stay home the next day so she wouldn't fail or be embarrassed. I even thought about writing a note explaining how this behavior was out of character for Lara and ask for extensions on both assignments. Ultimately, however, I realized the important lessons she would learn if she tried to face these challenges herself. She would figure out a way to handle the situation, I told her, and tucked her in for the night. She cried herself to sleep.

The next day, I dropped Lara off at school early and worried about her all morning. To my delight, that afternoon she was her usual buoyant self, even acting as if she didn't know what I was talking about when I asked about her day. She'd done the homework before class and did well on it. And a little creative problem solving prompted her to ask her forensics teacher if students could use props to hide their lines if they needed to. The teacher said yes, so Lara incorporated the act of reading a magazine into her skit, allowing her to look more natural as she accurately delivered her lines. In other words, she'd dealt with both situations and come away the better for it. I told her I was confident in her ability to solve similar problems in the future.

The importance of such mental inoculations was illustrated in a recent article in *The New York Times Magazine* discussing the constitution-building coaching strategies of Billy Fitzgerald. For three decades, Coach Fitzgerald and his no-nonsense, tough love style has been legendary in New Orleans, especially at the Isidore Newman High School. The result: year after year of winning baseball seasons.

Talk about effort-driven rewards! The author Michael Lewis described the grueling practice schedule the baseball team had to adhere to each season. Coach Fitz never bought into the noncontingent self-esteem movement. He has made clear to generations of students that rigorous training produces desirable results—baseball mastery in this case—while half-hearted efforts lead only to failure and loss. Michael Lewis not only survived Coach Fitz's strict regime, he went on to become a successful author of such best-selling books as *Moneyball* and, most recently, *Coach*, a book about Coach Fitz.

Now for the irony: At the same time that Isidore Newman alumni and former players were planning a fund-raising campaign to build a gym in honor of their esteemed coach, the headmaster's office was buzzing with complaints about Coach Fitz's "harsh" tactics. In one of Fitz's typical speeches, he pointed out specific examples of behavior that had led to the team's problems—not practicing enough, getting out of shape, blaming others for their failures. The speech prompted parents of the new millennium to call for Coach Fitz's dismissal because his lectures were leaving a "bad taste" in their children's mouths.

Robert Sternberg, an intelligence researcher and at the time the president of the American Psychological Association, called for an emphasis on the "other 3 Rs" of education—namely, reasoning, resilience, and responsibility. In his book *Optimizing Student Success in School with the Other Three Rs,* he challenged our educational system to incorporate resilience training. Life's path is strewn with obstacles, he explained, and at times these setbacks may seem like deal breakers. It takes a mighty sense of resilience to overcome them. He wrote:

> The conclusion I have reached is that what distinguishes those who are highly successful from others is, in large part, resilience in the face of humiliations, defeats and setbacks of various kinds. For those who do not have some kind of optimism—learned or otherwise—it often seems much easier just to start watching the world go by instead of actively participating in it. What we do not realize when we are younger is that almost all of us go through these periods of staggering defeat or, at least, uncertainty. The question is not whether you will go through it; it is how you will come out if it.

Sternberg's characterization of the passive nature of nonresilient people as they watch the world go by is, of course, highly reminiscent of someone suffering from depression. In Seligman's famed animal model of depression known as "learned helplessness," animals that were not allowed to escape during the initial exposure to a shock stimulus sat passively during subsequent testing, even when there were opportunities to escape.

Similarly, a person who's had bad luck with a few job interviews may find it difficult to keep searching and may eventually give up, even when new job opportunities arise. As people adopt a more passive approach, their brains begin to fail to recognize the relation between efforts and rewards. Previous tendencies to approach challenges with a plan of action become replaced by strategies for retreating in an attempt to avoid challenges, as the neural connections among the components of the effort-driven rewards circuit become short-circuited by fear and anxiety. With these diminished connections, effort-driven rewards fade from their emotional scene and the symptoms of depression—reduced pleasure, increased fatigue, decreased hope for the future—take over the emotional landscape.

There's no denying that being an active participant in life is the last thing on a depressed person's "to-do" list. However, if this approach does indeed build resilience and lift depression by fully engaging our brains, as my research indicates, we need to consider ways to slowly reintroduce depressed patients to active, full lifestyles. I will discuss a therapy designed to accomplish this goal in the next chapter.

THE POWER TO MAKE HEALTHIER CHOICES

Is it possible to learn how to fend off depression? Martin Seligman and his research team have made monumental strides toward answering this question. They have spent more than a decade systematically evaluating the merits of a school-based intervention program known as the Penn Resiliency Program.

In one study, the team identified fifth and sixth graders at risk for depression based on their current behavior. For three months, half the students met with the researchers for ninety-minute weekly sessions in which they worked on solving interpersonal problems, practiced effective coping techniques, and learned about being appropriately assertive. They also learned relaxation methods. The remaining students did not meet with the researchers. Six months after the sessions ended, fewer depressive symptoms were observed in the group that had received the training than in the control group. Two years later, the children who had not been exposed to the resiliency program were twice as likely to suffer from depressive symptoms.

According to Seligman, these resiliency-building intervention programs are essential. Once a young person experiences a depressive episode, she is more likely to become depressed in the future. "Arming children with anti-depressive thinking skills may short-circuit this cycle of depression and provide a cost-effective, longer-lasting, drug-free alternative to antidepressants," a recent article on the Penn Resiliency Program stated.

Research by Carol S. Dweck, a professor of psychology at Stanford University, also highlights the powerful effects effort can have in building children's resilience. In a fascinating study, Dweck and her colleagues exposed seventh-grade students, who had all done poorly in math during the previous school year, to an eight-session intervention program designed to teach them how their brains and intellect change incrementally as a result of their effort (e.g., studying, practicing). Compared to a group that received a comparable workshop focusing on study skills, the students who were given the resilience training dramatically improved their math grades, compared to the control group.

In her recent book, *Mindset: The New Psychology of Success*, Dweck emphasizes that in order to immunize children against feelings of helplessness, it's important to praise effort as opposed to talent. People who blame their failures on their lack of ability are easily discouraged when faced with setbacks. Those who blame their failures on a lack of effort are fueled by their setbacks and motivated to direct more effort toward challenges in the future.

There's no denying that it can be heart-wrenching to watch our children experience such growing pains. But given proper support and supervision, they'll have much better mental health forecasts throughout their lives if they learn how to deal with life's challenges through accurately calibrated effort-driven rewards.

Accurately calibrated is a key phrase here. It's just as important to know when certain efforts are not appropriate in a given situation. But overprotecting children prevents them from developing the critical ability to recognize when efforts will lead to failure. Being quick to intervene when your son pushes an older child on the playground may save him from being shoved or hit by the bigger kid that day. But if you let the children resolve this conflict themselves (watching closely from the sidelines), the inevitable shove by the larger kid will provide a powerful lesson he won't soon forget. Understanding the direct consequences of inappropriate social behavior will help shape your son's interactions in the future.

To shield their children from too much adversity, some well-intentioned parents resort to putting their kids on medications such as SSRIs. These drugs are like mental Band-Aids, only masking feelings of depression and anxiety. A healthy brain is an engaged brain, and a person who is not engaging her brain in coping with social anxieties at school, for example, may appear to be managing her anxiety by taking antidepressants. But the depressive symptoms will likely return when she goes off the drugs, unless she has made significant lifestyle changes. In fact, if a youngster is taking antidepressants throughout emotionally turbulent puberty, she will be deprived of the opportunity to recalibrate her coping strategies and effort-driven rewards as the challenges of elementary school morph into larger ones in middle and high school. If a child is sick and misses a few weeks of school, it is difficult to catch up with the academic skills taught during that period. It is no different for emotional skills. The last thing we want for our children is to have them facing adulthood with the coping skills of a sixth grader.

Taking SSRIs just because you feel that something's "not quite right" also diminishes the accuracy of your emotional gauges. It's not good to think that nothing you do makes a difference; on the other hand, it's not good to think you're always effective and can never make a mistake. The feeling that something isn't quite right is valuable when it prompts you to grab the child who is too close to traffic or, on a lighter note, notice that your pants are unzipped before entering a class for a serious lecture on coping with anxiety.

THIS IS YOUR BRAIN ON RESILIENCE

Although there is strong historical and theoretical evidence that resilience is critical for deflecting depression and maintaining mental health, bringing the concept into the laboratory is new.

Not surprisingly, research on the brain areas and the chemicals related to resilience consistently supports the importance of the effort-driven rewards circuit in explaining how it all fits together.

Christian Waugh, then a social psychologist at the University of Michigan and most recently a postdoctoral fellow at the Stanford Mood and Anxiety Disorders Laboratory, and his colleagues used fMRI brain scans to identify the brain mechanisms that affect resilience. Several hundred subjects who were not currently depressed were asked to complete a paper-and-pencil test measuring their resilience. Then fifteen of the most highly resilient subjects and fifteen of the least were chosen.

While they were in the fMRI scanner, subjects were shown slides of troubling images, such as burn victims, or more neutral images, like a wooden stool. The scans showed that both resilient and nonresilient subjects responded to the threatening slides with heightened activity in the right prefrontal cortex. After registering these emotionally charged images, the prefrontal cortex, a critical component of the effort-driven rewards circuit, likely alerted the other brain areas to be on high alert for impending threats.

Interesting differences were observed between the two groups. When additional neutral images followed the threatening slides, the nonresilient subjects continued to show increased prefrontal cortical activity, while the resilient people did not. After the brain scans, the subjects were asked to predict the number of times aversive and neutral slides were shown. The nonresilient subjects greatly overestimated the actual number of threatening slides, whereas the resilient subjects made more accurate estimations.

Although it's important to be on high emotional alert when there's a threat in your midst (the slide of the burn victim in this case), it's equally important to be able to turn off the high-alert response when it's no longer needed. Prolonged stress responses have toxic effects on our brains and bodies. Being able to turn off the stress response during recovery from a threatening situation appears to be an important building block of resilience. So how we perceive a threatening stimulus is very important. As Shakespeare's Hamlet once observed, "There is nothing either good or bad, but thinking makes it so."

Kevin Ochsner at Stanford University, an intellectual hotbed for resilience research, found that certain areas of the prefrontal cortex are important in the process of reappraising negative events. In his study, fifteen healthy women viewed aversive slides while in fMRI scanners. When asked to reassess these negative scenes, they showed increased activity in the cortical areas most associated with ongoing memory processes, cognitive control, and self-monitoring, and lower amounts of activity in the brain's high-alert areas such as the amygdala.

It's your prefrontal cortex that helps you figure out that your first attempt at asking for a raise failed because you were tired and your boss was in a bad mood and that a second, more energized pitch when your boss is feeling better may pay off. This reappraisal requires specific cognitive functions that allow you to weigh the influence of certain factors in determining success in a future attempt. The success of this cortical dependent, or top-down, emotional coping strategy provides additional support for the importance of the intervention/learning programs described earlier.

You don't necessarily need access to a coping strategy work-shop to build these top-down cognitive strategies or strengthen your effort-driven rewards mental muscles. Just remember that the information itself is the key "active" ingredient in this treat-ment approach. So, the good news is that if you're reading this book, or one like it, you are taking an important first step toward your mental health makeover.

Another key ingredient is learning from experience. Steven Maier and his colleagues at the University of Colorado found that rats that had prior experience with an escapable shock—that is, they encountered shock and found a way to escape it—had more prefrontal cortex activity when exposed to a subsequent inescapable shock than animals without that valu-able earlier experience. The processing abilities of the pre-frontal cortex enabled these animals to "reappraise" the danger and determine that it might be worth another escape attempt. In fact, if that area of the cortex is temporarily deactivated, the more experienced rats show less resilience, confirming the im-portant role this problem-solving/processing area of the brain plays in this critical attribute.

As mentioned in a previous chapter, Maier also discovered that the prefrontal cortex can enhance resilience by suppressing the activation of a brainstem area responsible for secreting the neurochemical that is so often associated with depression—serotonin. It's been demonstrated that increased resilience is associated with *decreased* activation of the serotonergic neu-rons. As Barry Jacobs's work at Princeton suggests, activation of serotonergic neurons may be important to cultivate a coping response after a threat has been perceived. But if a threat isn't perceived by a quick-thinking, reappraising prefrontal cortex, there's no need to call in the stress and coping neural troops, thus avoiding the ravages of allostatic load.

Lower levels of activity in the prefrontal cortex have been observed in people suffering from post-traumatic stress disorder (PTSD), a condition in which stressful situations wear down natural resilience. Compromised activity in this area may make it difficult for these patients to reappraise the events in their lives once the trauma has passed. Typically, the aversive event was so emotional that the brain continues in its high-alert mode even when the circumstances have changed and appear safer. By continuing at high alert, the brain basically becomes unable to discern different threat levels accurately, so it cannot respond appropriately. Everything becomes an emergency, and the patient's response is similarly overblown. The ability to dial back the brain's "threat detector" to a reasonable level so that every new threat can be evaluated appropriately is a vital aspect of resilience.

Two chemicals that play leading roles in resilient responses to chronic stress are DHEA and Neuropeptide Y (NPY). Animals with higher levels of peripheral DHEA (dehydroepiandrosterone) exhibit less intense emotional responses to stressful experiences. DHEA also seems to protect the brain from some of the harmful effects of the stress hormone cortisol. Hence, the conclusion: the higher the levels of naturally occurring DHEA, the higher the resilience.

When injected into the amygdala (the fear center) of the rat brain, Neuropeptide Y reduces anxietylike responses even when the animals are subsequently exposed to stressful stimuli. One of the most abundant neurochemicals in the brain, which is involved in other essential systems such as determining how much we eat, Neuropeptide Y also appears to play a significant role in enabling the animal to keep the brain's "fight or flight" sympathetic nervous system in check. In fact, people suffering from PTSD have lower levels of Neuropeptide Y than healthy controls. Indeed, the patients exhibiting the most severe PTSD symptoms had the lowest NPY levels.

In our research into flexible coping strategies, my students and I were interested in whether these resilience neurochemicals were different in the more resilient flexible copers (our term for flexible coping rats). Further, would it be possible to determine if these flexible coping rats would "reappraise" a challenging situation? To find out, we headed back to the laboratory.

GAINING RESILIENCE THROUGH FLEXIBLE COPING

Given these research findings, our task in the lab seemed straightforward: Profile rats for coping strategies, expose them to our chronic unpredictable stress model for several weeks, and figure out a way to "ask" them about their reappraisal and self-monitoring strategies by conducting several behavioral assessments. (We've yet to find a paper-and-pencil test they'll respond to!) Then, measure the body and brain's response to the stress by assessing their blood pressure, peripheral stress hormone levels (obtained from fecal samples), and Neuropeptide Y levels in the brain.

The flexible copers "told" us that they were more in tune with their environment because they changed their behavior, especially in the swim task. This consisted of placing a rat in a small swim tank such as an aquarium, a common behavioral assessment for depressionlike symptoms such as persistence and "learned despair" (a laboratory term for giving up). Typically, rats that start floating the earliest and keep floating as opposed to those who vigorously swim to find an escape route are considered the most likely candidates for depression.

While the flexible copers were the most active in their first three-minute swim—searching desperately for an escape route—they were the least active during the second swim. In other words, the flexible copers were the most optimistic during the first trial, in that they spent more time searching for an escape. But does that mean they were also the most depressed in the second and third trials because they just floated?

I think not. In my opinion, they made the most appropriate choice. After spending the first session surveying the environment and finding no escape route, they opted simply to wait out the swim time by floating the second time around. Why expend all that energy dog-paddling furiously around the tank when they had already learned that swimming did not lead to the desirable consequence of escaping the water? Thus, the change in behavior was well suited to the environmental condition. The passive and active copers caught on by the third swim. The flexible copers led the reappraisal thinking pack.

One of the most surprising findings was that when exposed to unpredictable stressors at unpredictable times, the flexible copers' stress hormones were much higher than the other groups, suggesting that their stress response did indeed depend on the nature of the stressor. When exposed to the more predictable stress of running, they had lower stress hormones. So when stress is unpredictable, it seems adaptive for the stress response to be "ready" to respond.

In fact, all the rats' resting heart rates increased by 30 percent during this stress experiment. Such a dramatic increase, if experienced in our real world of unpredictable stress, could have dangerous consequences. Still, the flexible copers had a lower systolic blood pressure. They also had much healthier stress hormone/DHEA ratios, characterized by higher levels of DHEA. And they were loaded with the resilience neurochemical Neuropeptide Y. In fact, we found five times more in the brains of the flexible copers than in those of the active copers.

The convergence of hormonal, cardiovascular, brain, and behavioral data confirms that being flexible appears to be the healthiest option when dealing with life's stressors. And of course, being more in tune with the environment gives us more control over our surroundings. The more control we have, the easier it is to select the appropriate response strategies to stressful events, and finding the most effective way to head off threats appears to be key to resilience.

Other areas of the brain are also involved in resilience. In addition to the prefrontal cortex, the striatum (the component of the effort-driven rewards circuit controlling our movement) is critical in executing the physical response to the stress-producing events in our lives. Then there's the brain's pleasure/reward center, the nucleus accumbens. George Koob, perhaps the foremost expert in this area of the brain, provides some important clues about the role of reward in resilience. Working at the Scripps Institute, Koob is trying to understand how psychoactive drugs, such as cocaine and heroin, take our brain's pleasure center hostage by completely changing nature's rules for effort-based rewards. People who take these drugs circumvent having to work for rewards by getting a shortcut to pleasure. Just as robbing a bank provides an immediate payoff of unearned money, these drugs rob the accumbens of valuable, yet unearned, dopamine and pleasure. In other words, using such drugs "cheats" the effort-driven rewards circuit and disrupts healthy responding.

When the direct connections between efforts and rewards no longer exist, the addict is not motivated to engage in behavior important for his survival, such as maintaining social relationships, healthy eating habits, or clean, safe living conditions. Such vital endeavors now take a backseat to getting the next hit of the drug of choice, which continues to rob the brain's pleasure center time after time.

Koob's laboratory work on addiction confirms the importance of healthy, well-placed effort-driven rewards (as opposed to drug-facilitated shortcuts) in the maintenance of mental health. In fact, he recognizes the value of slower-paced brain rewards, the way nature intended. He spends a good deal of his free time tending his fruit orchard. He experiences an abundance of "natural" pleasure from the long-term process of planting, watching, pruning, and harvesting the fruit (in this case, literally the fruits of his effort-driven rewards). Such activities help keep the brain's reward system more closely in tune with the kinds of responses that lead to the healthiest outcomes, and allow the higher-evolved prefrontal cortex to make the smartest choices.

A well-maintained effort-driven rewards system seems to provide the fundamental components for resilience. Failure to nurture any aspect of the circuit can result in ineffective responding, inaccurate assessments of the situation at hand, or a diminished motivation to choose the healthiest response paths, which can lead to depression. Limited intellectual capacity, inexperience with how actual efforts lead to tangible desirable consequences, or an altered sense of reward that is out of step with appropriate effort will all contribute to a coil breaking under the pressure instead of springing back into shape.

Perhaps these observations explain why so many celebrities seem to suffer from an overabundance of addiction problems and mental breakdowns. Although their efforts lead to rewards in the earlier stages of their careers, as they gain celebrity status, those rewards—money, resources, constant social attention and adoration—become less contingent on appropriate responses. Effort-driven rewards in these cases, in which it appears that these people have everything one could hope for, lose their effectiveness. This leads to a search for pleasure from alternative sources such as drugs, alcohol, food, or risky behavior. Of course, anyone can become an addict. It doesn't matter if the effort-driven rewards circuit is distorted due to celebrity status or losing a job; once reward-robbing drugs are onboard, resilience quickly yields to the emergence of mental illness.

GAINING STRENGTH—AND RESILIENCE—IN NUMBERS

The most glorious of all human responses are often in response to the needs of others. Literature is filled with stories of heroic gestures to win the love of another, medals are awarded to those who put their lives on the line to save others, and parents have successfully endured unimaginable hardships to create better lives for their children.

As discussed in the previous chapter, our brains are geared to respond to those around us. That's why when social bonds are broken, we become more vulnerable to depression and other illnesses. Accordingly, we will, in times of mental health, go to great lengths to keep our social lives intact, providing another interesting window through which we can glean valuable knowledge about resilience.

Meet Razza, the wily rat who outsmarted a host of Ph.D.s. Part of a study designed to learn more about how to eradicate wild rats from the surrounding islands, Razza was equipped with a radio collar and released on the shores of Motuhoropapa, one of the Noises Islands northeast of New Zealand. Scientists at the University of Auckland intended to follow the behavior of this solitary rat to learn more about how he and his mates inhabit these islands.

Razza's radio signal told them that he explored the entire island before settling into one area. When the scientists set out traps to catch him, however, he eluded them despite the radio-tracking device. After ten weeks, the scientists lost the signal. Not willing to be outwitted by a rat, even a really clever one, the team of experienced scientists tried every trick they knew—live traps, snap traps, buried traps, trained dogs—to catch him.

But Razza was incredibly resourceful and persistent—and very "in tune" with his environment. Each time he detected or smelled a "trap," he found a clever way to elude it. This is resilience at its best—persistent and strong well-calibrated effort coupled with constant evaluations and reappraisal.

I can only imagine the SWAT team of scientists with their radios, antennas, and backpacks filled with advanced equipment—all to catch this single tiny rodent. Eventually, they relocated his signal on yet another island, which meant that Razza had swum over four hundred meters across the open water, the first rat on record to cover such a distance in the water (and remember, swimming is considered a severe stressor in the laboratory!). Most interesting of all, the scientists credited his heroic effort to his need for "conspecifics"—that is, rat friends, most likely of the female persuasion. Just as Tom Hanks's character set out to find civilization on his homemade raft in Cast Away, Razza set out swimming to find another island in hopes of finding a little companionship.

After eighteen weeks, Razza was finally caught. If there ever was a rodent superhero, he has to top the list. In fact, the New Zealand author Witi Ihimaera wrote a children's book, *The Amazing Adventures of Razza the Rat*. Razza's story confirms that persistence and resilience are important tools for immunizing ourselves against depression. Again, we see that true resilience is nothing but ordinary magic. Razza hadn't received special training from the FBI or Scotland Yard, but he had become resilient, able to actively sort through alternatives.

The ties between social endeavors and effort-driven rewards can also be seen in a study exploring social cooperation, which activates the effort-driven rewards circuitry and leads to resilience. Based on real-life police interrogation dramas, the experiment known as the prisoner's dilemma is designed to determine if two people will cooperate to gain the biggest reward. Of course, there are three possible outcomes: Both subjects or accomplices cooperate or decide not to—or one may cooperate and the other refuse. The reward in these scenarios is dependent on the responses.

In a laboratory version of the prisoner's dilemma game, women were given choices about cooperating with another female subject to gain a monetary reward. fMRI scans indicated that when both women responded in a mutual fashion to help the other, the brain areas responsible for social cooperation generated a lot of buzz in the effort-driven brain reward circuit. The nucleus accumbens, striatum (specifically, the caudate nucleus), and various areas of the prefrontal cortex were all activated. Although other response strategies were also profitable, the subjects reported more subjective pleasure when both subjects cooperated.

Daily positive social interactions diminish the stress in our lives by facilitating the effort-driven rewards circuit to overcome obstacles in order to maintain this positive social status. But, of course, our social relationships aren't always positive. For many people, social support from family and friends is unpredictable; making matters worse, they haven't experienced sufficient control over their lives to establish strong effort-driven rewards gauges. These living contexts, also known as neighborhoods, represent another clue in the investigation of resilience.

RESILIENCE IN THE 'HOOD

Although generations of American children grew up listening to the late Mr. Rogers singing about "a beautiful day in the neighborhood," the reality is that many neighborhoods are anything but beautiful—and that leads to substantial stress in children. Over thirty years ago, Justin M. Joffe, a professor of psychology at the University of Vermont, tested the effects of growing up in two different types of "neighborhoods" by measuring the emotional responses in rats. In the contingent environment, the rats were trained to press levers to deliver their food, water, and lighting. In the noncontingent environment, the animals received the same amount of food, water, and lighting as the others but had no control over the delivery of these resources. The contingent environment group could easily make associations between efforts and rewards, strengthening the effort-driven brain reward circuit.

Then Joffe went further by testing the rats' emotional responsiveness by placing them in a novel environment known as an open field. His researchers counted the number of fecal boli the rats dropped (thought to be a sign of anxiety) and observed their general activity. The contingent group appeared more resilient, since they seemed less stressed when faced with the challenge of being in the unfamiliar environment—they pooped less and explored more than the other group. Subsequent esearch suggested that the perception of control in one's neighborhood early in life has long-lasting effects on emotional health.

What about humans? Carolyn Cutrona and her colleagues at Iowa State University looked at the impact of neighborhood characteristics on building resilience against depression in children, and their findings concur with the lessons learned from Joffe's rat environments. Given the same income level, family stress level, and other environmental factors, people living in an adverse neighborhood will be more likely to suffer from depression when faced with a significant challenge down the road, such as job loss.

For example, when African American women who had experienced a negative life event within the previous year were assessed for depression, those living in the high-stress neighborhoods were six times more likely to develop depressive symptoms than those living in low-stress areas. Reasons for the higher rates of depression included lack of resources, hopeful role models, and social norms for effective coping.

Although adverse neighborhoods add a layer of risk for depression, certain personal variables among the residents—such as personal mastery (which refers to one's perception of having control over life's events) and optimism—help protect against depression. Certainly, effort-driven rewards build a sense of personal mastery as successful interactions with one's environment add up and are internalized. Plus, the development of the problem-solving prefrontal cortex leads to broader thinking about life's challenges, opening the door for a more optimistic style of thinking.

FROM AN AGGRESSIVE UNDERACHIEVER TO AN ACCLAIMED NEUROSURGEON

Several years ago I discovered *Gifted Hands,* a book written by Ben Carson, director of pediatric neurosurgery at Johns Hopkins University, and became captivated by his narrative. Although it wasn't intended to be a children's bedtime story, I read the book to my daughters so they could also benefit from Carson's inspirational life lessons. An African American raised by a single mother in the adverse conditions of inner-city Detroit, Carson certainly didn't show early signs of promise.

For one thing, his intellectual abilities—also known to be important in resilience—seemed to be lacking. In the fifth grade, Ben was deemed the "dumbest" student in his classroom. He was especially bad at math and recalled taking tests on which he received a zero. How humiliating it was to have to call out those scores to his teacher! The other children relentlessly ridiculed this "dumb" kid. His future looked bleak, a negative outlook reinforced by his often aggressive behavior. It appeared that Carson would be lucky just to stay out of jail as he grew into adulthood.

In his case, the research suggesting the importance of having at least one supportive parent proved pivotal. His mother, a nearly illiterate woman who had married at the age of thirteen, held down two jobs to support her two sons and became determined that they would not end up doomed to menial work or, worse, jail. She repeatedly told her sons that they could do anything they wanted in life. When Carson was in the fifth grade, she announced that the boys were watching too much TV and told them they could watch only three shows a week. Although barely literate herself, she also told her children to go to the public library each week, read two books, and write reports on each one for her to "evaluate."

To meet their mother's demands, the boys were forced to spend less time hanging out with their peers. At the same time, they both discovered entirely new worlds through the books they read. This literary adventure, coupled with the school's giving him a free eye exam and glasses (apparently Carson had very bad vision—another factor contributing to his poor grades), resulted in his transformation from the worst student to one of the top students by the seventh grade.

Carson soon became interested in medicine. He persisted through financial and social challenges, received a scholarship to attend Yale University, and later went to medical school at the University of Michigan. After spending a summer operating a crane, he realized that his brain was adept at controlling his hands and he had a unique eye-hand coordination that worked in a three-dimensional context. This led him to consider the specialization of neurosurgery.

Today, at Johns Hopkins, he makes priceless contributions to our society by giving children a second chance at life. He removes brain tumors, extracts large portions of the brain hemispheres responsible for generating epileptic seizures (a procedure known as a hemispherectomy), and has even separated conjoined twins sharing skull tissue. Carson's meticulous use of his hands to gently navigate the complex terrain of the brain continuously strengthens his effort-driven rewards circuit.

In retrospect, Carson's mother should receive an honorary degree in psychology for the brilliant strategies she used to foster intellectual capacity and motivation in her sons. (Her younger son became an engineer.) Without the aid of a scientific education, a family therapist, or even the ability to read parenting magazines, this amazing woman perfected a winning resilience formula by combining nurturing parental support, high expectations, and opportunities for intellectual engagement—all against a backdrop of an optimistic attitude that her sons could do anything they wanted to in life.

I began this chapter by considering the importance of ordinary magic in resilience—and Ben Carson's story elegantly exemplifies this approach. No one swooped in to save Ben and his brother from their impoverished neighborhoods of Detroit. Instead, a wise and loving mother provided the vaccination and continued "booster shots" to ensure their resilience.

While it appears that humans possess the natural adaptiveness to withstand many of life's challenges, landing firmly on your feet may also require an awareness of the weaknesses as well as the strengths present in all of us. Indeed, stories of children who gain resilience through their adverse experiences are remarkable. But far from treating these healthy approaches to setbacks as magical or miraculous, we need more systematic studies of resilience. Scientists still have a lot to learn from these real-life superheroes.

Occasionally, life's challenges are too overwhelming, and even the most resilient people succumb to depression. These symptoms should be recognized as our brain's way of telling us something is wrong either in our environment or in the way we're interacting with it. The next step is to identify effective ways to get back on the resilient path of mental health. Therapeutic approaches that emphasize the value of our actions and expectations (as emphasized in effort-driven rewards) can be powerful behavioral elixirs for the treatment of depression. We'll explore these more active therapeutic approaches in the next chapter.

8

Nonpharmacological Treatments for Depression: A Little Less Talk and a Lot More Action

REGARDLESS OF HOW emotionally resilient you are, you're not totally immune to experiencing depressive symptoms from time to time. None of us is. And if depression sets in and you need professional help, one of the biggest challenges is identifying the most effective treatment strategy. The irony, of course, is that depression impairs the very cognitive skills—thinking, concentration, and problem-solving abilities—that are critical to making such an important decision.

Someone who meets the criteria for depression has a serious condition that deserves attention. While depression is often considered the common cold of mental illness, it's among the most debilitating psychiatric disorders. In fact, depression is the number one cause of disability in the world. With so many people affected, it is imperative that both patients and mental health professionals be able to identify the treatments that will yield the most significant improvements.

As I reported earlier, when various therapies were compared, both interpersonal and cognitive-behavioral therapies were just as successful as taking antidepressants, but without the unwanted side effects, such as sleep disturbances, sexual dysfunction, and discontinuation syndrome (Big Pharma's euphemistic term for withdrawal symptoms), associated with SSRIs. Psychoanalytic therapy, fashioned after Freud's theories, was the only therapy investigated that produced no better results than the control placebo.

No single therapy can claim a 100 percent recovery or cure rate. Approximately half of depressed patients respond positively to antidepressant medications, yet one study reported that 81 percent of those who took SSRIs relapsed during the year following treatment. In contrast, only 25 percent of those who received cognitive therapy relapsed during the year after treatment, according to a seminal report in the journal *Psychological Science in the Public Interest* in 2002, written by Steven D. Hollon from Vanderbilt University and his colleagues. This provides further evidence of how much more attractive this type of therapy is than antidepressants.

In general, combining therapies works better than using just one type. Taking antidepressants while engaging in cognitive behavioral therapy may result in a faster recovery, with less potential for relapse following the termination of treatment.

Still, despite this research, drugs remain the most popular therapeutic approach. In 2004, one in ten American women reported taking antidepressants, most often prescribed by their general physicians rather than psychiatrists. Considering the potential problems associated with SSRIs, these rates seem alarmingly high. That year, the Centers for Disease Control and Prevention reported that the use of antidepressants had almost tripled over the last decade.

Did people suddenly become three times more likely to suffer from depression? Was there some cataclysmic event that threw millions into the grip of this mood disorder? Did the world economy collapse? Well, *no*. But the pharmaceutical industry *was* spending approximately $6 billion annually marketing to physicians, not to mention funneling billions more ad dollars into consumer magazines and TV commercials.

Perhaps the fastest-growing group of new consumers are college students. One survey of twenty-nine thousand students reported that 28 percent of males and 38 percent of females were currently taking an antidepressant. Typically, they began using these in high school.

Just last semester, after hearing my lecture on the neurobiology of depression, a student mentioned that she had been diagnosed with depression as a sophomore in high school. Over the years, she's been prescribed an antidepressant sampler platter—Paxil, Prozac, Zoloft, Lexapro, Effexor, Wellbutrin, and Cymbalta. When she started college, her doctor added attention deficit hyperactivity disorder (ADHD) to her diagnosis, so she is currently taking medications for this condition as well. Most recently, her doctor speculated that she may suffer from borderline personality disorder, but no additional meds have been prescribed. Still, it's difficult to believe that such a high-functioning twenty-year-old has needed so much medication.

In the same small class, another student reported that during a recent visit to her pediatrician, she'd mentioned that she was feeling a little anxious at college, providing no further details. She was shocked when her doctor, without conducting a psychological interview or a specific diagnostic assessment, told her that she was suffering from depression and recommended that she take an antidepressant for a full year to determine its effects on her condition.

My students aren't necessarily a representative sample of the college population, but they do provide insight into the kinds of pressure many young people face as doctors, school psychologists, and parents push them to take these mind-altering medications. All too often, it's in order to deal with normal, everyday stressors that could be better handled in other ways. Although research suggests that both cognitive-behavioral and interpersonal therapy are just as effective as drug treatments, many people find that their insurance coverage for psychotherapy is limited. So seeking this kind of help requires more out-of-pocket expenses than merely taking medication, which is covered. Even if a patient is fortunate enough to have adequate insurance coverage for therapy sessions, he or she has to find the best therapist with the most effective strategy, and that's not easy, either.

When it comes to dealing with depression, it's important to find a type of therapy that engages both your brain and your body. Before I describe two active approaches—behavioral activation therapy and old-fashioned exercise—let's examine more traditional talk therapies used to treat grief, which is often associated with depression. As we discussed previously, significant traumas such as the loss of loved ones are potent triggers for the onset of depression. In learning about how certain therapeutic approaches affect these people at risk for depression, we can learn more about treatment strategies that offer the best hopes for lifting depression, regardless of its original cause.

Contrary to popular belief, talking about the traumas of your life may not help you to move from depression to mental health. In fact, in some cases this approach may impede your natural path to resilience and recovery. After conducting research focusing on predictors of depression following grief, Susan Nolen-Hoeksema, a professor of psychology at Yale, commented, "People who were prone to focusing on themselves, worrying about their feelings and not doing things specifically to lift their moods, such as talking with other people or engaging in activities they enjoyed, were more prone to still be depressed six months later." This research highlights the importance of taking specific actions to protect yourself from looming depression at your most vulnerable times.

Understanding more about preventing depression in vulnerable people is also extremely important for physical well-being. A recent study comprising two hundred fifty-four thousand subjects from sixty countries, conducted by the World Health Organization, reported that compared to other chronic illnesses, depression appears to be the most disabling disease in the world. In a subsequent interview about the study, Somnath Chatterji, one of the lead researchers, said, "Compared to the chronic physical illnesses of angina, arthritis, asthma, and diabetes, depression produces the most decline in health. Having depression over and above a physical illness significantly worsens health even further."

With depression posing such a threat to our mental and physical health, it is more important than ever that effective strategies be identified for both the prevention of depression in high-risk people and the eradication of symptoms once they emerge.

TOO MUCH TALK?

In the early 1990s, audiences were enthralled with the Academy Award–winning movie *The Prince of Tides,* based on the book by Pat Conroy, a tale of how a New York City psychoanalyst (played

by Barbra Streisand) conducted mental excavations on her patient, teacher and football coach Tom Wingo (played by Nick
Nolte). In session after session, the psychoanalyst worked to uncover important clues about a horrible attack on Tom's family
when he was a boy.

"Success" came when the memories were ultimately recov-
ered fully intact, accompanied by all the original raw mental pain
and anguish Tom had experienced decades earlier. Streisand's
character appeared intelligent and motivated as she led her
patient back in time to the most horrific event of his life.

At some point, Americans became enamored of the notion
of talk therapy as a way of treating trauma. They accepted that
this was both necessary and beneficial to help prevent a patient
from developing a debilitating mental illness down the line. If
someone experiences a traumatic event, he's encouraged to talk
about it, preferably with a mental health professional. In fact, if
a person seems to be functioning adaptively after experiencing a
traumatic event, she is often considered impaired or mentally
stunted. So we've come to view the ability to cope even only
somewhat well, which frankly should be viewed as a positive, in
the exact opposite way.

It's an interesting perception. A woman who loses a loved
one stumbles emotionally a bit but manages to continue working and taking care of her family. In the distorted world of mental health perspectives, we view her as dysfunctional. Why? Part
of the answer probably lies in how the media portray characters
enmeshed in trying circumstances. TV shows have led us to
expect drama—the affected person breaks down emotionally,
embracing her grief in a verbal way, and then rises back up to
meet the challenge. Only then do we consider her on the path
to emotional recovery. Everyone else is just in denial—an

emotional time bomb waiting to explode. But is this true? Nolen-Hoeksema's work suggests that this woman is on the path to mental health and much less likely to experience depression than those who are still paralyzed with grief.

Robert Neimeyer, a professor of psychology at the University of Memphis, has devoted his career to understanding grief and bereavement. When he began to question the effectiveness of grief counseling, he turned to the published studies and concluded that these grief interventions were "typically ineffective, and perhaps even deleterious, at least for persons experiencing a normal bereavement." In fact, in one study 38 percent of those receiving grief therapy were worse off than the control group that received no treatment.

George Bonanno, a psychologist at Columbia University, refers to the notion that people must work through their grief after experiencing a horrible life event to regain their mental health as the *Grief Work Assumption*. He traces this idea back to Freud, who wrote that every bereaved person should review memories and hopes associated with their sense of loss. Freud's therapeutic approach became more and more accepted throughout the twentieth century despite the fact that there was very little empirical evidence to support it.

When Bonanno and his colleagues started looking more closely at the efficacy of the Grief Work Assumption, he also found the approach ineffective. It actually seemed to impede recovery in some cases. Research suggests that cognitive-behavioral therapeutic approaches are more effective for conditions such as post-traumatic stress disorder that often follow exposure to traumatic events.

Many other researchers outside of the United States agree. Wolfgang Stroebe, Hank Schut, and Margaret Stroebe, psychologists at Utrecht University in the Netherlands, concluded that although a subset of people experience a "complicated grief" response that deviates from the norm and responds positively to grief therapy, there was little evidence confirming that induced disclosure of painful emotions is an effective coping strategy for bereavement.

Even so, from Columbine to 9/11 and every type of trauma in between, the grief therapy approach has been applied as a blanket intervention. Yet Bonanno and other experts worry that this practice may actually undermine the brain's natural resilience processes and lead to increased depression and anxiety disorders.

Our culture's ideas about dealing with trauma—in a manner that prevents the bereavement from developing into a paralyzing depression—are confusing. If a person survives an attack without breaking down emotionally, he is viewed as resilient and heroic. But if someone fails to suffer some form of an emotional breakdown after losing a loved one, he is considered pathological. There are even some developmental psychology theories that suggest that such bereaved individuals must have been emotionally distant from their loved one. Otherwise, how could they continue to function after such a loss? But a study assessing relationships of married couples three years prior to the death of a spouse found no evidence that emotionally resilient spouses were cold or indifferent in their relationships.

Living in New York City during the 9/11 terrorist attack, Bonanno seized the opportunity to learn more about natural resilience in the face of such a disaster. He and his colleagues assessed nearly twenty-eight hundred area residents during a six-month period following the attack. Resilience, defined as having no more than one symptom of PTSD (e.g., feelings of anxiety, flashbacks, sleep disturbances, exaggerated startle responses, difficulty concentrating), was observed in 65 percent of the sample. Although those who experienced the most intense exposure to the attacks were more likely to express PTSD symptoms, the resilience numbers never fell below one-third. These statistics support our earlier discussion on resilience—survivors with more financial resources, education, and social support exhibited enhanced resilience.

In fact, Bonanno's research points to resilience as the natural response to disaster. He and his colleagues argue that these studies should be considered when arguing against "the wholesale prophylactic psychological interventions in the aftermath of trauma."

In a recent *New York Times* article, the psychologist Lauren Slater described the swarms of therapists that descended on New York City after the Twin Towers attack. One psychologist told her that all this talk made some people worse, leaving them retraumatized by the interventions. Richard Gist, a community psychologist, trauma researcher, and associate professor at the University of Missouri, who provided psychological services following the collapse of the Hyatt Regency pedestrian skywalks and the United Airlines crash in Sioux City, Iowa, in the 1980s, had similar reactions to this undiscriminating grief therapy:

"Basically, all these therapists run down to the scene, and there's a lot of grunting and groaning and encouraging people to review what they saw, and then the survivors get worse. I've been saying for years, is it any surprise that if you keep leading people to the edge of a cliff they eventually fall off?"

So what alternatives are there to this approach?

Achieving Hardiness Through Effort-Driven Rewards

Although the empirical results are in, many experts are frustrated that the multimillion-dollar trauma industry continues to thrive—even though the evidence fails to show that it protects against the emergence of depression. But the grief intervention approach seems to be here to stay for the time being, as thousands of trauma recovery centers and the burgeoning self-help industry are committed to talking out our emotional pain. Meanwhile, there's plenty of research directing the therapeutic pendulum toward therapies that help the patients move from their trauma to a path that leads to resilience rather than debilitating depression.

Research suggests that having a meaningful purpose in life, appreciating one's surroundings and outcomes, and learning to grow from one's experiences are keys to developing "hardiness" that will keep people off the proverbial psychiatric or psychological couch.

Dusty Miller, a psychologist in Northampton, Massachusetts, began using a more proactive therapeutic approach some years ago. Early on, Miller found herself on the other side of the therapist's couch as a patient working through her anxiety after being sexually abused by her father. When she began therapy as an undergraduate student at Cornell University, she was told that her memories were actually wishful thinking. Decades later, other therapists said that her recollections were true and she needed to reach into her mental reserves and uncover every detail. As she revisited the memories of her abuse, however, her despair led to physical symptoms such as fever and chronically aching joints.

Finally losing patience with her therapists' insistence that she had to get worse before she got better, she opted for less talk and a more active form of therapy—tennis lessons. "Tennis was so grounding and taught me so much grace and helped me to regulate my anxiety. It was tennis, not talk, that really helped."

She channeled her new insights into her own work by directing her patients away from their anxiety and toward taking positive, proactive steps. She refrains from asking how they're feeling in group therapy sessions—knowing this will lead to hours of conversation—and merely asks what strengths they plan to focus on. She has also started a trauma resource center for low-income women. The traditional quiet rooms and couches have been replaced with a kitchen full of utensils so the women can work with their hands instead of dwelling on the demons of their pasts. There's also a computer room where they can type résumés and learn computing skills, and an attic full of clothes to help them move into the workplace.

Miller powerfully reinforces the importance of effort-driven rewards in her therapeutic approach. Talk therapy, she found, served only to magnify the toxic stress and anxiety associated with her patients' painful histories. But the opportunity to engage in physical tasks that produced meaningful results, such as preparing food for their children or going on job interviews that led to employment, enabled the women to reestablish connections between their efforts and rewards. As a result, their anxiety was reduced and they once again felt as though their efforts were worthwhile.

This anecdotal evidence suggests that replacing talk therapy with physical activity that leads to visible, meaningful consequences—that is, effort-driven rewards—in a patient's current life is more beneficial when treating trauma, anxiety, and depression in a clinical setting. In order for them to pass our scientific litmus test, however, we need more empirical evidence to gauge the success of these real-time active therapies.

Taking Effort-Driven Rewards to the Therapist's Couch

In 2006, I published the effort-driven rewards theory in a neuroscience journal. Soon after the article was published, I received an e-mail from Christopher Martell, a psychologist who, in addition to having a private practice, is a clinical associate professor at the University of Washington. My ideas, he wrote, complemented a type of therapy—he called it "behavioral activation therapy"—that he had been researching and implementing for several years. As I learned more about this emerging therapeutic approach, I could easily see how it transfers the principal components of effort-driven rewards to clinical practice and provides the perfect opportunity to test the theory with depressed patients.

Although behavioral approaches to treating depression have been around as long as cognitive therapies, they've never been widely used in clinical practice. Generally, these methods emphasize that depression results from a person experiencing few rewards, most likely due to problems in his environment or poor social skills. Using the behavioral approach, the psychologist works to restructure a person's behavioral responses and perhaps even alter the person's environment (moving to a different neighborhood to avoid reminders of past drug consumption, taking the mini-fridge out of the bedroom to cut down on snacks) to enhance the number and quality of life's rewards. Behavioral therapy is easily combined with cognitive therapy to include strategies that help restructure thought processes. The idea is to prevent fears and anxieties from blocking a person's achieving goals and experiencing the resulting pleasure. Although many attempts have been made to apply behavioral approaches to therapy, no real breakthroughs occurred until a surprising finding surfaced about a decade ago.

When Neil Jacobson and his colleagues at the University of Washington conducted a thorough analysis of the effectiveness of various cognitive therapies, they found that behavioral strategies that focused on enhancing the patient's activity level were just as successful in treating depression as the full-blown cognitive-behavioral treatment package. Jacobsen was intrigued. How could only one component of this complex treatment approach be so critical to improving a patient's outcome?

Working with Christopher Martell and others, Jacobson developed a comprehensive behavioral activation approach that focused on how the patient's interactions with the environment help shape his actions. This form of therapy emphasizes the importance of connections between efforts and rewards as critical factors in the treatment of depression. Whereas psychoanalysis was derived from Freud's observations about the unconscious mind, behavioral activation therapy was based on successful strategies and research in the field of psychology.

What's known as *avoidance behavior* and its role in reinforcing bad habits that lead to depression symptoms is at the heart of this methodology. Say someone reports to her therapist that she is depressed because she can't find a fulfilling job or a romantic relationship. She may find herself in this situation because it's much easier to avoid the anxiety associated with failing to get a job offer or a second call after a date if she never applies for the job or goes out on that first date—avoidance behavior at its best (or worst!).

In the short term, this kind of behavior seems to elevate her mood. She may think, "Whew, now I don't have to deal with that rejection. What a relief!" In the long run, of course, it's a mood depressor because she still finds herself facing unemployment, with no significant romantic partner to provide support.

This reminds me of the passive and active rats I've investigated in my laboratory. Passive animals, always freezing up or avoiding a challenge, were more likely to have higher baseline stress hormones and lower levels of resilience-related neurochemicals than the more adaptive, flexible coping rats. In a University of Chicago study, the shy rats that consistently avoided exploring a new toy placed in their cages had higher stress hormones and more anxious behavior and ultimately lived significantly shorter lives than their bolder counterparts.

For our patient's depression to lift, her avoidance behavior must be replaced with more adaptive behavior. That involves effectively interacting with her actual environment (not just an imaginary or wishful one), so that tangible, meaningful results can be reliably produced. In other words, adaptive behavior is dependent upon effort-driven rewards.

Though I've talked extensively about building and maintaining resilience against the onset of depression, the story changes once a person is actually suffering from depression. The emotional stakes are higher and so the effort-driven rewards need to be strategically supervised to allow the patient to gain—or regain—control over the challenges that are causing her so much anxiety and mental anguish.

In behavioral activation therapy, the client's attention is focused away from the idea that her symptoms are the result of a biological defect or deficiency. Ironically, therapeutic models that emphasize such defects as the source of depression divert attention away from the context of a person's life, which is usually the most critical source of emotional pain. Further, this notion of a chemical imbalance ignores the one thing that a person may have the most control over—her ability to change the circumstances of her life (break up with an abusive boyfriend, spend more time with her friends, spruce up her house so she can get more money if she sells it).

As Martell and his colleagues note: "We become so preoccupied with internal biological or psychological 'things' that we miss the flow of transactions between people and the worlds in which they live."

Indeed, in this new approach, depression is simply seen as the result of certain actions that are more likely to yield punishment (rejection, guilt) than rewards (acceptance, sense of accomplishment). Continuing to sit on the couch each weekend will further alienate a person from meeting people and forming valuable, meaningful friendships. As the effort-driven rewards circuit is triggered less and less, the underlying brain circuitry responsible for the physiological experience of pleasure and rewards becomes compromised. This leads to less motivation to interact with the world—in other words, the downward spiral of depression.

Persistent depressive behavior alters the effort-driven brain reward circuit in ways that can change the connections and sensitivity of the circuit, along with some of the brain's supporting systems (the hippocampus and other constituents of the emotional limbic system). As I experienced after my mother's death, cognitive functions such as problem solving, planning, hope, and optimism diminish as depression enters the emotional scene.

The effort-driven rewards theory dovetails with behavioral activation therapy in unique and interesting ways. People suffering from depression can be coached to modify the contexts of their lives so that the effort-driven rewards circuitry can once again become engaged. The phrase *use it or lose it* comes to mind. The increased pleasure resulting from the nucleus accumbens once a person engages in a meaningful activity (also activating the striatum) fires up the effort-driven rewards circuit, adding a new spark to the activity of the prefrontal cortex, a person's best hope for making the decisions that will lift the depression. It appears that the effort-driven brain reward circuit facilitates the neural implementation of behavioral activation therapy.

Still, this type of therapy is not easy. In some respects, it's similar to dealing with phobias. Exposure therapy (another form of behavioral therapy) is clearly the most effective treatment for this disorder. But being exposed to the root of a phobia—spiders, snakes, heights—is the patient's worst nightmare. Think about a spider? Maybe. But touch one, no thank you! For this reason, many people opt to live their entire lives with their dysfunction rather than face their worst fears—yet another example of how avoidance behaviors work.

Although often not as extreme as confronting a deep-seated phobia, becoming active and social again is hardly at the top of the to-do list for someone who's depressed. After all, if you've sunk into a state of hopelessness, inactivity, rumination, and withdrawal, the very thought of reengaging with your family, your job, or your friends can be daunting.

That's why a behavioral activation therapist creates a highly structured environment. Throughout therapy, the clinician works as a coach, encouraging patients to actively learn to identify areas of low positive reinforcement and high punishment. For example, the therapist might direct a struggling student to the realization that studying in the dorm room with friends who are talking and playing music is not leading to an understanding of the material, thus leading to low grades and high anxiety. But as often as possible, the therapist places the client at the helm of her treatment protocol. This is essential for gaining a sense of control and seeing that, once again, one's efforts lead to rewards. The therapist makes recommendations but does not tell the client what to do.

As a patient in this type of therapy, you will be asked to keep daily charts to track your activities and feelings, so that the steps leading to positive emotions can be identified and repeated, while those that result in negative emotions are reduced or eliminated. The idea is to move you from simply reacting to what's happening around you to a more proactive approach. You'll be given "practice" assignments so that you can experiment with the best response strategies before putting them to the test in truly meaningful ways.

In their book *Depression in Context*, Christopher Martell, Michael Addis, and Neil Jacobson describe Henry, a fifty-four-year-old executive who had been laid off from his job two years before starting behavioral activation therapy. Unable to find a position in a related field, he had to settle for a warehouse job to support his wife and son. Henry scored in the severely depressed range when he took the Hamilton Rating Scale for Depression (a paper-and-pencil assessment of depression).

After reading about this therapeutic approach, his clinician asked him to identify any bad habits that may have exacerbated his depressed feelings. Henry said that he avoided being around his son or wife because he was worried that they would ask him to do something he didn't want to do. Instead, he'd stay in bed pretending to be asleep or sit on the couch and watch television. This made his wife angry and his son retreat to his room.

Henry also said that they used to do things as a family but didn't anymore because they didn't have the money.

The therapist outlined the life events that led to Henry's depression: losing his job; seeing friends get good jobs when he didn't; having to accept a low-paying, unchallenging position; being forced to sell their house and rent a smaller house in a less desirable neighborhood. Then the therapist identified some of the secondary behaviors that resulted from these depression-triggering events—staying in bed, watching TV, avoiding spending time with his loved ones and friends due to embarrassment about his situation. Henry agreed that these behaviors made him feel worse. And they certainly didn't increase his chances of finding a more challenging job or spending meaningful time with his family.

At this point, the therapist attempted to "activate" Henry by focusing on changing these correctable secondary behaviors. He mapped out possible strategies on a whiteboard and asked for input from Henry, making sure that he understood the reasoning behind each suggestion.

In behavioral activation therapy, following each session, clients are given an assignment—behavioral baby steps—that focus on modifying the secondary behaviors. In Henry's case, he and his therapist agreed that spending some amount of time a day working on a project with his son or helping his wife out around the house would improve his relationships and begin to improve the appearance of his home. He might also make a concerted effort to socialize with his old friends.

A little trick to make sure the client carries out these plans—instead of avoiding them—is to think about outside-in behavioral prompts as opposed to inside-out prompts. For example, Henry may have said that he'd call his friends when he felt like going out with them (inside-out approach). But it's easy to anticipate that a depressed patient may never feel like socializing. So his therapist suggested that Henry contact a friend and tell him that he'd appreciate a call the next time the gang got together (an outside-in approach). After being invited out for a beer, Henry would probably be more likely to spend time with his friends.

A client who is working on increasing exercise as a secondary behavior might pack a workout bag the night before and place it in the car, or join a class that meets at certain times each week, and ask a friend to accompany her to the gym on some of those nights—providing several outside-in, environmental prompts for achieving her goal.

This outside-in approach, although challenging at the beginning, can eventually help lift depressed emotions once the client begins to engage in the behavior. Henry reported that as he worked on these secondary behaviors, it became clearer how they could mitigate some of the critical underlying factors causing his depression. For example, improving his home situation made him feel less like a failure and increasing his social contacts helped him network and find a better job.

The therapist tracks how well the treatment is working by administering the Hamilton Depression Scale at each session. By the time a client scores in the nondepressed range, he also has a whole new set of behavioral coping strategies to help him stay there.

So how does behavioral activation therapy fare when compared to the so-called gold standard of depression therapies—SSRIs? Recently, Sona Dimidjian at the University of Washington and several colleagues conducted a study in which 240 subjects diagnosed with major depression were randomly assigned to either an antidepressant group (paroxetine), a placebo control group, a cognitive therapy group, or a behavioral activation group for sixteen weeks.

The antidepressant and behavioral activation groups were comparable in their ability to improve symptoms across all levels of severity. But in the subgroup of the most severely depressed patients, behavioral activation therapy significantly outperformed the SSRI group as well as the cognitive or placebo group.

When it came to adherence to therapy, however, there was no contest. Nearly four times more patients in the antidepressant group dropped out of the study than those using the cognitive and behavioral activation therapies. One reason may have been the drug side effects; subjects reported reduced sexual libido, insomnia, gastrointestinal distress, and dry mouth. Finally, behavioral activation therapy brought a higher number of subjects to remission—that is, to the point of improvement where they no longer exhibited the symptoms of depression.

Generally, in about 50 percent of cases, SSRIs eventually change the neurobiology of the patient enough to stir him out of the depressed state, but then what? Unless the doctor prescribing the medication also instructs the patient on how certain habits, circumstances, and thought processes lead to the symptoms of depression (which is unlikely, considering that most of these prescriptions are not written by mental health professionals), the person may easily find himself right back in a depressed state when the drug treatment ends.

In her study, Dimidjian explained that behavioral activation helps depressed clients increase their activities in the kinds of structured ways that enable them to connect directly with the real and tangible sources of the rewards in their lives (that is, to reestablish lost effort-driven rewards). It also gives them the insight and tools to solve their problems after the treatment stops. Antidepressants, on the other hand, activate the brain in more generalized ways so that a person eventually feels like taking positive steps on his own behalf. But there's no life coach, no strategies, no goals, no awareness of behavioral pitfalls, just generalized activity that may or may not lead to permanent change.

Using a military analogy, behavioral activation therapy is like a smart brain missile targeted at a specific destination (the effort-driven brain reward circuit), whereas antidepressants are the equivalent of bombing the entire city, ultimately hitting the target but affecting many other areas (the physiological functions throughout the brain and body) with many unwanted side effects.

JUMP-STARTING EFFORT-DRIVEN REWARDS AND RELIEVING THE SYMPTOMS OF DEPRESSION WITH EXERCISE

Admit it, if you went to your physician complaining of depression and she asked you to consider joining an exercise class, you'd question her professional training. After all, you could have gotten the same advice by opening a magazine or watching a television talk show. Hold your judgment, though, because the research is in and it points overwhelmingly to the positive effects of exercise on mental health, especially depression. In fact, the therapeutic potential for this activity deserves a second look—and more than a little respect.

In the mid-1980s, a few experimental reports demonstrated the effectiveness of exercise in treating depression. In one study, Lisa McCann and David Holmes at the University of Kansas were interested in whether exercise training had more therapeutic value than relaxation in the treatment of depression. They recruited depressed undergraduate women and assigned them to one of three groups: an exercise training group that participated one hour of aerobic exercise two times a week, a relaxation training class that met for the same amount of time, or a control group that received no training. To make it more interesting, both training groups were told that their assigned treatment (exercise or relaxation) was effective in helping people overcome stress, a prominent cause of depression, as discussed in chapter 5. By telling the subjects that their "treatment" would mitigate stress, they were controlling for expectations about the effectiveness of each treatment.

After ten weeks, the exercise group demonstrated considerably more improvement in their depression symptoms than the other two groups. Plus, the exercise group had significantly higher aerobic capacity scores than the other two groups; so these side effects yielded concrete benefits to health and fitness. This landmark study represented the first empirical evidence that strenuous exercise could be an effective treatment for depression.

As psychiatric pharmaceuticals gained momentum in the 1990s, researchers wondered how exercise would fare in direct comparison. In 1999, James Blumenthal and his colleagues at Duke University recruited older patients (fifty and over) for either a sixteen-week program consisting of exercise, the SSRI sertraline Hcl (Zoloft), or combined exercise and antidepressant therapy.

Interestingly, at the end of the study there were no differences among the groups. This means that exercise held its own in the treatment of depression. The researchers did note a faster initial response in the drug group for the most severely depressed patients along with a faster response rate for the combination therapy in the less severely depressed patients.

But by the end of the sixteen weeks, the exercise group had caught up on the improvement scales. And, once again, patients in the exercise or exercise/drug combination groups demonstrated greater improvements in aerobic capacity than the drug group. Oxygen is an important fuel for the brain, so enhanced aerobic capacity also sharpens mental functions and enhances the brain's resilience. Thus, if exercise treatment ultimately results in the same improvement without the negative side effects, this therapeutic approach deserves consideration as a viable treatment option for depressed patients.

More recently, in an interesting assessment of the effectiveness of a single "dose" of exercise, John Bartholomew and his colleagues at the University of Texas at Austin exposed subjects to either thirty minutes of exercise or quiet rest, and then determined any changes in their self-reported mood states. Both interventions reduced stress, tension, and feelings of depression and anger. However, the exercise group reported an increase in the more positive emotions relating to subjective well-being and vigor.

So what is exercise doing to the brain? Does it influence the effort-driven rewards circuitry by building resilience and hardiness and thus fighting the severity of depression symptoms? The answer is yes. The finding in the Bartholomew study that exercise leads to more pleasurable emotions suggests that exercise may activate the brain's pleasure center, which is so critical to the effort-driven rewards circuit. Animal research shows that running increases sensitivity to the reward neurochemical dopamine. Furthermore, a review of the effects of exercise on our cognition or thought processes reveals selective but robust improvements on executive-control processes, which allow us to schedule, plan, monitor, and coordinate our tasks. Of course, the prefrontal cortex, another component of the effort-driven rewards circuit, controls these functions. Thus, it's likely that this brain area is altered in some way with exercise as well. And what about that third component of the circuit—the striatum? Considering that this area coordinates our bodies' movements, this is probably the most actively engaged component of the circuit during exercise.

Exercise has other potential brain benefits, too. We've already discussed the enhanced rates of neurogenesis (the production of new neurons) consistently found in rats engaged in running. Because we can verify the existence of these new cells in a brain only during an autopsy, it's obviously been difficult to determine if these rodent studies are the same for humans. One creative study, however, conducted by Rusty Gage from the Salk Institute and Scott Small from Columbia University got around this challenge by using MRI technology to map cerebral blood volume in people before and after a three-month exercise program. Sure enough, they found increased blood volume, and we know from research on rodents that increased cerebral blood flow is a reliable indicator of new cell growth.

William Greenough at the University of Illinois has also demonstrated that rats housed in cages with running wheels develop increased capillary density in the cerebellum, another area of the brain involved in motor coordination. More capillaries translate into more blood delivery to the brain, with all the accompanying increases in oxygen and glucose.

Another way that exercise may treat depression is through stress reduction. Rod Dishman, a researcher in the University of Georgia's Department of Exercise Science, has spent the better part of his career producing elegant results supporting this thesis. Indeed, I conducted my very first research project in collaboration with Dishman's laboratory when I was a biopsychology graduate student. We found that students who had undergone an intense six-week exercise program handled a stressful mental task with fewer signs of stress than the control nonexercising group.

In a recent review, Dishman chronicled several ways that exercise boosts the all-important allostatic processes—that is, it enhances the body's ability to respond to physiological challenges with an ideal level of efficiency, thus creating a buffer against the effects of chronic stress. The hippocampus is the area of the brain that responds to stress hormones, which makes it vulnerable during stressful times and depression. It's protected by exercise-generated boosts in mitochondrial proteins (which are the cell's power plants) and by enhanced protection against toxic invaders to the brain such as oxygen free radicals. In addition to the creation of new cells, exercise also increases brain growth factors.

Finally, the repetitive movement of running increases serotonin in the brainstem, suggesting that exercise may be nature's way of delivering antidepressants in the form of tiny bursts of serotonin to the brain during meaningful physical movements. In a recent *Newsweek* article on the effects of exercising on the brain, John J. Ratey, M.D., an associate professor of psychiatry at Harvard Medical School, commented, "Dopamine, serotonin, and norepinephrine—all of these are elevated after a bout of exercise. So having a workout will help with focus, calming down, impulsivity—it's like taking a little bit of Prozac and a little bit of Ritalin." But, of course, without the side effects.

Still, the positive effects of exercise are diffuse—not unlike the effects of SSRIs. Behavioral activation therapy, on the other hand, makes clearer connections between effort and specific rewards, which confirms the importance of effort-driven rewards in rebuilding mental health when you're faced with depression. Exercise likely activates the same brain growth factors (neurochemical-like fertilizers that facilitate the formation of important connections within the many brain circuits) generated in SSRI therapy, which takes some time but eventually makes you feel better. But exercise has the added benefit of improved cardiovascular health and tighter abs.

The pendulum is definitely swinging toward active rather than passive therapeutic approaches for depression. Research suggests that a depressed patient who undergoes some form of cognitive-behavioral therapy (especially behavioral activation therapy) in addition to starting an exercise program and seeking social support will activate her brain in significant ways that will improve her symptoms.

Of course, it's difficult for someone suffering from depression to make these informed decisions. Even small proactive steps take effort, something that is not easy to muster when you're under the cloud of depression. As Andrew Solomon, author of *The Noonday Demon,* describes it, "Depression starts out insipid, fogs the days into a dull color, weakens ordinary actions until their clear shapes are obscured by the effort they require, leaves you tired and bored and self-obsessed. . . ."

After my mother died, I vividly remember not having the energy to do anything but look out the window endlessly. The serendipitous vacuuming provided baby effort-driven rewards steps that stirred me from these motionless trances. I was fortunate to have stumbled across this unique therapy at that memorable flea market. But not everyone is as lucky as I was, and for far too many of us, the approach to treating depression is much less systematic than treating medical ailments.

When you strain a muscle, you may take painkillers indefinitely and ignore the physical therapist's recommendation to start physical rehabilitation. After all, those rehabilitative exercises are often painful in the beginning (and tempting to avoid!). However, you need to endure the pain in order for the muscle to heal efficiently and appropriately. It's the same with depression. Realizing that the best treatment may not be the easiest or most convenient would serve patients well and help change the landscape of therapeutic approaches in our society.

Research clearly seems to reinforce the importance of physical effort and effort-driven rewards in maintaining our emotional well-being and combating or preventing depression. But then, scientific literature doesn't always dictate or even influence our lifestyles or social and medical policies. In the next chapter, I'll consider the contemporary patterns of effort-driven rewards emerging in our lifestyles, as well as the long-term effects of such practices on the ongoing evolution of our brains. A serious look at where our society is headed may encourage us to take a more serious look at our current lifestyles.

9

Effort-Driven Rewards and
Our Evolving Brains

I CURRENTLY SERVE AS THE DEPARTMENTAL chair for the psychology department at Randolph-Macon College, and I refer to myself as a behavioral neuroscientist. But my true roots lie in the field of ethology, the scientific study of behavior in an animal's natural setting. I began my training at the "University of My Backyard" in Mobile, Alabama, where I loved observing frogs, lizards, and other animals. I even tried incubating the prized bird eggs I'd discovered hidden among gigantic magnolia trees behind our house.

I was curious about whether sand crabs from the nearby Gulf of Mexico would adapt to the grass in my yard (they didn't). How could it be that when I grabbed a lizard by the tail, the tail would often separate from the lizard's body? As the lizard scurried to safety, the bodyless tail would wiggle in my hands for some time. Wow! Was that a way to distract the predator (me) while the animal ran to safety?

During these childhood ethological adventures, I knew nothing about actual research in the discipline. I didn't even know what research was! That is, until one memorable night when I was twelve years old and my parents had a local game warden over for dinner. For his job, he had been encouraged to take courses about animal behavior at a local community college. Other than my schoolteachers, I didn't know many people who'd attended college, so I was intrigued. I have vivid memories of sitting at the top of the stairs and straining to hear every word he said.

As I eavesdropped, our guest talked about what he was learning in class. One scientist, he said, took little goslings away from their mothers and then exposed them to various items such as boots with different designs on them. I remember everyone's excitement and laughter when he described the motherless goslings following around a balloon floating in the lake or polka-dot boots worn by the scientist. "Those silly birds thought the balloon was their mother," he proclaimed.

I now know that the scientist in question was the Nobel Prize–winning ethologist Konrad Lorenz. Each time I teach my own comparative animal behavior course, I describe his work on these critical windows for imprinting parental-like bonds. During a certain period of time, the goslings register the first thing they see as "mom." I continue to be just as enamored of his research as I was on that evening more than three decades ago.

Niko Tinbergen, who shared the Nobel Prize in medicine with Konrad Lorenz and Karl Von Frisch in 1973, was another founding father of ethology. In addition to contributing valuable research on the triggers of aggression in the stickleback fish, he outlined the criteria that should be met when scientists try to understand a biological phenomenon. To develop a thorough understanding of these phenomena, he wrote, we should understand the mechanisms, development, function, and evolutionary history associated with specific behaviors. Can we use this evolutionary perspective to determine the potential value of using effort-driven rewards as a way to maintain a buffer against the onset of depression?

EFFORT-DRIVEN REWARDS IN AN EVOLUTIONARY CONTEXT

Throughout this book, I've talked about effort-driven rewards from Tinbergen's four criteria. I've discussed the accumbens-striatal-cortical circuit and related neurochemicals as the underlying mechanisms of effort-driven rewards, which help alleviate depressive behavior. From a developmental perspective, I've explored the importance of strengthening the connections between effort and positive consequences early in a child's life to foster a healthy resilience in the face of the inevitable setbacks to come. I have suggested an adaptive, or beneficial, function for physical effort that contributes to effort-driven rewards, especially when that effort involves acquiring important resources related to survival.

But what about the evolutionary history of effort-driven rewards? Can this behavior be found in other mammalian species? If so, we'd have further evidence of the biological relevance of effort-driven rewards throughout evolution. Identifying a strong biological tendency for these rewards throughout the animal kingdom would help us understand why the abrupt removal of these behavioral patterns has wreaked havoc on our emotional lives.

A quick tour through the animal world yields rich evidence of effort-driven rewards. One dramatic example is the response of bowerbirds, a little bird found in both Australia and New Guinea, to the challenge of finding a mate. Male bowerbirds

build elaborate towering nests, complete with unique decora-
tions (eggshells, butterfly wings, shiny seashells) to impress the
ladies. Females have very high expectations when it comes to
choosing their mates. Males not only must display impressive
architectural and carpentry skills, but once the female arrives,
the male must engage in a winning "courtship display." He flits
back and forth in his carefully constructed bower and flicks his
wings, while imitating the calls of other birds during his
courtship rituals.

Bowerbirds are the nest-building champions when it comes
to birds and mammals, but all nest building can be viewed as a
form of effort-driven rewards. There's no immediate gratification from nest building, however. It takes time before the eggs
will be laid or a potential mate flies by.

A more prevalent form of effort-driven rewards can be seen in
the foraging strategies used by most animals. Mammals spend
considerable amounts of their waking hours searching for food.
These efforts range from the spider monkey's methods of locating
and harvesting ripe fruit despite fierce competition to an inner-city
rat's technique of following humans and consuming their garbage.
Clearly, the brain's ability to initiate and sustain effort directed
toward acquiring important resources has been an essential
response to the challenges of survival in mammalian evolution.

Martin Seligman provided another dramatic example of the
importance of effort-driven rewards in the evolution of animals.
When I e-mailed him a copy of the article I had published that
described the effort-driven rewards theory, he reminded me
about the importance of avoiding shortcuts to rewards so that
more gratification is associated with more effort directed toward
the prizes in our lives. He also reminded me of a story he'd
included in *Authentic Happiness,* in which he'd described the

lengths to which a professor of his went to entice an exotic Amazonian pet lizard to eat.

The professor had tried feeding the lizard mangos, lettuce, ground pork, and flies, but the lizard refused to eat anything and looked as if it were wasting away. One day, the professor brought in a ham sandwich, and, as usual, when he tossed it to the lizard, there was no response. While reading the newspaper, the professor dropped a section on the floor, which happened to land on top of the sandwich. The lizard approached the newspaper, shredded it, and devoured the sandwich. The lizard's simple and reflexive brain had evolved in such a way that it required the animal to engage in physical effort before it could feed itself. No shortcuts for our reptile friends!

Of course, our brains are much more complex than the reptile brain, but we still carry evolutionary reminders of our ancestral past. I was fascinated to read in *Newsweek* about a retailing challenge Wal-Mart faced when it first opened stores in China. Although American consumers are happy to purchase prepared cuts of meat that have been sitting in cellophane wrapping, the Chinese are not. People from this more agrarian culture demanded fresh meat that they had a "hand" in preparing.

Wisely, Wal-Mart adapted to the cultural differences and introduced fish and turtle tanks. This gives customers the opportunity to exert effort toward catching their own food, which is cleaned by a shop person. The satisfied customers then toss their bloodstained bags of carp into their shopping cart beside other household items and cosmetics. That's something you would never see in an American store.

Another way to understand the biological importance of a response is to observe what happens when an animal is deprived of the opportunity to express it. During times of food deprivation, all of our attention is focused on acquiring nourishment to relieve the hunger. This is also true for drinking, sleeping, socializing, and other important behavioral responses. We can learn about their importance by observing fluctuating rates of effort-driven rewards under various environmental conditions.

Raccoons, which are the poster mammal for effort-driven rewards, provide some insight. Deemed "ecological opportunists of the first order" by the zoologist Dorcas MacClintock, these animals run their handlike paws along the bottom of the riverbank, identify food, retrieve it, manipulate it to secure the edible portions, and then consume it. They are very successful in adapting to new environmental challenges and currently thrive in many environmental niches ranging from Panama to Canada.

In a now famous article written by two students of the late famous behaviorist B. F. Skinner, Marian and Keller Breland wrote about leaving the ivory tower of academe to apply their knowledge about animal responses to training them for military and entertainment purposes. When they tried to train raccoons to put coins in a piggy bank for an upcoming television commercial, the couple was initially successful using food rewards to motivate the raccoons' behavior. However, after a while, they noticed that the raccoons started to make mistakes, especially when given more than one coin. They would grab the coins, start rubbing them together in a miserly fashion, take them over to their water dish, and swish them around a bit before eventually dropping the coins in the bank.

The Brelands had similar results when trying to get pigs to drop a coin in the piggy bank. After training created strong associations between the coins and food rewards, the pigs started dropping the coins on the floor and manipulating them with their noses as they do when they are rooting around in the mud for their food.

These annoying distractions didn't make for good television, but the Brelands recognized their importance. They called this type of response instinctive drift. When a response has biological relevance for an animal, even if it learns to obtain the rewards without making the response, the animal will drift toward the original means of obtaining rewards. This behavioral recalibration suggests that this is an important response for the brain, and healthy functioning may be disrupted if these predisposed responses are not allowed to be expressed. In other words, if exerting effort to obtain rewards was important in the lives of our ancestors, the abrupt removal of these responses from our contemporary behavioral repertoires would disrupt the brain's functions, manifesting itself as depression or other anxiety-related disorders, such as obsessive-compulsive disorder.

Anecdotal evidence from captive raccoons also reinforces the importance of evolved effort-driven rewards response patterns. Some raccoons experience such excessive stress while being held in zoo cages, they start washing their food obsessively—as if increased rates of effort-driven rewards may compensate for a lack of control in their environment. One captive maternal raccoon washed her newborn cub so much that she ultimately drowned him.

During a recent trip to Costa Rica to observe primates, I was delighted one evening when a pair of raccoons entered the open-air restaurant where my family and I were eating dinner. For me, this was definitely "dinner and a show." It almost seemed as if these masked animals had arrived to provide a final confirmation of the value of effort-driven rewards for mental health as I was completing the manuscript for this book. Apparently, the raccoon "couple" had smelled the toast that was warming in the toaster oven and were motivated to retrieve a piece from the large bread-basket. Talk about resilience and persistence! They strutted into a large human-filled dining room and didn't seem frightened when the waiters shooed them out the door. They returned time and time again until they successfully retrieved a piece of toast from the breadbasket. Each time, they used a different strategy. At one point, one raccoon was peering over a wall, seemingly as-sessing the situation (or serving as a distraction while his partner in crime scurried under the "bread table") when a waiter walked up with a cloth napkin and actually swatted the raccoon on the nose. The raccoon merely closed his eyes and leaned back each time the napkin came hurling toward his face.

Their clever manipulation of the world around them, coupled with their strong social ties (some raccoons are monogamous), leave no doubt in my mind why this species has successfully adapted to such a diverse array of natural habitats—providing further evidence that effort-driven rewards do indeed lead to enhanced resilience and creative problem solving.

Lessons learned from animal models reinforce the evolution-ary value of experiencing well-placed effort-driven rewards throughout all of our lives. In addition to intellectual pursuits that are important for our mental health, engaging in personally meaningful activities that provide effort-driven rewards (crafts, cooking, chores, gardening, scrapbooking) appears to be valu-able for maintaining healthy mental functioning. If you feel yourself being pulled to these activities, listen to your emotional instinctive drifts. Filling those voids in our emotional lives may save us a lot of money in filling antidepressant prescriptions!

And what if you don't feel drawn toward such physical activi-ties? As humans, we can be extremely flexible in how we respond so that we may not be as emotionally lost as raccoons when their resource-seeking rituals are suppressed. But adding such activities engages the accumbens-striatal-cortical circuit as well as various higher-order motor circuits—in addition to providing cardiovascular benefits. Those of you who feel the pull of your brain nudging you to engage in more physical effort to produce life's important resources are fortunate (embrace your instinctual effort-driven rewards drifts!). You are less likely to fall prey to the temptation of our effortless society and less likely to become depressed. For those who don't feel the need to be more active, as discussed in previous chapters, merely possessing knowledge about healthy levels of physical effort may provide the necessary motivation to prevent a sedentary lifestyle, which puts you at risk for developing depression. This is not a trivial point. As we get farther and farther away from a lifestyle that requires physical effort, our instinctual drifts may slowly fade away, increasing our brain and body's vulnerability to heightened anxiety and depression.

GETTING YOUR BRAIN ENGAGED

During conversations with my brother, Doug, I'm always reminded of how important it is to maintain healthy emotional responses. Doug's a doctor who specializes in infectious diseases, and he often has to tell several patients a week that they have HIV/AIDS. Of course, the diagnosis is no longer a death sentence because this disease, similar to diabetes, can be managed throughout one's life. But when patients are initially told they've tested positive, they are almost always overwhelmed with fear and panic. Their responses range from catatonic trances lasting hours to suicidal attempts, Doug says. So he has to watch his patients very closely after he gives them this news.

After walking his patients through emotional minefields each week, my brother finds that he needs to recalibrate his anxiety level to maintain his emotional equilibrium. His effort-driven reward of choice is planning and preparing an incredibly elaborate gourmet meal to share with as many friends as he can squeeze around his dinner table each Sunday evening. "For me, cooking is therapeutic because it's something I enjoy doing and it's totally different from my medical practice," he says. "I experience immense pleasure from all aspects of preparing these meals—looking through cookbooks to select just the right recipes, thinking about how each dish will complement the other items on my dinner menu, then actually preparing the food. During these culinary mental retreats, the stress of my practice never enters my mind."

The methodical process of planning, shopping for, and preparing these weekly gastronomical adventures allows my brother to reestablish his optimal emotional baseline so that he's ready for the next week of patients. In his mind, the more challenging the recipe, the more control he gains over the uncertainty in his world. The lively conversation and laughter throughout his multicourse dinners also serve as stress busters.

I've been on the receiving end of many of these impressive meals myself, and I can add that his culinary efforts are extremely rewarding for his guests as well. In fact, engaging in effort-driven rewards that ultimately make others feel good is probably especially appropriate for someone who has chosen a career devoted to helping others heal. But not all M.D.s cook away their stress and anxiety. A close friend of my brother's, who specializes in internal medicine, recently told him that after a stressful week of working with patients, ironing for several hours each Saturday is her ticket to mental health.

Some of us use effort-driven rewards as a preventive for keeping job-related anxiety at bay; others find that these rewards work even in the midst of a full-blown depression by helping to recalibrate emotional gauges that are spinning out of control. Adrienne Martini, a journalist and communications professor in upstate New York, discovered that knitting rescued her from the depths of postpartum depression.

Scientists aren't certain what triggers this kind of depression, but because it appears after a woman gives birth, when there's a drastic alteration of several reproductive hormones, most experts speculate that this unique variety of depression is related to an abrupt endocrinological shift. Regardless of the reason, approximately half of new mothers experience "maternal blues," a transient depressed mood lasting a few days. In about 14 percent of cases, however, the symptoms persist and a major depression ensues. Being depressed, especially for new mothers, who are learning a whole new regime of caring for a helpless little baby, is daunting and requires appropriate and immediate interventions in serious cases.

Although Adrienne was well aware of the depression that characterized her Appalachian family history, she was unprepared for the wave of anxiety and sadness that hit after having her first child, Maddy. Her life was completely satisfying before she gave birth—a supportive spouse, fulfilling career, spirited friends—but having Maddy caused her balanced life to tilt off its emotional axis.

In her book *Hillbilly Gothic: A Memoir of Madness and Motherhood*, Martini writes about spending what she calls "quality time" on a psychiatric ward after giving birth, reminding her that she couldn't escape her family history. "My own hillbilly gothic roots are riddled with emotional instability," she wrote.

"Rather than send a layette, my family gifted me with a tendency for clinical depression."

Could effort-driven rewards realign Adrienne's hormonal and emotional confusion? After she came home from the hospital, the antidepressants calmed her enough to enable her to take care of her daughter. However, she still didn't feel like herself. She had been a sporadic knitter before she had Maddy, and now she decided to pick up her needles again, figuring she could work on some unfinished hats during the quiet times when her daughter was sleeping in her lap. "My neglected hats proved to be the perfect panacea. Their simplicity was ideal and the monotony a moving meditation. . . . I began to feel like Dr. Seuss' Bartholomew Cubbins, knee-deep in 500 hats. I gave a few as gifts, some to charity, and one still waits for the perfect owner."

In Adrienne's case, the effort-driven rewards boosted the effects of the antidepressant so that she felt like herself once again. Now that she was aware of the therapeutic effects of effort-driven rewards, she was better prepared for the birth of her second child. She recently told me that she knitted her way through labor, putting her needles aside only when the nurses insisted that she focus on the delivery of her emerging son. She didn't experience severe depression the second time around. "My knitting takes the edge off, so I can deal with the chaos in my life."

I didn't have to look far from my office to find more support for the healing properties of meaningful action that, in this case, replaced the need for antidepressants. Jack Trammell, director of the Learning Center at Randolph-Macon College, helps students with learning-related challenges, a growing problem on college campuses across the country. On a daily basis, he gives them guidance about how to deal with their learning disabilities.

After growing up on a farm in Kentucky, Jack married and moved to Richmond in his twenties, leaving his agrarian roots far behind. He took an office job as a manager for a rental car office, which replaced his daily farming chores. Meanwhile, he was spiraling into depression. At home, instead of mowing his lawn or gardening, he paid someone to do his yard work. As he retreated to his "cave" office in the basement each evening, he proceeded to test the waters of professional writing, a skill he developed with proficiency; he has written several books and articles about southern history.

But by the time Jack was in his early thirties, he found the pleasure in his life diminishing; he told me he never felt as fulfilled as he had living on the farm in Kentucky. In addition to being dissatisfied at work, he found himself in an unhappy marriage. He was soon diagnosed with depression and put on antidepressants.

In a bold moment, Jack took drastic measures to recapture the passion of his youth as well as become less dependent on medication. He decided that going back to his agrarian lifestyle would help him recover his mental health and stability. He remarried and purchased an old farm in Louisa County, Virginia—twenty acres for gardening and raising animals. There, his children have no time for TV or video games, as they come home and quickly run outside to tend to chores that include taking care of a slew of animals—horses, donkeys, chickens, dogs, and cats. Also, during these redefining times, Jack completed his Ph.D. in the School of Education's Research and Evaluation Track at Virginia Commonwealth University.

Today, Jack is more fulfilled in his career working with college students, and he can't wait to get home to his farm and family each evening. His decision to recalibrate his life by moving to the farm stabilized the emotional turbulence in his life, so he's no longer taking antidepressants. "The farm has in essence become an antidepressant," he explains. "Even when I feel paralyzed with fatigue, anxiety and worry about my complex life, the animals still need to be fed, and they don't care about the expensive unexpected car repair or the problems at work that must be resolved. By tending to their needs, it forces me outside myself, and requires me to physically exert myself. Inevitably, I always feel better after feeding the chickens."

The stories told by Doug, Adrienne, and Jack illustrate the diverse ways effort-driven rewards can recalibrate your emotional gauges. Regardless of the task—knitting, cooking, ironing, or farming—these physical efforts can help you gain resilience against the onset of depression as well as help treat the problem once it sets in. If used in conjunction with other traditional therapies such as antidepressants, effort-driven rewards can help you recover from an existing bout of depression. We also learn from these enlightened and engaging people that regardless of how cognitively stimulating our lives are, we still have instinctual drifts toward these physical endeavors. Indeed, we need our effort-driven rewards "vitamins" to protect us from our emotional vulnerabilities. As observed across the animal world, physical effort remains an important element of mental and physical well-being.

LIVING THE VIRTUAL LIFE

"So where are we going from here?" asked a student after a lecture about the evolution of the human brain. I'd just explained the important role that meaningful movement played in generating the resources that allowed our ancestors to survive. What will happen if our society continues to engage in less and less physical activity, skipping the labor to enjoy the fruit, this insightful student wondered. Will we become massive blobs sitting in front of our computer screens? Will we eventually develop one huge digit to activate electronic inputs?

Or maybe we'll have "virtual life" programs streamed into our consciousness, without having to go through all the trouble of actually living unpredictable, sometimes treacherous lives. To live an entirely virtual existence, we don't need to fast-forward thousands of years. Some of us are doing it already. Joel Stein recently wrote in *Time* magazine about Second Life, an online virtual ethos available to anyone willing to download the program and sit in front of their computer for hours and hours. "After all, if Second Life is a virtual community in which you can look however you want, do whatever you want and use the fake name you want, then I could make all my fantasies come true." He reported that in the last two months of 2006, more than eight hundred thousand people had visited the site.

Clearly there's a potentially serious conflict between the evolution of our brains and life in contemporary society. What impact will our ever advancing technology have on the mental health of future generations if incentives to challenge themselves physically and mentally are taken away?

If effort-driven rewards are indeed important for maintaining mental health, each new technological advance that reduces the need for our physical engagement may compromise the integrity of the accumbens-striatal-cortical circuit. As we keep discovering ways to bypass the natural effort-driven rewards with shortcuts, are we robbing our brains of the opportunities to experience pure, natural rewards in the context in which they evolved? Remember that shortcuts to rewards are not as pleasurable as encountering the rewards the old-fashioned way—as nature intended.

Arthur C. Clarke, author of the famous science-fiction movie *2001: A Space Odyssey,* seems to be warning us about getting too comfortable and dependent on electronic technology. The fictitious Hal, the computer that controlled the spacecraft *Discovery* on its voyage across the solar system, was the product of human hands. However, as the story progressed, this wonder machine started to control the humans instead of the other way around. "Hal had been created innocent; but all too soon, a snake had entered his Electronic Eden," wrote Clarke.

Although the story line for this movie was generated nearly a half-century ago, we still appear to be far from having computerized robots gaining conscious awareness and attempting to gain control over humans. But there are concerns about the electronic Eden we have created for ourselves and what this may be doing to our brains and mental health.

Remember how vacuuming helped me recover from depression after my mother's death? It's just one small example of a type of effort that can lead to tangible rewards. But today we have the Roomba Vacuuming Robot, which would threaten my vacuuming antidepressant for future generations. Now you no longer even have to be in the room to clean your floors. This prototypical household robot, traveling back and forth across the designated preprogrammed space, does the job for you, relieving you from having to exert any effort at all.

In fact, in the January 2007 issue of *Scientific American,* Microsoft's Bill Gates wrote the cover story about the not-so distant future of robots (and their interactions with computers, of course) in the American household. A large diagram depicted his vision of the future homeowner using his home computer to oversee and coordinate multiple home robots. A long-armed robot was shown folding clothes in the laundry room, an upright mobile robot was dispensing food and medicine to Grandma, who was bedridden (poor Grandma—no therapeutic social contact for her!), and a lawn-mowing robot is cutting the grass.

There is no doubt that our culture is redefining the relation between effort and rewards at a pace that is difficult for our brains to keep up with. A recent survey of how we reward effort monetarily reinforces this confusion. When determining how long and how much effort it takes for certain people in different professions to earn a thousand dollars, it was reported that the talk show host Howard Stern earns this amount in twenty-four seconds; the actor Brad Pitt in four minutes, forty-eight seconds; and the athlete Kobe Bryant in five minutes, thirty seconds. Professions representing the more traditional effort-driven rewards of our ancestors (e.g., efforts related to agriculture and keeping our shelters/homes safe and free of threatening germs) reflected a very different story. For example, it takes farmers 57 hours and janitors 103 hours to earn a thousand dollars.

Forms of entertainment that require no physical effort also appear to be altering our activity levels at a rapid pace. The Centers for Disease Control and Prevention recently asked a sample of nearly two hundred twenty thousand people how many times a week they engaged in vigorous leisure-time activity lasting at least ten minutes. A whopping 61 percent reported that they never engaged in that amount of activity; and only 11 percent reported five or more activity bouts per week. More women reported inactivity than men.

Teen activity levels are also troubling. In 2003, the number of male high school students engaging in thirty minutes of moderate "regular" activity (not requiring one to break a sweat) five days each week—or, on at least three days per week, engaging in twenty minutes of vigorous activity that does result in a sweat—declined from 76 percent in the ninth grade to 67 percent in the twelve grade. For girls, only 57 percent of ninth graders were physically active, whereas only half of the twelfth graders reported healthy rates of activity.

Even a low-key physical education program for thirty minutes each day would yield a 100 percent compliance with this recommended amount of physical activity that is so important for our mental and physical health.

Given the therapeutic value of exercise, these cultural trends help to explain rising rates of depression in contemporary society. The gender difference in activity levels of these high school students suggests that the diminished activity levels for women, which are believed to contribute to their increased vulnerability for depression, begin early in a female's life and may contribute to increased rates of this disorder later in their lives.

Technological advances have made many positive contributions to our lives, and we will continue to redefine how we live in the context of such technology. At the same time, we must persist in questioning the impact of these advances in terms of our health and environment. Using a body comprising muscles and nerves that evolved to travel no faster than the speed of walking (and occasionally running), for example, leads to problems when this same biological system is placed behind the wheel of a car that travels 70 mph to work every day. It's just one of the countless ways in which our bodies (and minds) have to adjust to the speed and physical discordance of modern living.

Moving Toward an Evolutionary Theory of Effort-Driven Rewards and Depression

Many current therapies for biological conditions such as depression have been discovered serendipitously. Serotonin took the spotlight as a major factor in depression following the accidental discovery that drugs altering this neurotransmitter also altered patients' moods. At that point, a whirlwind of activity went into developing more effective drugs. Considerably less attention has been directed toward gaining a thorough understanding of depressive symptoms and their biological relevance. There's potential for even more targeted treatments if we address these medical questions from a theoretical perspective.

Let's consider for a moment the brain's motor systems, and why movement seems to play such a pivotal role in effort-driven rewards and building resilience against depression. On the surface, it may sound surprising to suggest that physical effort has such a strong influence on mental health. However, we've already seen how much of the brain's landscape and energy are directed toward physically guiding our bodies.

The importance of motor circuits in developing a buffer against depression was also evident in the pioneering work of Paul MacLean, the neuroscientist who described and named the brain's emotional limbic system. As early as the 1950s, he was thinking about the role of the brain structures he referred to as the "basal ganglia and company." At the time, no one could identify a function of these areas, which comprise the components of the effort-driven rewards circuit known as the striatum and also contain the largest amount of tissue in the brain.

MacLean's curiosity motivated him to design a research project at the National Institutes of Health with lizards and primates to determine the actual function of the basal ganglia and its related parts. His work revealed that these brain areas controlled the expression of natural, unlearned movement patterns such as aggression and reproductive behavioral rituals. This area was also important in organizing and carrying out the daily routines of life. MacLean commented that people with the neuromuscular condition Huntington's disease reported that they couldn't maintain their daily routines any longer, although, interestingly, they could mimic them if allowed to observe others engaging in the specific behavior. It was engaging in the behavior spontaneously that they found so challenging.

As we consider symptoms of depression, we see that a diminished sensitivity of this striatal area may lead to difficulty initiating the routines of our lives, such as grooming, socializing, preparing food, and cleaning. On the other hand, overactivation of these structures can lead to problems as well. Jeffrey Schwartz, a neuropsychiatrist at UCLA, found that the basal ganglia structure known as the caudate was most closely linked to obsessive-compulsive disorder, which is marked by excessive expression of life routines, such as grooming and daily checking rituals. Thus, a more comprehensive understanding of effort-driven rewards and their biological relevance is essential to provide valuable information when behavioral responses are decreased in depressed patients or increased in those with obsessive-compulsive disorder.

In their book *Why We Get Sick*, Randolph Nesse and George Williams, at the University of Michigan Medical School and the State University of New York at Stony Brook, respectively, persuasively illustrate the importance of understanding the evolutionary context of responses. They wrote that we can more responsibly treat a fever once we understand that it's an adaptive response. Body temperature rises to kill an invading infectious agent such as a flu virus or harmful bacteria. Some studies have shown that taking acetaminophen to reduce a fever actually prolongs the symptoms of the illness, compromising a sophisticated evolved mechanism that fights off unwelcome guests such as an invading pathogen. If a high fever persists, however, fever-reducing drugs can be beneficial.

We can think about anxiety as an *emotional fever*, alerting us to impending threats to our emotional or physical well-being. But, just as a fever can get so high that it itself may lead to damage, anxiety levels may become so excessive and exaggerated that they no longer accurately predict real dangers. This is typically when mental illness enters the emotional scene. There are many kinds of anxiety, ranging from specific phobias to the more diffuse generalized anxiety disorder. Depression is also associated with heightened levels of anxiety that leads to the avoidance behavior I talk about in chapter 8.

In Nesse and Williams's opinion, it's unfortunate that psychiatry has generated so many diagnostic categories of symptoms, without providing a theoretical context for them. "By trying to find the flaws that cause disease without understanding normal functions of the mechanisms, psychiatry puts the cart before the horse," they state.

For example, anxiety is a powerful defense that kept our ancestors from approaching dangerous predators and engaging in social conflict. Anxiety responses also allowed early humans to be responsive parents as they attended quickly to the cries of children who were sick or in life-threatening situations. Knowing more about the evolutionary context and adaptive nature of this response, as well as the mechanisms and development of anxiety, helps us understand this biological phenomenon and treat extreme levels of anxiety that may lead to depression in a more responsible manner.

Nesse and Willams use an interesting analogy to illustrate the importance of putting a biological phenomenon into an evolutionary context before rushing to treat it. Let's say a mouse went to a mouse psychiatrist and complained about all the anxiety it experienced when it encountered cat odors. Knowing that cats present an imminent threat to the survival of mice, the mouse psychiatrist would never prescribe a drug that would reduce this anxiety because it would rob his patient of a very important survival skill—eluding cats that want to eat him for dinner!

It may not seem logical to think about depression as being good for us. But if we approach this mood disorder in the same way we do other medical challenges (coughs, and fevers, for example), we may begin to understand why these symptoms evolved. Just as a fever alerts the immune system to impending biological threats, decreased pleasurable responses help us detect threats to our emotional health. Just as physical pain stops us in our tracks and forces us to consider what is threatening our health, the mental pain of depression may also serve as a warning that a person needs to drop back and reassess the situation.

It is not adaptive to continue doing things that consistently lead to losses or unrealized goals. If a depressed person can make a more accurate assessment of the elements of his problem, he will be better equipped to embrace more proactive strategies. Behavioral activation treatment, described earlier, approaches depression from this perspective. So, for example, if your job gives you financial rewards but the long hours and extensive travel diminish your time with family and friends—and make you feel guilty and unhappy—you may want to reassess your career path to create a better and more satisfying work-life balance. And at the same time, you may gain the effort-driven rewards bonus of having more time to do that yard work that calms your nerves.

It appears that at least in some cases, certain components of anxiety and depression play an important role in maintaining our emotional and physical lives. Being more tolerant of appropriately negative emotions may provide meaningful insights into our mental health. And being more mindful of these responses may alert us in a more efficient manner when the symptoms have become *inappropriately* intense.

In some cases, experiencing anxiety and depression may actually help you maintain your emotional health. If you are more accepting of your negative emotions, you'll find it easier to gauge when they've become overly intense and you need to seek help.

According to E. O. Smith, "We must accept the possibility that depression is an evolved psychological trait. That is, in our evolutionary past, individuals who exhibited at least some of the symptoms of depression must have experienced some slight advantage over those who did not exhibit the trait. As strange as it sounds, individuals who were depressed at least some of the time had a fitness advantage compared with those who were perennially perky."

Justin Joffe at the University of Vermont confirmed this idea when he recently suggested that we need to start viewing our brains' sometimes bizarre and pathological responses to our world being turned upside down as an adaptive, rather than maladaptive, response. If we don't experience some alteration in our mental health when threats occur during the course of our daily lives, it would likely mean that our brains are not functioning normally.

In Joffe's view, just as an immune system would be seen as malfunctioning if it failed to generate a fever when faced with an immunological threat, our brains would be malfunctioning if they failed to respond in disruptive ways during threatening situations. "Only if the brain was impaired in some manner would the organism fail to respond to stress by showing pathological changes—in short, you'd have to be sick not to be crazy," he wrote.

What about those cases when depression seems to pop out of the blue, unrelated to any kind of threat? Well, we can't be consciously aware of every threat our body and brain perceive—or it may be that we do not immediately recognize them as threats. When you first start experiencing depressive symptoms, it may become clear to you, after reflecting on your current lifestyle or visiting your physician, that your altered diet, sleep habits, activity level, an overactive immune system, or even an alteration in hormonal or neurochemical levels is presenting a real medical challenge. After making appropriate modifications, the depression lifts because the threats—even the ones that are not clearly visible to you as mental threats—have been removed.

So why are we masking these uncomfortable but important feelings with drugs? Often, our choice to medicate ourselves immediately when stress hits likely dampens our resilience on many fronts. Taking SSRIs to lower anxiety or lift depression just because we feel that something's "not quite right" in our lives diminishes the accuracy of our emotional gauges.

I hope that a fuller appreciation of the evolutionary value of feelings of anxiety and sadness will make you more tolerant of your fluctuating moods. Instead of becoming frightened or ashamed when you feel the symptoms of depression emerging, you can try to figure out the origin of the symptoms. This may help you remove the source of the anxious or depressed feelings before the symptoms develop into a full-blown debilitating depression episode. Or if depression is already on your emotional scene, understanding how the symptoms manifest in your daily life may direct you to the most appropriate treatment strategy.

Of course, as discussed in the last chapter, carrying out such analyses and making informed decisions about treatment strategies are difficult for someone in the throes of depression. Having a loved one or friend point you toward an effective treatment is critical. Anything that can be done to help you engage in activity and social interactions will help jump-start the effort-driven brain reward circuit and work toward diminishing the paralyzing symptoms of depression, all the while building resilience to ward off the next bout.

Depression should never be taken lightly, but I find that, at times, some well-placed humor enables my students to view problems in a different way. A short piece published in the satirical newspaper *The Onion* helps us appreciate the importance of anxiety in our lives and the potential threat to our rich emotional fabric when all such emotions are removed:

THE PFIZER "ZOLOFT FOR EVERYTHING" AD CAMPAIGN

Zoloft for Everything campaign will employ print and TV ads to inform potential users about the "literally thousands" of new applications for Zoloft. Among the conditions the drug can be used to treat: anxiety associated with summer swimsuit season, insecurity over sexual potency and performance, feelings of shame over taking an antidepressant, and a sense of

hollowness stemming from losing an online auction. . . .
Do you find yourself feeling excited or sad? No one should
have to suffer through those harrowing peaks and valleys.

How can you take this information about effort-driven rewards, which is emerging from the scientific literature, and
build resilience or lift your looming episodes of depression? In
the next chapter, I'll give you some practical ways to apply this
new research to prevent depression or lift it once it has set in.

10

The New Rx for Preventing
and Lifting Depression

A S I AM WRITING this final chapter, I'm in Rio de Janeiro attending the annual meeting of the International Behavioral
Neuroscience Society. I'm trying to focus on the latest neuroscientific advances being presented, but my attention keeps wan-
dering outside the hotel's confines to the fascinating streets of
this colorful city and its diverse and passionate population.

On the surface, the culture of Rio appears to be the perfect
lifestyle antidote to our stressed-out, information-craving way of
life. The Brazilians seem to embrace life's passions that we too
often suppress. Dancing, public displays of affection, and
leisurely lunches along the beach are just what the emotion doctor ordered. When some of my students who attended the conference approached one of the many musical performances along
the street, onlookers were positive they were American. "Why?"
they asked. "Because you're not dancing," the locals replied.

Too often in this country we suppress movement even though
our brains are craving to respond to the music of life with free-
style moves and passion. And what is the cost of such emotional

restraint in a physiological system that is often experiencing massive amounts of stress? The symptoms of depression.

Of course, that's my tourist's-eye view of Rio. Ironically, Brazilians find themselves in an epidemiological transition today as they experience an increase in deaths from cardiovascular disease. A close analysis of the risk factors points to inactivity. In fact, sedentary lifestyles contribute to two million deaths per year worldwide, and the U.S. government alone spends approximately $24 billion annually addressing the same problems. So a campaign to increase the physical activity of Brazilians seemed like the best buy among public health options.

In São Paulo, a city of thirty-four million, a communitywide intervention program known as the *Agita São Paulo Experience* was launched in 1996 to encourage citizens to get "one step ahead" by participating in thirty minutes of activity every day. Interestingly, the program's premise is completely consistent with factors that contribute to resilience, namely, increased physical activity, enhanced mental enrichment, and stronger social ties.

Brazilians are encouraged to be more active at work, in school, or during their leisure activities. Even tourists are urged to climb stairs, dance, or walk. In Rio, a law was passed to establish "healthy streets," where traffic can be interrupted so that Brazilians are able to exercise on the streets safely. Imagine a society that legislates "dancing in the streets"! Here's an approach that differs greatly from the more pharmaceutical-oriented mindset that dominates the U.S. culture's attempts to address obesity and depression.

After four years of the Agita São Paulo campaign, approximately 55 percent of residents were meeting the thirty-minute activity recommendation. Those aware of the program and the risk of living a sedentary lifestyle were twice as likely to be active as those who were unaware of the program. These statistics stand in sharp contrast to the U.S. figures presented in the previous chapter. The World Health Organization hopes that this program will serve as a model for other cultures threatened by the negative health consequences of a sedentary lifestyle.

Of course, mental health also needs to be addressed from a personal perspective. In fact, I view the work in my laboratory as a form of emotional forensic investigation. I like to call it *ESI* (*Emotional Scene Investigators*), after the popular TV show *CSI* (*Crime Scene Investigators*). As we've investigated the perpetrator known as depression, we've considered the mystery of rising rates in modern society. We've explored the effectiveness of SSRIs and whether low serotonin levels alone are really guilty of triggering depression, and we've discovered that this neurochemical is hardly the only culprit. It may be an accomplice, but the real perpetrator in the case of depression is our sedentary lifestyle, which fails to engage our brains and bodies in meaningful ways.

Just as important, we've uncovered the factors that contribute to building resilience against the onset of depression. Doing a variety of activities that keep the effort-driven rewards circuit humming and engaged is the equivalent of an extreme workout for our brains, solidifying the connections that make up the circuit and enhancing the activation of our responses in the future. Brain activation leading to meaningful responses is a powerful antidote for the symptoms of depression so often characterized by passivity and avoidance.

TOOLS FOR YOUR EMOTIONAL TOOL KIT

As more and more research is conducted, I hope that my proposed effort-driven rewards circuit will provide a springboard for the development of effective new treatment strategies. In the meantime, the existing scientific literature points to several things all of us can do now to build resilience against the onset of depression. Being aware of the importance of taking meaningful action and knowing how to monitor your own emotional compass will help you make the appropriate adjustments, despite the ups and downs of everyday life. What follows are some tools to keep in your emotional tool kits. These will help you determine your current mental health profile so you can focus on the best ways to build resilience for the inevitable challenges life will throw your way.

INCORPORATE EFFORT-DRIVEN REWARDS INTO YOUR LIFE

Effort-driven rewards generate activity in several key areas of the brain. The prefrontal cortex is activated as you plan to engage in an activity, and the striatum is involved as you activate the necessary movements. The brain's reward center regulates the amount of psychological satisfaction you'll experience while you're in the process of doing and completing the activity that results in a meaningful, tangible outcome.

Regardless of whether your effort-driven reward of choice involves the scarf you've knitted for your niece, the casserole you've cooked for a sick neighbor, the vegetables you've harvested from your garden, or the piece of pottery you've made for your husband's birthday, you have activated the accumbens-striatal-cortical circuit. This enables you to carry out the actions that lead to a successful final outcome and the subsequent pleasure you experience.

The trick is to identify the types of effort you enjoy the most and to consistently include these activities in your life. You may not have time to engage in effort-driven rewards daily, but they should become part of your regular routine so that you are constantly reminded that your efforts can produce rewarding results. If doing carpentry, making jewelry, or decorating cakes makes you feel good after a stressful month at work, imagine how therapeutic it could be if you did it more often.

A key component of effort-driven rewards is that they enhance your sense of control. Of course, there are many areas of your life that can't be micromanaged, and some situations and relationships generate immense stress. But you can buffer these negative emotions by taking advantage of those aspects of your life that you can control. The ability to use our hands in complex ways separates us from other primates and allows us to be resourceful when dealing with the daunting environmental pressures we encounter. Even when your hands create products less directly related to survival, such as jewelry and art, they tap into the fascinating and unique characteristics of the human mind relating to hope, creativity, celebration, and aesthetic awareness. Hope and optimism, along with other positive emotions, signify our unique ability to plan for the future—a meaningful and rewarding future (very different from the depressed mental state)—and they provide a buffer against the onset of depression as they build emotional resilience.

It's also important to remember the complexity of deceptively simple everyday tasks. Chopping, stirring, and cooking activate areas of the brain responsible for motivation, planning, problem solving, decision making, manual dexterity, and pleasure. This contrasts significantly with the passive act of taking a pill to deal with depression, especially when the pharmacological-induced change in neurochemistry occurs out of the context of meaningful actions.

MAINTAIN AN ACTIVE LIFESTYLE

Even though exercising doesn't tap into the accumbens-striatal-cortical circuitry as directly as the more traditional effort-driven rewards I've discussed throughout the book, it certainly enhances the brain's ability to build resilience and lift depression. Exercise triggers the release of endorphins that give you an emotional boost and help generate the brain's fertilizer chemicals, also known as neurotrophic factors, that lead to enhanced cognitive abilities. Increased cardiovascular health resulting from consistent exercise translates into increased oxygen for the brain, yet another physiological benefit.

Exercise leads to a more generalized boost to your emotional health (realigned serotonergic or other neurochemical systems), much like the long-term effects of antidepressants. But, of course, jogging and other aerobic activities have no negative side effects and can help enhance cardiovascular health and weight loss. If you feel a sense of pride and accomplishment from your workouts, your exercise regimen may be as beneficial as effort-driven rewards, even though exercise is generally not as effective a means to gain control over the threats in your day-to-day environment. As I discussed earlier, exercise provides a general boost to your mental health by increasing an exercise-induced neurochemical cocktail. But when you run three miles on a treadmill, you don't produce something tangible that you can see, feel, and use, and that's an important component in maximizing the mental effects of effort-driven rewards. However, playing sports that involve complex planning and movement of the hands and body, such as baseball, basketball, or tennis, may provide both exercise and a healthy dose of effort-driven rewards.

Making a mental note of just how wonderful it is to meet your workout goal puts you closer to experiencing the pleasure that more tangible outcomes may produce. If you just go through the motions when you're on the treadmill, you might tone your leg muscles but not feel that overwhelming sense of accomplishment or increased control over your life. Coming away from the gym or the playing field feeling frustrated about your performance obviously doesn't generate emotional rewards. Your best bet is to engage in activities that generate a good workout and effort-driven rewards, or some meaningful combination (for example, gardening can be a great physical workout that will eventually lead to putting dinner on the table).

Consider purchasing an inexpensive pedometer to determine exactly how active you are each day. Make sure you compare your activity level to reputable data charts to determine the healthiest number of steps you should take daily depending on your age. Your physician can also provide helpful information about setting activity goals based on your current health status.

You might find yourself opting for the farthest parking spot from the grocery store, taking the stairs instead of the elevator, and encouraging your friends to take walks just to be able to write down that high number of steps each night. When you check the chart, you'll know for certain exactly how your activity compares to others in your age category.

DEVELOP EFFECTIVE COPING STRATEGIES

Above and beyond incorporating effort-driven rewards and healthy levels of activity into your life, you need to be mindful of how effective your coping strategies are. Current research has moved beyond the classic Type A and Type B personality styles to an emphasis on passive and active coping responses. Research suggests that it's best to be flexible when responding to demanding situations and even to minor stressors.

Always being passive may benefit animals that are susceptible to being attacked by predators, but for humans, that avoidance response can be just the trigger that throws us into the downward spiral of depression. On the other hand, persistent active coping, especially accompanied by hostility, is toxic to the cardiovascular system.

If you notice that you reflexively avoid challenges or always lash out when you feel even remotely threatened, this is a warning sign that you are not coping in the most effective way. Of course, some situations require avoidance or fast action. Walking away before you say some things that will anger your boss or responding aggressively when a stranger grabs your child are both effective coping strategies.

Staying flexible and responding in a way that's appropriate to the situation at hand indicates a heightened awareness of the impact of your actions, whatever the challenge you face. Throughout evolutionary history, mammals with the capacity to adjust their coping responses depending on the circumstances were more likely to respond to the dynamic demands of new environments.

Although research on flexible coping strategies is in its infancy, experiments with flexibly coping rats suggest that their neurochemical makeup is different from those of passive and active copers. Their baseline and stress-exposed levels of adrenal hormones and neurochemicals such as Neuropeptide Y (known as a resilience neurochemical) are much healthier than in the other animals.

Interestingly, recent research has found that college students who were better at manipulating their emotional reactions (that is, being able to appear happy or sad upon demand) exhibited less distress by the end of their second year of college.

Being more in control of one's emotional expression, rather than reflexively expressing happiness or sadness, was shown to be the most beneficial reaction. So let's hear it for the "poker face." Whether you're being challenged by a spouse, a stranger on the street, or an opponent in a poker game, having control over your emotional responses gives you the upper hand over those who react reflexively.

Effective, fine-tuned coping strategies are also influenced by effort-driven rewards and exercise. In the experiment I described in chapter 2, the working rats that had experience with effort-driven rewards persisted longer in responding to a challenge than the trust fund rats (the ones that had never worked for their rewards).

Also, how physically fit you are determines how much energy you have to respond in an emergency. If you're late for an important appointment, you can't make a run for it if you're not in good shape.

To determine how effectively you cope, I recommend collecting some forensic evidence. Kits that measure levels of stress hormone (cortisol) can be obtained through your physician or from reputable biomedical companies. You can also assess your levels of the resilience hormone DHEA. By carefully following the instructions and then comparing your results to the ranges provided by your physician or the kit manufacturer, you can get feedback about how your brain's stress axis is responding to the pressures and aggravations in your life.

The best time to collect such data is when things are going well, so that this hormonal profile becomes your emotional health baseline. When you redo the tests during more emotionally or physically vulnerable times, you can compare the levels. Also, it's good to monitor your cardiovascular fitness on a regular basis.

Purchase a small blood pressure monitor at your local drugstore so you can keep a record of your heart's response during both calm and turbulent times. Show your chart to your physician.

The value of knowing when your body is experiencing mounting stress levels (and approaching allostatic load) is that it alerts you to the need to compensate by incorporating more effective coping strategies. You always want to stop stress before it takes root in your brain. Remember, elevated cortisol levels are found in half of depressed patients, and stressful events often precipitate the emergence of depression. So responding quickly to persistently high levels of cortisol or increased blood pressure may prevent depression. Also, understanding more about times when your cortisol/DHEA ratios are at their healthiest levels will help you identify the coping strategies and lifestyle changes that lead to the greatest level of resilience.

When I teach my neurobiology of stress class, I ask my students to keep a *stressography,* a journal in which they keep track of the stressors in their lives and how they respond to them. In addition to writing about their psychological responses, they also monitor their blood pressure and stress hormones levels. They continue these daily entries as they incorporate new resiliency interventions into their routines (such as an exercise program or meditation to help them turn off their stress response and relax). It's a way to help them determine for themselves how effective their coping strategies are.

My goal is to teach my students to monitor their emotional health in a proactive way so that they're more sensitive to drastic changes that may require professional help. Using such a rich set of emotional data can help a therapist make a more informed decision about the best approach to treat an emerging emotional illness.

BUILD YOUR SOCIAL SUPPORT NETWORK

We're highly social mammals. Our brains are built to detect the subtleties of social interactions reflected in facial expressions, social contact, hand gestures, and other physical clues. Friendly, supportive social contact not only enriches our brains but also serves as a buffer against the toxicity of stress. Premature babies receiving massage grow at a faster rate than nonmassaged preemies. And challenges to adults' immune systems are less threatening in those who report supportive social contact.

Clearly, a rich social life increases our chances of living a healthy life and responding to challenges in effective ways. Having someone remind us to take our heart medication, go out and take a walk, or skip the third helping of apple pie ultimately leads to better health and increased longevity. Getting that stress-busting oxytocin booster as we interact with our significant others, children, and friends also helps to curb the toxicity of stress.

We must also be more vigilant about the impact that cell phones, iPods, computers, and other technological wonders are having on our nervous systems designed for social interaction. Although we may be in virtual contact with an impressive number of people each day, our actual face-to-face contact (reading someone's facial expressions or shaking someone's hand) with people is rapidly diminishing. Using so many shortcuts in our social communications will likely take a toll on our emotional health in the coming years.

FOSTER RESILIENCE IN YOUR CHILDREN

Resilience in the face of adversity is not a gift you're born with or a magical ability. It's a learned response acquired by experiencing real-life challenges—including those we overcame and those that overcame us. When children learn how to get back on their feet after taking an emotional tumble, the confidence gained will make them better able to cope with the next challenging situation. Until they begin to gain a sense of control over their world, they will not develop accurate emotional gauges and effective coping strategies.

In addition to standing back and letting a child stumble every now and then, parents can facilitate the development of resilience by teaching them how to work through problems. Having more cognitive resources will lead to more adaptive problem solving when faced with inevitable dilemmas. A practical way to avoid stress and the onset of depression is to make more reasonable, measured decisions throughout our lives that keep us out of harm's way. Although stress can't be avoided, being resilient by incorporating effective coping strategies provides us with an essential buffer.

Allowing kids to engage in rough-and-tumble play also provides young children with the chance to test their physical and emotional powers in the real world. A study conducted by Jaak Panksepp, a behavioral neuroscientist at Washington State University and author of *Affective Neuroscience: The Foundations of Human and Animal Emotions,* showed that when juvenile rats are deprived of the ability to roughhouse, they compensate by spending even more than the usual amount of time wrestling and playing when they are finally presented with their rat playmates.

As we've seen, anytime this kind of rebound reaction occurs, it implies that the behavior that's been deprived is important for survival. Considering that play contributes to the physical, social, and emotional well-being of children, it's easy to see how important it is for a developing mind. In fact, Panksepp argues that the systematic reduction of free time and recess in the elementary school schedule leads to more emotional and cognitive difficulties in children, including an increase in attention deficit hyperactivity disorder (ADHD). Others have suggested that the increased time pressures in our children's lives have resulted in higher levels of anxiety, which can lead to depression.

Supportive and nurturing relationships provide a social buffer during tumultuous periods. Close relationships trigger the release of oxytocin and provide valuable role models for future social relations. The most effective parents provide the appropriate emotional safety nets while encouraging a child's independence and intellectual development.

SEEK ACTIVE FORMS OF THERAPY ONCE DEPRESSION EMERGES

When depression strikes, it's important to seek treatment that activates the brain in healthy ways. Before choosing a strategy, question the therapist or physician about a treatment's effectiveness as reported by research. What percentage of patients respond positively to a particular drug or therapy? How long will the treatment last, and when should you expect to notice a difference in your depressive symptoms? What is the likelihood of experiencing side effects? What percentage of patients relapse once the treatment is terminated? If you are not satisfied with the answers, seek a second opinion and a more suitable option.

Behavioral activation therapy, described earlier, is relatively new. To find therapists in your area who offer this approach or the similar cognitive-behavioral therapy, go to the Web site maintained by the Association for Behavioral and Cognitive Therapies (www.abct.org).

Once you choose a treatment strategy, make sure you understand the course of action your therapist proposes. Depression should be verified by an accepted assessment inventory so that progress in recovery can be quantitatively assessed at key points throughout the treatment process. An official diagnosis of depression should follow only an appropriate assessment, not an informal conversation or self-diagnosis.

An injured muscle can recover only after uncomfortable muscular rehabilitation and persistent use. Recovering from mental injuries/illnesses is no different. So the most effective therapies involve hard work and not just a passive response from the patient. Just as diabetes patients successfully manage their disease by monitoring their blood sugar levels, taking their insulin, and maintaining a healthy weight, the responsibility and accountability of the patient is no different for mental illness. So don't avoid therapies that involve persistent effort on your part. Playing an active role in your recovery will leave you with a set of skills to incorporate into your coping behavior repertoire.

Embrace the Full Spectrum of Emotions

Negative emotions aren't at the top of anyone's wish list. Even so, it's imperative that you acknowledge the importance of negative emotions in your emotional inventory. For example, anxiety can alert you to potential threats in your emotional life before they become actual ones or jump-start the resilient brain into action before depression becomes an unwelcome guest in our emotional lives. Being mindful of subtle signs of increased tension and financial pressures at the office may prompt you to start searching for a job before your boss informs you that yours has been eliminated due to downsizing. Although many people take drugs to alleviate feelings of anxiety, it's important to realize how masking feelings in this way can confuse your emotional gauges.

Researchers recently investigated rats' typical responses to the traumatic experience of confronting a live rattlesnake. Not surprisingly, a rat in such a situation can have an escape response, a freeze response, or a cautious form of locomotion known as the stretch attend response that is frequently observed during risk assessment. When the researchers gave the antidepressant Prozac to a second group of rats and exposed them to a snake, they didn't show the appropriate fear and defensive responses. The antidepressant rats carried on as if nothing were out of the ordinary.

Experiencing anxiety is never desirable, but when a natural predator wants to eat you for lunch, it's probably not the best time to feel relaxed. Only animals that register the emotional version of a high security alert will be able to recognize the danger and identify the best escape strategy.

Anxiety can also help us reach out to others. Recently, we did an experiment in my lab investigating the genesis of nurturing responses in rodents. We observed how male California mice that already had parenting experience approached an unrelated mouse pup that was distressed from being restrained in a wire mesh container (the pup tent). These paternal rodents, known for their family values, showed more activity in an area of their brains involved in the production of anxiety than their deadbeat-dad mouse counterparts. The increased activity observed in the presence of an isolated foster pup may facilitate the impressive nurturing they provide for their own pups. Amazingly, they do everything the mother does other than deliver and nurse the pups. As seen in these Mr. Moms, certain forms of anxiety prompt us to respond to the needs of others.

It is also important to understand that experiencing anxiety when things go wrong is an appropriate response. In fact, if we didn't feel anxious or even exhibit transient symptoms of depression during times of significant loss, we would have to question the accuracy of our emotional gauges. It's when anxiety or depression persists well beyond the period of loss or threat that you need to seek professional help.

Remember the Importance of Context

The role that context plays in maintaining resilience or lifting depression is extremely important and always worth considering. For instance, having difficulties at the office may be less traumatic when you go home each evening to a loving family. And, as I've mentioned, taking a drug that alters your neurochemistry without considering what's happening in your life is not the best way to activate the brain in positive ways. Further, it's important to take into account your physical health when considering the cause of depressive symptoms; many times, these symptoms are the result of an illness.

In a recent global survey conducted by the World Health Organization, depression is shown to be much more likely to occur in people with an existing chronic disease such as asthma, diabetes, or arthritis. This study confirms the strong connections between the brain's emotional circuits and the body's immune functions and helps explain why depressed patients often experience physical as well as emotional pain. So, as symptoms of acute and chronic illnesses are treated, the depression symptoms should lift as well.

Let me give you another example of the importance of context. The experience of those living in London during the Nazi blitzkrieg bombings reminds us of the importance of context in considering stress and depression. We might assume that more bomb raids would mean more stress. But an article published in

1942 reported that although the suburbs received fewer bombing attacks, those living in the suburbs developed more stress ulcers than Londoners. The reason? The London bombings were very predictable—they came at the same time every evening. The suburban bombings were sporadic, occurring only once a week or so, but the residents never knew when they would happen. The predictability (or temporal context) of the stressors in our lives determines just how much negative impact they will have on our emotional health.

On a lighter note, there are simple ways to relieve the tension in the stressful contexts of our lives. Going to the dentist produces a lot of stress in most of us. Researchers at the neurologic clinic at the University of Vienna have found that the infusion of an orange citrus odor calms patients' anxiety. Even rats show a tendency to relax in the presence of citrus aromatherapy. Rats exposed to a sweet orange aroma for five minutes before navigating a complicated maze exhibited bolder exploratory responses than the rats with no aromatherapy exposure. Thus, the environment around us is a critical variable in determining the severity of our stress responses in different situations.

Just as a forensic investigator pays as much attention to the scene of the crime as to the victim, an informed emotional detective will always consider the context of a person's life before attempting to understand the underlying causes and impact of chronic stress or depressive symptoms. The most effective therapists maximize the effectiveness of medications by providing the appropriate context for the brain changes that can lift depression. Taking a drug in conjunction with undergoing cognitive-behavioral therapy or behavioral activation therapy, and adding an exercise program into the mix, will have more impact than merely taking a drug.

So often, however, context is not taken into account when treating depression, especially when antidepressants are administered by a physician rather than a mental health professional. Using a drug while in the midst of a full-blown depression episode will never be as effective as combining the drug with meaningful responses such as effort-driven rewards.

POISED TO MAKE A DIFFERENCE

Throughout this book, my goal has been to increase the number of windows from which we view mental health by presenting information from many disciplines—anthropology, neuroscience, psychology, psychiatry, psychopharmacology, and ethology—and by considering the impact of the dramatic changes in our environment over the past century. Regardless of the cause of depression, it's important to know that well-placed effort-driven rewards, physical health, effective coping skills, and cognitive enrichment can lift us from the downward spiral of chronic stress and depression and help us build more resilience to offset stress down the line.

I've shown you ways to become your own best mental health advocate. Being mindful of your day-to-day mental health status will help alert you when the symptoms of stress and depression begin to appear. With this early-warning system in place, you can take steps to activate your brain in healthy ways to deflect and lift looming depression.

Acknowledgments

I am grateful to my friend Katherine Ellison, a talented journalist and author, who became interested in the research I, along with my colleague Craig Kinsley, conducted on the parental brain. It was Kathy who, while writing her book *The Mommy Brain,* convinced me that a professor of neuroscience and psychology could write a book for a popular audience. Her supportive guidance gave me the confidence that this book could become a reality. I am also indebted to the deft skills of my agent, Michelle Tessler, who saw potential in the premise of the book and took a chance on a rookie author. My editor at Basic Books, Jo Ann Miller, provided wisdom and guidance as she supported my desire to convey the stories about science in this book in the same way I would to my students—something for which I am very grateful. And the day-to-day interactions with my freelance editor, Stephanie Abarbanel, were priceless as she rescued the manuscript from unnecessary intellectual side trips and excessive scientific jargon. I appreciate her endless enthusiasm for the message of this book, especially when I started to feel overwhelmed by the project.

Writing this book has been a true cognitive adventure as I have searched for clues to the ongoing mystery of depression in several disciplines—including psychology, behavioral neuroscience, pharmacology, psychiatry, anthropology, ethology, physiology, sociology, and philosophy. As I have stepped out of my academic and research comfort zones, I have been indebted to several amazing scholars, researchers, and clinicians who have taken the time to answer my questions about the neurobiology of mental illness and health over the past several years. Others have graciously considered my ideas about effort-driven rewards and flexible coping strategies, and provided invaluable feedback. These investigators include Stanley Ambrose, Gregory Berns, Eberhard Fuchs, Doug Gurley, David Healy, Kim Huhman, Justin Joffe, Jonathan Kanter, George Koob, Leah Krubitzer, Jeffrey Lacasse, Jonathan Leo, Jeffrey Lorberbaum, Paul MacLean, Steven Maier, Christopher Martel, Susan Nolen-Hoekesema, Jaak Panksepp, Robert Sapolsky, Jeffrey Schwartz, Martin Seligman, Ron Shane, and Christian Waugh.

Science is a cumulative and collaborative process. The ideas I propose in this book are based on the fascinating research of the many researchers who have contributed to the neuroscience and biomedical scientific literature. If I have misrepresented any of these findings, I apologize. It was my intention to incorporate as much research as possible from a diverse array of scientific areas as I gathered clues about depression. My goal is to provide a springboard for future research.

I am grateful to my undergraduate and graduate mentors at Samford University in Birmingham, Alabama, and the University of Georgia—including Janice Teal, Lelon Peacock, Roger Thomas, Brad Bunnell, and Dan Estep—for instilling in me a healthy respect for the historical foundations of a scientific question, as well as the importance of utilizing relevant and meaningful animal models to provide the most valuable information about brain functions. My education continued when I joined the faculty of Randolph-Macon College and began collaborations with Craig Kinsley at the nearby University of Richmond. I appreciate Craig's willingness to work with such a "green" neuroscientist nearly twenty years ago and I cherish our ongoing collaborative relationship to this day. Many of the studies described in this book began as scribbles on a napkin at our favorite Mexican restaurant—our heated conversations evolved into research proposals, joint research projects with our undergraduates, and, eventually, exciting results.

Of course, one's education is a continuous process, and I am fortunate to work in a wonderful intellectual climate at Randolph-Macon College. My top-notch colleagues in the Psychology Department—Alva Hughes, Kristen Klaaren, Mike McKay, Susan Parker, and Bob Resnick—often listen to endless descriptions of animal/brain observations emerging from my lab and provide valuable feedback on a constant basis. Additional support, in the form of answers to questions and loans of equipment and chemicals, regularly comes from my colleagues in the Biology and Chemistry Departments, especially from Art Conway, David Coppola, Jim Foster, and Serge Schreiner. And I have learned from my colleagues across the entire campus—regardless of their disciplines—and appreciate their continuous curiosity about what the "rat lady" is doing in the basement of the science building. Outside of the laboratory, administrative assistant Barbara Wirth has kept me straight by issuing timely warnings of approaching deadlines and enthusiastically executing the "business" of the Psychology Department.

I am fortunate to have received support for the behavioral neuroscience laboratory through the years, especially from the Chenery Research Professorship, the Rashkind Family Foundation, and the Walter Williams Craigie Fellowship at R-MC. I am indebted to our current president, Robert Lindgren, for recognizing the value of undergraduate neuroscience research and responding to the changing needs of the behavioral neuroscience laboratory. Additionally, gratitude is extended to the R-MC board of trustees, the Duff family of Fredericksburg, Virginia, and the generous support of Macon and Joan Brock over the years. On a broader scale, special thanks are extended to the National Science Foundation and the National Institute of Mental Health for providing financial support for various studies described in the book.

There is no question in my mind that I am most indebted to my many undergraduate students over the years. There are too many to mention in this brief section, but I continue to learn from those who have gone on to earn their Ph.D.'s—Sabra Klein, Hendree Jones, Charles Cook, Erin Doudera Clabough, Sara Buckelew Anderson (M.D.), Catherine Lowry Franssen, Robin Diehl Lacks, Catherine Aurentz Griffith, Thomas Campbell, Erica Glasper, and Stacie Lin—and are kind enough to educate their old professor when I now turn to them for answers to questions. Most of the stress, depression, and coping studies described in this book were conducted by my most recent group of undergraduates—Kelly Tu, Ashley Everette, Mollee Farrell, Torrie Higgins, and Darby Fleming—all of whom recently left their undergraduate "nest" to attend graduate school. My current student Ashly Crockett continues to develop rat models of depression to assess brain responses to flexible coping strategies. Most of my research students participated in R-MC's Schapiro Undergraduate Research Fellowship (SURF), so generously supported by Ben and Peggy Schapiro.

My most heartfelt appreciation is extended to my family. This project would never have left the ground without the help of my supportive husband, Gary, who was always the first person to read each chapter in its roughest form. Many cups of coffee were required to navigate some of those long and winding neurobiological stories. In each chapter, his advice was right on the mark and was critical in keeping the book appropriate for a mainstream audience. Our relationship is truly a team effort, and I value his many contributions toward the well-being of our home and family. I am especially grateful that now that it has run its therapeutic course for my mental health, he has once again taken over the vacuuming in the house! (This last statement will make sense after you read chapter 1.) An emotional hug of gratitude is extended to my wonderful daughters, Lara and Skylar, who have taught me so much about the positive emotions that can be generated from the amazingly complex human brain. I appreciate their continued support during this writing process as their mom worked on "the book" late at night and on too many weekends. I hope that one day they'll read this book and understand why, on more occasions than they liked, I proclaimed that cleaning their rooms provided a valuable mental boost, as it developed their brain's effort-driven rewards circuit!

Notes

CHAPTER 1 DEPRESSION STRIKES DEEP

3 Diagnostic and Statistical Manual (DSM-IV); American Psychiatric Association, 2000.

4 *"You are falling away . . .":* Solomon, 2001, p. 27.

5 *relentless beat of drug marketing:* Lacasse and Leo, 2005.

5 *are depression rates higher than ever?:* Parker et al., 2001; World Health Organization, 2005; Un, 2004; Kessler et al., 2003; Vedantam, 2004; Vedantam, 2006.

7 *effort-driven rewards circuit:* Lambert, 2006.

10 *the science of mental illness:* Lambert and Kinsley, 2005.

12 *"moral" treatment of the mentally ill:* Hothersall, 1995; Whitaker, 2002.

12 Madness in America: Whitaker, 2002.

13 *Kirkbride's success rate:* Tomes, 1994; Whitaker, 2002.

13 *Dix's successful lobbying:* Lambert and Kinsley, 2005.

13 *Sigmund Freud introduced psychoanalysis:* Shorter, 1997.

14 *"nothing but a conquistador":* Carroll, 2003.

14 *German psychiatrist Emil Kraepelin:* Shorter, 1997.

15 *effectiveness of drugs for depression:* Richelson, 2001; Valenstein, 1998.

16 *Harvard psychiatrist Joseph Schildkraut:* Schildkraut, 1965.

16 *introduction of fluoxetine:* Richelsen, 2001.

16 *low levels of serotonin:* Cheetham et al., 1991.

17 *Pedro Delgado . . . tryptophan-free diet:* Delgado, 2000.

18 *tianeptine, a drug that:* Fuchs et al., 2002; Fuchs, 2005.

18 *meta-analyses of previously conducted:* Taylor et al., 2006.

19 *success rates of antidepressants:* Arroll et al., 2005.

19 *efficacy rates of antidepressants:* Hollon et al., 2002.

19 *Interpersonal talk therapy:* Mardowitz and Weisman, 2004.

20 Let Them Eat Prozac: Healy, 2004.

20 *"Good Drugs or Good Marketing?"* Dobbs, 2004; Arroll et al., 2005.

21 *Freedom of Information Act:* Kirsch et al., 2002a; Kirsch et al., 2002b.

21 *professionals in the field have expressed:* Lacasse and Leo, 2005; all quotes from Table. Also, personal communication with Lacasse and Leo, March 2006.

22 *forty years since the discovery:* Richelson, 2001.

22 *the FDA takes care of this:* Lacasse and Leo, 2005; Lacasse, 2005.

CHAPTER 2 WHY *ARE* WE SO DEPRESSED? THE LIFESTYLE PARADOX

26 *ten times more likely to suffer major depression:* Klerman et al., 1985; Seligman, 1990.

26 *later corroborated in a second study:* Robins et al., 1984.

27 Little House on the Prairie: Wilder, 1953.

27 Goodnight Moon: Brown, 1947.

29 *effort-driven rewards:* Lambert, 2006.

29 *"Life during the agricultural period":* Eaton et al., 1988; Eaton et al., 1996, p. 1734.

32 *accumbens-striatal-cortical network:* Lambert, 2006.

32 *effort-driven rewards circuit is kept humming:* Knutson et al., 2001; Carelli et al., 2004.

33 *likely stimulates neurogenesis:* Santarelli et al., 2003.

33 *The Trust Fund Rats:* Lambert et al., 2006.

36 *effort-consequence disconnect as* learned helplessness: Seligman and Maier, 1967; Seligman and Weiss, 1980.

36 When Culture and Biology Collide: Smith, 2002, p. 13.

37 *more of us are knowledge workers than physical laborers:* Fisk, 2001.

38 *food budget on food prepared in restaurants:* Fisk, 2001.

41 *"I missed picking fresh greens from the garden. . . .":* Kingsolver, 2007, p. 143.

42 *Research shows that the Amish spend:* Bassett et al., 2004.

42 *According to the U.S. Public Health Service:* Egeland and Hosteller, 1983; U.S. Public Health Service, 2005.

42 *depression rate in the Amish:* Seligman, 1988; Egeland and Hosteller, 1983.

43 *prevalence rate of depression in China:* Parker et al., 2001.

43 *Chinese population still live in rural areas:* Graham and Lam, 2003.

43 *women are twice as likely to experience depression:* Nolen-Hoeksema, 2001; Nazoo, 2005.

44 *Nigerian women engage in farming:* The Post Colonial Web, 2005.

44 *depression in Amish women:* Egeland and Hostetter, 1983.

44 *Working mothers who have husbands:* Lennon, 1994.

44 *repetitive actions that lack meaningful outcomes:* Bassett et al., 2004.

CHAPTER 3 BUILDING THE EFFORT-DRIVEN REWARDS BRAIN CIRCUIT: USE IT OR LOSE IT

47 Frontal Lobotomy and Affective Behavior: Fulton, 1951.

47   *He called this emotional circuit the limbic system:* MacLean, 1996.

48   *MacLean demonstrated that our emotional behavior:* MacLean, 1964; Lambert, 2003.

48   *"walking through a cathedral":* personal communication with the author, May 2000.

48   The Amygdala: Aggleton, 2000.

52   *accumbens . . . integrating emotional and motor functions:* Kelley, 1999.

52   *inputs and outputs as a motive circuit:* Kalivas et al., 1999.

53   *interactions among the accumbens, the striatum's motor:* Groenewegen et al., 1999.

53   *accumbens-striatal-cortical circuit:* Lambert, 2006.

55   *preferred tasks that required less effort:* Cardinal et al., 2001.

55   *work harder for the larger prize:* Walton et al., 2002.

56   *active group showed greater activity:* Zink et al., 2004.

57   *Dopamine, the primary neurotransmitter:* Neill and Justice, 1981.

57   *rodent version of an unpredictable sales career:* Salamone et al., 1994; Cousins et al., 1996; Richardson and Gratton, 1998.

58   *serotonin, the neurochemical darling of the depression industry?:* Amat et al., 2005.

59   Who Moved My Cheese?: Johnson, 1998.

59   *trained rats to lick a citric acid solution:* Neigh et al., 2004.

60   *conducted fMRI scans of unmedicated depressed:* Tremblay et al., 2005.

62   cingulate cortex . . . *processing emotionally relevant stimuli:* Maddock et al., 2003.

62   *cingulate cortex processes "reward-prediction" errors:* McCoy and Platt, 2005.

63   *"The problem with depression":* Kliff, 2007.

64   *increased blood flow to the amygdala in men's brains:* Kilpatrick et al., 2006.

64   *women engage in cognitive rumination:* Nolen-Hoeksema et al., 1999.

65   Calvin and Hobbes: Watterson, 1995.

66   *average American spends three to four hours a day watching TV:* The Source Book for Teaching Science.

66   *Hibernating bears provide valuable insights:* Tsiouris, 2005.

67   The Hibernation Response: Whybrow and Bahr, 1988.

CHAPTER 4   GIVING THE BRAIN A HAND

70   *for at least a million years:* Allman, 1999.

70   *Maria Montessori, born in 1870:* Montessori, 1965.

71   *tapping into a deep reward system:* Lilard, 1990.

73   *Montessori-trained children were more energetic:* Rathunde and Csikszent-mihalyi, 2005.

73 *Csikszentmihalyi introduced the term* flow: Csikszentmihalyi, 1990;
    Debold, 2002.

75 *Montessori intervention for Alzheimer's:* Mahandra et al., 2006.

75 *hand gestures are "windows into our thought processes":* Wachsmuth, 2005;
    McNeill, 2005.

76 *Spencer Kelly at Colgate University:* Kelly et al., 2004.

77 *areas of the brain controlling hand gestures:* Wachsmuth, 2006.

77 *first toolmakers, earning the nickname "handy man":* "The Mind's Big Bang,"
    2001.

77 *John Shea, an anthropologist:* "The Mind's Big Bang," 2001.

78 *Ambrose hypothesizes that some cataclysmic natural disaster:* Ambrose, per-
    sonal communication with the author, July 2007.

79 *involvement in the fine-motor control of language:* Greenfield, 1991.

79 *handiwork requiring complex brain circuitry:* Kuhn et al., 2001.

80 *"The only thing that separates . . .":* Internet Movie Database.

80 *the use of our hands to produce:* Sheratt, 1997, p. 279; Wynn and Coolidge,
    2003.

80 *The earliest settlers in the Americas:* Time Magazine, 2006.

82 *when Gustav Fritsch and Eduard Hitzig began to unlock:* Taylor and Gross,
    2003.

84 *The actions leading to rewards:* Tricomi et al., 2004.

85 *bilateral coordination necessary to perform tasks:* Disbrow et al., 2001.

85 *hands generate a sense of self:* Krubitzer, personal communication with the
    author, June 2006.

86 *"The types of jobs where people actually make something":* Kollatz, 2005,
    p. H16.

87 *Knitting has long been considered mentally therapeutic:* Macdonald, 1988.

87 *Robert Reiner, a clinical psychologist:* personal communication with the
    author, December 2007. *Craft to Heal:* Molson, 2005.

88 *Hip New Yorkers are knitting:* New York Times, 2005.

88 Chicks with Sticks: Lenhard, 2006.

88 *Dr. Steven Knapp's academic pedigree:* Kinzie, 2006.

89 *"It's nice to have a spread of activity . . .":* Kinzie, 2006, p. B03.

CHAPTER 5 COPING EFFECTIVELY WITH STRESS

92 *observations that link stress to depression:* Sapolsky, 2004.

92 *Harvard physiologist Walter Cannon:* Cannon, 1935.

92 *Selye noticed that when rats:* Selye, 1936.

93 Stress of Life: Selye, 1952.

94 *rats were subjected to chronic social stress:* Rygula et al., 2005.

98 *cortisol levels and depression:* Strickland et al., 2002.

98 *post-traumatic stress disorder:* Young and Breslau, 2004.

98 *a new concept,* allostasis: McEwen, 2000.

100 *sweet-smelling blooms known as kudzu:* Baldwin, 2003; Shores, 1996.

102 Why Zebras Don't Get Ulcers: Sapolsky, 1998.

103 *cells are produced in the hippocampus each day:* Schmidt-Hieber et al., 2004.

103 *chronic stress also changes the topography of the brain's hippocampus:* Woolley et al., 1990; Watanabe et al., 1992.

103 *chronic stress in rats reduced the branching points:* Lambert, 1998.

104 *individuals reveal hippocampal shrinkage:* Sheline et al., 1996; Sheline, 1999; Bremner et al., 2000.

104 *oversecretion of stress hormones:* Sapolsky, 2000; Sapolsky, 2001.

104 *excitotoxicity:* Magarions et al., 1999.

104 *hormones and neurochemicals that inhibit neurogenesis:* Jacobs et al., 2000; Henn and Vollmayr, 2004.

104 *demise of the hippocampus:* Lehrer, 2006.

105 *indirect effect of altered neurogenesis:* Duman et al., 2001.

105 *Electroconvulsant seizures in animals . . . increased rates of neurogenesis:* Duman, 2004; Sapolsky, 2004.

105 *transcranial magnetic stimulation:* Sapolsky, 2004.

106 *mimic the impoverished conditions:* Brunson et al., 2005.

106 *these women had exaggerated stress responses:* Heim et al., 2001.

107 *positive outcome to short-term stress:* Parker et al., 2006.

107 *moms immediately step up their grooming:* Meaney et al., 1985.

107 *small doses of stress:* Parker et al., 2006.

108 *Type A or Type B responders:* Rosenman et al., 1975.

108 *Hostile people consistently respond:* Dahlstrom et al., 1983.

108 *Research with serotonin levels by Barry Jacobs:* Jacobs and Fornal, 2000; Jacobs et al., 1990.

109 *have been shown to develop fewer stress ulcers:* Koolhaas et al., 1999.

109 *engaging in a form of self-medication:* Jacobs, 1994; Jacobs and Fornal, 2000.

109 *day-to-day stressors in our lives:* Cavigelli and McClintock, 2003.

111 *coping strategies in the midst of life's annoying little stressors:* Campbell et al., 2003.

111 *by some Danish piglets:* Geverink et al., 2002; Geverink et al., 2004; Spoolder et al., 1996; Hessing et al., 1993.

112 *active copers had lower levels of baseline cortisol:* Schouten and Wiegant, 1997.

112 *assessing the temperament styles of guppies:* Neese and Williams, 1994.

113 *explore active and passive response styles to stress:* Korte, Koolhaas, Wingfield, and McEwen, 2005.

113 *neither active nor passive coping strategies:* Lambert et al., 2006.

114 *The flexible copers were the most vigorous:* Fleming et al., 2007.

115 *less allostatic load and stress-related activity:* Lambert et al., 2007.

115 *journalist Terry Anderson was kidnapped:* Anderson, 1993.

CHAPTER 6 OUR SOCIAL BRAINS

120 *characteristics that separate mammals from reptiles:* MacLean, 1996; MacLean, 1985.

120 *interpersonal therapy:* Hollon et al., 2002.

120 *consequences of social isolation:* Paul, Ayis, and Ebrahim, 2006.

121 *social isolation was associated with depressed:* Iliffe et al., 2007.

122 *evolutionary purpose of langauge:* Dunbar, 1996.

123 *Touch is the first sensory system:* Slater and Lewis, 2007.

123 *body's two square meters of skin:* Jacobs and Schmidt, 1999.

123 *growth and maturation of institutionalized children in Romania:* Parker and Nelson, 2005.

123 *curious little rodent known as the prairie vole:* Young and Want, 2004.

124 *isolating these highly social prairie voles:* Grippo et al., 2007.

125 *"reach out and touch someone" commercials:* Sheppard, 1980; Arlen, 1980.

126 *students in South Korea:* Gellene, 2006.

126 *Elizabeth Gould:* Stranahan et al., 2006.

128 *pup-preferring moms:* Mattson and Morrell, 2005; Mattson et al., 2001.

128 *fMRI scans on mothers:* Lorberbaum et al., 2002.

128 *mothers merely gazed at their own children:* Bartels and Zeki, 2004.

128 *Retrieving, nursing, cleaning:* Kinsley and Lambert, 2006.

128 *cradle her baby with her left arm:* MacLean, 1996.

129 *the social hormone oxytocin:* Moberg, 2003.

129 *the Brahms Lullaby each day:* Standley, 1996.

130 *rodent moms are emotionally bolder:* Kinsley and Lambert, 2006.

130 *second-time moms:* Love et al., 2005.

130 *more sophisticated attention task:* Higgins et al., 2007.

131 *the males care for their offspring:* Everette et al., 2007.

132 *vasopressin, in the prefrontal cortex:* Kozorouitskiy et al., 2006.

132 *anal-genital licks:* Menard et al., 2004; Plotsky et al., 2005.

132 Touch: Field, 2001.

133 *Mothers were observed interacting:* Ferber, 2004.

133 *women who felt social isolation:* Nielsen et al., 2000.

134 *heal more quickly when they have a roommate:* Ashley et al., unpublished manuscript.

134   *social contact seems to improve immune functions:* Glasper and DeVries, 2005.

134   *Ronald Glaser and Janice Kiecolt-Glaser:* Kiecolt-Glaser et al., 1984.

134   *which helps mitigate the stress response:* Grewen et al., 2005.

134   *social contact is negatively affected by marital arguments:* Kiecolt-Glaser et al., 2005.

134   *Social contact and touch:* Weze et al., 2005.

135   *deep pressure massages to infants:* Field et al., 1986.

135   *social contact on dogs:* Coppola et al., 2006.

135   *healing effects work both ways:* Friedmann, 1995.

135   *positive interactions with pets:* Odendaal, 2000.

136   *experiment using cynomolgus monkeys:* Lam et al., 1991.

136   *olive baboons in the Serengeti:* Sapolsky, 2004.

136   The Noonday Demon: Solomon, 2001.

137   *"And then when they have mastered . . .":* Solomon, 2001, p. 36.

139   *dentists have noted that depressed patients:* Friedlander et al., 1993.

139   *hens that were allowed to take dustbaths:* Vestergaard et al., 1997.

139   *rodent version of a hair salon consultation:* Mineur et al., 2003.

140   *increased incidences of grooming in rats:* Sanchez et al., 2001.

140   *brain's reward center when they licked:* Champagne et al., 2004.

141   *grooming his face, head, and neck:* Taira and Rolls, 1996.

141   *groom the arm of the experimenter:* Falk, 1958.

CHAPTER 7 THE BUILDING BLOCKS OF RESILIENCE

143   *interviewed Katherine Sherwood:* Lambert and Kinsley, 2005.

145   *more like ordinary magic:* Masten, 2001.

145   *"Resilience appears to be a common phenomenon . . .":* Masten, 2001, p. 227.

145   *Research on children:* Masten, 2001.

146   *aspiring screenplay writer Joe Dee:* Schwartz, 1996; personal communication with Joe Dee, May 2003.

146   *"helicopter moms":* Shellenbarger, accessed 2007.

147   *"self-esteem movement":* Seligman, 1996.

148   *self-efficacy help facilitate a student's adjustment:* Silverthorn and Gekoski, 1995.

148   *Stanford University psychologist Albert Bandura:* Bandura, 1997.

148   *humans were born as a* tabula rasa: Benjamin, 1993.

148   *"How necessary health is to our business":* Benjamin, 1993, p. 4.

148   *Jonas Salk was also concerned about the importance of fostering resilience:* Seligman, 1996.

150   *Coach Fitzgerald and his no-nonsense, tough love:* Lewis, 2004.

151 *"The conclusion I have reached"*: Sternberg and Subotnik, 2006, p. 26.

151 *Robert Sternberg, an intelligence researcher*: Sternberg and Subotnik, 2006; Sternberg, 2003.

152 *Seligman's famed animal model of depression*: Seligman, 1998.

152 *therapy designed to accomplish this goal*: Martell et al., 2001.

153 *school-based intervention program*: Gillham et al., 1995.

153 *"drug-free alternative to antidepressants"*: Cutuli et al., 2006, APA online, 2007; Cutuli et al., 2006.

153 *a recent article on the Penn Resiliency*: Cutuli et al., 2006

154 *an eight-session intervention program*: Blackwell et al., 2007.

154 Mindset: The New Psychology of Success: Dweck, 2006.

156 *Christian Waugh, then a social psychologist at the University of Michigan*: Waugh et al., 2006.

157 *When asked to reassess these negative scenes*: Ochsner et al., 2002.

158 *animals to "reappraise the danger*: Amat et al., 2006.

158 *Barry Jacobs's work*: Jacobs and Fornal, 2000.

159 *people suffering from post-traumatic stress disorder*: Lanius et al., 2001.

159 *higher levels of DHEA*: Cohen et al., 2007.

159 *DHEA also seems to protect the brain*: Charney, 2004.

159 *When injected into the amygdala*: Charney, 2004.

160 *Profile rats for coping strategies*: Fleming et al., 2007.

161 *more predictable stress of running*: Lambert et al., 2006.

162 *George Koob, perhaps the foremost expert in this area of the brain*: Moyers on Addiction; personal communication with George Koob.

164 *Meet Razza*: Russell et al., 2005.

166 The Amazing Adventures of Razza the Rat: Ihimaera, 2006.

166 *laboratory version of the prisoner's dilemma game*: Rilling et al., 2002.

167 *Justin M. Joffe, a professor of psychology at the University of Vermont*: Joffe et al., 1973.

168 *neighborhood characteristics on building resilience*: Cutrona et al., 2006.

168 *Reasons for the higher rates of depression*: Elliott, 2000.

169 Gifted Hands: Carson, 1990.

CHAPTER 8 NONPHARMACOLOGICAL TREATMENTS FOR DEPRESSION: A LITTLE LESS TALK AND A LOT MORE ACTION

173 *depression is the number one cause of disability*: Murray and Lopez, 1997; Hollen et al., 2002.

173 *when various therapies were compared*: Hollon et al., 2002.

174 *81 percent of those who took SSRIs*: Hollon et al., 2001.

174 *seminal report in the journal* Psychological Science: Hollon et al., 2001.

174 *combining therapies works better:* Hollon and Shelton, 2001.

174 *one in ten American women:* Vedantam, 2004.

175 *pharmaceutical industry* was *spending:* Wolfe, 2003.

175 *fastest-growing group of new consumers:* Kadison and DiGeronimo, 2004.

177 *"People who were prone to focusing":* Stanford News Release, 1994.

177 *depression appears to be the most disabling:* Reinberg, 2007; Moussavi et al., 2007.

177 *"Compared to the chronic physical":* Reinberg, 2007.

179 *woman is on the path to mental health:* Stanford News Release, 1994.

179 *began to question the effectiveness of grief counseling:* Neimeyer, 2000; Bonanno, 2004.

179 Grief Work Assumption: Bonanno, 2004.

180 *people experience a "complicated grief " response:* Stroebe et al., 2005.

180 *undermine the brain's natural resilience:* Bonanno, 2005.

180 *developmental psychology theories:* Bowlby, 1980.

180 *emotionally resilient spouses:* Bonanno et al., 2002.

180 *Living in New York City during the 9/11 terrorist attack:* Bonanno et al., 2006.

181 *"wholesale prophylactic psychological interventions":* McNally et al., 2003.

181 *swarms of therapists:* Slater, 2003.

181 *"Basically, all these therapists":* Slater, 2003.

181 *"keep leading people to the edge of a cliff ":* Slater, 2003.

182 *Dusty Miller, a psychologist:* Slater, 2003.

183 *"It was tennis, not talk, that really helped":* Slater, 2003.

184 *the effort-driven rewards theory:* Lambert, 2006.

184 *he called it "behavioral activation therapy":* Martell, personal communication with the author, 2006.

184 *person experiencing few rewards:* Lewinsohn et al., 1976: Hollon et al., 2002.

185 *conducted a thorough analysis of the effectiveness:* Jacobson et al., 1996.

185 *developed a comprehensive behavioral activation approach:* Martell et al., 2001.

185 *behavioral activation therapy was based on successful strategies:* Levanthal and Martell, 2006.

186 *shy rats that consistently avoided:* Cavigelli and McClintock, 2003.

187 *"preoccupied with internal biological":* Martell et al., 2001, p. xxvi.

189 *Henry, a fifty-four-year-old executive:* Martell et al., 2001.

191 *240 subjects diagnosed with major depression:* Dimidjian et al., 2006.

193 *Lisa McCann and David Holmes:* McCann and Holmes, 1984.

194 *sixteen-week program consisting of exercise:* Blumenthal et al., 1984.

195 *single "dose" of exercise:* Bartholomew et al., 2005.

195 *running increases sensitivity to the reward:* Fordyce and Farrar, 1991.

195   *robust improvements on executive-control processes:* Colcombe and Kramer, 2003.

196   *MRI technology to map cerebral blood volume:* Pereira et al., 2007.

196   *increased capillary density in the cerebellum:* Black et al., 1990.

197   *my very first research project:* Gurley (now Lambert) et al., 1987.

197   *exercise boosts the all-important allostatic processes:* Dishman et al., 2006.

197   *John J. Ratey, M.D., an associate professor of psychiatry at Harvard Medical School, commented:* Carmichael, 2007.

198   *"Depression starts out insipid":* Solomon, 2001, p. 17.

CHAPTER 9 EFFORT-DRIVEN REWARDS AND OUR EVOLVING BRAINS

202   *Nobel Prize–winning ethologist Konrad Lorenz:* Lorenz, 1937.

202   *Niko Tinbergen, who shared the Nobel Prize in Medicine:* Tinbergen, 1974.

202   *aggression in the stickleback fish:* Tinbergen, 1952.

202   *criteria that should be met:* Dewsbury, 1978.

203   *response of bowerbirds:* Borgia, 1995.

204   *Martin Seligman provided another dramatic example:* Seligman, personal communication with the author, December 2006.

204   Authentic Happiness: Seligman, 2002.

205   *retailing challenge Wal-Mart faced:* Naughton, 2006.

206   *"ecological opportunists of the first order":* MacClintock, 2002.

206   *very successful in adapting:* Zeveloff, 2002.

206   *a now famous article written by two students:* Breland and Breland, 1961.

207   *One captive maternal raccoon:* Lydall-Watson, 1963.

209   *my brother, Doug:* Doug Gurley, personal communication with the author, 2007.

211   *Adrienne Martini, a journalist and communications:* Martini, 2006; Martini, 2003; Martini, personal communication with the author, July 2007.

212   *"I began to feel like Dr. Seuss'":* Martini, 2003.

212   *Jack Trammell, director of the Learning Center:* Trammell, personal communication with the author, July 2007.

215   *"After all, if":* Stein, 2006.

216   *"Hal had been created":* Clarke, 1993, p. 151.

216   *Microsoft's Bill Gates:* Gates, 2007.

217   *recent survey of how we reward effort monetarily:* Dykman, 2006.

217   *engaged in vigorous leisure-time activity:* Pleis et al., 2006.

217   *Teen activity levels are also troubling:* Centers for Disease Control and Prevention, 2005.

219   *pioneering work of Paul MacLean:* MacLean, 1989.

220   *Jefffrey Schwartz, a neuropsychiatrist at UCLA:* Schwartz, 1996.

220   Why We Get Sick: Neese and Williams, 1994.

221   *"By trying to find the flaws"*: Neese and Williams, 1994, p. 230.

223   *According to E. O. Smith*: Smith, 2002.

223   *"We must accept the possibility"*: Smith, 2002, p. 126.

223   *Joffe . . . confirmed this idea when*: Silvestri and Joffe, 2004.

224   *"Only if the brain was impaired"*: Silvestri and Joffe, 2004, p. 508.

225   The *Pfizer "Zoloft for Everything" Ad Campaign*: The Onion, 2003.

CHAPTER 10   THE NEW RX FOR PREVENTING AND LIFTING DEPRESSION

228   *campaign to increase the physical activity*: Coitinho et al., 2002; Matsudo et al., 2002.

232   *Exercise triggers the release of endorphins*: Dishman et al., 2006.

233   *how effective your coping strategies*: Fleming et al., 2007.

234   *less distress by the end*: Bonanno et al., 2004.

236   *elevated cortisol levels are found*: Sapolsky, 2004; Sapolsky, 2000.

237   *Premature babies receiving massage*: Field et al., 1986.

238   *rough-and-tumble play*: Panksepp, 1988.

239   *increased time pressures in our children's lives*: Ginsberg, 2007.

241   *rats' typical responses to the traumatic experience*: Ubali et al., 2007.

241   *As seen in these Mr. Moms*: Everette et al., 2007.

242   *In a recent global survey*: Moussavi et al., 2007.

242   *living in London during the Nazi blitzkrieg*: Stewart and Winser, 1942.

243   *infusion of an orange citrus odor*: Lehrner et al., 2000.

243   *than the rats with no aromatherapy exposure*: Faturi et al., 2007.

References

Aggleton, J. P. (ed.). (2000). *The Amygdala: A Functional Analysis*. New York: Oxford University Press.

Allman, J. M. (1999). *Evolving Brains*. New York: W. H. Freeman.

Amat, J., Baratta, M. V., Paul, E., Bland, S. T., Watkins, L. R., and Maier, S. F. (2005). "Medial Prefrontal Cortex Determines How Stressor Controllability Affects Behavior and Dorsal Raphe Nucleus." *Nature Neuroscience*, 8, 365–371.

Amat, J., Paul, E., Zarza, C., Watkins, L. R., and Maier, S. F. (2006). "Previous Experience with Behavioral Control over Stress Blocks the Behavioral and Dorsal Raphe Nucleus Activating Effects of Later Uncontrollable Stress: Role of the Ventral Medial Prefrontal Cortex." *Journal of Neuroscience*, 26, 13264–13272.

American Psychiatric Association. (2000). *Diagnostic and Statistical Manual of Mental Disorders* (4th ed.). Washington, DC: American Psychiatric Association.

Anderson, T. (1993). *Den of Lions*. New York: Ballantine Books.

APA online. (2003). "School-Based Program Teaches Skills That Stave Off Depression." Retrieved Nov. 1, 2007, from www.pwychologymatters.org/gillham.html.

Arlen, M. (1980). *Thirty Seconds*. New York: Farrar, Straus & Giroux.

Arroll, B., et al. (2005). "Efficacy and Tolerability of Tricyclic Antidepressants and SSRIs Compared with Placebo for Treatment of Depression in Primary Care: A Meta-Analysis." *Annals of Family Medicine*, 3, 449–456.

Ashley, H. E., McNamara, I., Morgan, M., Klein, S. L., Glasper, E. R., DeVries, A. C., Conway, A., Tu, K., Kinsley, C. H., and Lambert, K. G. "Sex and Social Housing Influence Wound Healing and Anxiogenic Responses in Chronically Stressed." Manuscript in preparation.

Baldwin, J. (2003). *Kudzu in America*. Virginia Beach, VA: Suntop Press.

Bandura, A. (1997). *Self-Efficacy: The Exercise of Control*. New York: W. H. Freeman and Company.

Bartels, A., and Zeki, S. (2004). "The Neural Correlates of Maternal and Romantic Love." *Neuroimage*, 21, 1155–1166.

Bartholomew, J. B., Morrison, D., and Ciccolo, J. T. (2005). "Effects of Acute Exercise on Mood and Well-Being in Patients with Major Depressive Disorder." *Medicine and Science in Sports & Exercise*, 37, 2032–2037.

Basset, D. R., Schneider, P. L., and Huntington, G. E. (2004). "Physical Activity in an Old Order Amish Community." *Medical and Science in Sports and Exercise*, 36, 79–85.

Benjamin, L. T. (1993). *A History of Psychology in Letters*. Dubuque, IA: Wm. C. Brown Communications, Inc.

Black, J. E., Isaacs, K. R., Anderson, B. J., Alcantara, A. A., and Greenough, W. T. (1990). "Learning Causes Synaptogenesis, Whereas Motor Activity Causes Angiogenesis in Cerebellar Cortex of Adult Rats." *Proceedings of the National Academy of Sciences*, 87, 5568–5572.

Blackwell, L. S., Trzesniewski, K. H., and Dweck, C. S. (2007). "Implicit Theories of Intelligence Predict Achievement Across an Adolescent Transition: A Longitudinal Study and an Intervention." *Child Development*, 78, 246–263.

Blumenthal, J. A., Babyak, M. A., Moore, K. A., et al. (1999). "Effects of Exercise Training on Older Patients with Major Depression." *Archives of Internal Medicine*, 159, 2349–2356.

Bonanno, G. A. (2004). "Loss, Trauma, and Human Resilience: Have We Underestimated the Human Capacity to Thrive After Extremely Aversive Events?" *American Psychologist*, 59, 20–28.

Bonanno, G. A. (2005). "Resilience in the Face of Potential Trauma." *Current Directions in Psychological Science,* 14, 135–138.

Bonanno, G. A., Galea, S., Bucciarelli, A., and Vlahov, D. (2006). "Psychological Resilience After Disaster." *Psychological Science*, 17, 181–186.

Bonanno, G. A., Papa, A., Lalande, K., Westphal, M., and Coifman, K. (2004). "The Importance of Being Flexible: The Ability to Both Enhance and Suppress Emotional Expression Predicts Long-Term Adjustment." *Psychological Science*, 15, 482–487.

Bonanno, G. A., Wortman, C. B., Lehman, D. R., Tweed, R. G., Haring, M., Sonnega, J., Carr, D., and Neese, R. M. (2002). "Resilience to Loss and Chronic Grief: A Prospective Study from Pre-Loss to 18 Months Post-Loss." *Journal of Personality and Social Psychology*, 83, 1150–1164.

Borgia, G. (1995). "Why Do Bowerbirds Build Bowers?" *American Scientist*, 83, 542–547.

Bowlby, J. (1980). *Loss: Sadness and Depression*. Vol. 3: *Attachment and Loss*. New York: Basic Books.

Breland, K., and Breland, M. (1961). "The Misbehavior of Organisms." *American Psychologist*, 16, 681–684.

Bremner, J. D., Narayan, M., Anderson, E. R., Staib, L. H., Miller, H. L., and Charney, D. S. (2000). "Hippocampal Volume Reduction in Major Depression." *American Journal of Psychiatry*, 157, 115–118.

Brown, M. W. (1947). *Goodnight Moon*. New York: Harper & Row.

Brunson, K. L., Kramar, E., Lin, B., Chen, Y., Colgin, L. L., Yanagihara, T. K., Lynch, G., and Baram, T. Z. (2005). "Mechanisms of Late-Onset Cognitive Decline After Early-Life Stress." *Journal of Neuroscience*, 25, 9328–9338.

Campbell, T., Lin, S., DeVries, C., and Lambert, K. (2003). "Coping Strategies in Male and Female Rats Exposed to Multiple Stressors." *Physiology and Behavior*, 78, 495–504.

Cannon, W. B. (1935). "Stresses and Strains of Homeostasis." *American Journal of Medical Sciences*, 189, 1–14.

Cardinal, R. N., Pennicott, D. R., Sugathapala, C. L., Robbins, T. W., and Everitt, B. J. (2001). "Impulsive Choice Induced in Rats by Lesions of the Nucleus Accumbens Core." *Science*, 292, 2499–2501.

Carelli, R. M., and Wightman, R. M. (2004). "Functional Neuroanatomy in the Accumbens Underlying Drug Addiction: Insights from Real-Time Signaling During Behavior." *Current Opinion in Neurobiology*, 14, 764–768.

Carmichael, M. (2007, Mar. 26). "Health: Can Exercise Make You Smarter?" *Newsweek*. Retrieved Nov. 1, 2007, from www.newsweek.com/id/36056.

Carroll, R. T. (2003). *The Skeptic's Dictionary*. Hoboken, NJ: John Wiley and Sons.

Carson, B. (1990). *Gifted Hands*. Grand Rapids, MI: Zondervan Publishers.

Cavigelli, S. A., and McClintock, M. K. (2003). "Fear of Novelty in Infant Rats Predicts Adult Corticosterone Dynamics and an Early Death." *Proceedings of the National Academy of Sciences*, 100, 16131–16136.

Centers for Disease Control and Prevention. (2005). *2005 Youth Risk Behavior Survey*. Atlanta: National Center for Chronic Disease Prevention and Health Promotion. Retrieved May 15, 2007, from www.cdc.gov/nchs/data/hus/hus05.pdf#data13.

Champagne, F. A., Chretien, P., Stevenson, C. W., Zhang, T. Y., Gratton, A., and Meaney, M. J. (2004). "Variations in Nucleus Accumbens Dopamine Associated with Individual Differences in Maternal Behavior in the Rat." *Journal of Neuroscience*, 24, 4113–4123.

Charney, D. S. (2004). "Psychobiological Mechanisms of Resilience and Vulnerability: Implications for Successful Adaptation to Extreme Stress." *American Journal of Psychiatry*, 161, 195–216.

Check, E. (2006). "Comfortably Numb." *Nature*, 443, 629–630.

Cheetham, S. C., Katona, C. L. E., and Horton, R. W. (1991). "Post-Mortem Studies of Neurotransmitter Biochemistry in Depression and Suicide." In R. W. Horton and C.L.E. Katona (eds.), *Biological Aspects of Affective Disorders* (pp. 192–221). London: Academic Press.

Clarke, A. C. (1993). *2001: A Space Odyssey*. New York: Roc Trade Paperbacks.

Cohen, H., Maayan, R., Touati-Werner, D., Kaplan, Z., Mater, M., Loewenthal, W., Kozlousky, N., and Weitman, R. (2007). "Decreased Circulatory Levels of Neuroactive Steroids in Behaviourally More Extremely Affected Rats Subsequent to a Potentially Traumatic Experience." *International Journal of Neuropsychopharmacolgy*, 10, 203–209.

Coitinho, D., Monteiro, C. A., and Popkin, B. M. (2002). "What Brazil Is Doing to Promote Healthy Diets and Active Lifestyles." *Public Health Nutrition*, 5, 263–267.

Colcombe, S., and Kramer, A. R. (2003). "Fitness Effects on the Cognitive Function of Older Adults: A Meta-Analytic Study." *Psychological Science*, 14, 125–130.

Coppola, C. L., Grandin, T., and Enns, R. M. (2006). "Human Interaction and Cortisol: Can Human Contact Reduce Stress for Shelter Dogs?" *Physiology and Behavior*, 87, 537–541.

Cousins, M. S., Atherton, A., Turner, L., and Salamone, J. D. (1996). "Nucleus Accumbens Dopamine Depletions Alter Relative Response Allocation in a T-Maze Cost/Benefit Task." *Behavior and Brain Research*, 74, 189–197.

Csikszentmihalyi, M. (1990). *Flow: The Psychology of Optimal Experience*. New York: Harper & Row.

Cutrona, C. E., Wallace, G., and Wesner, K. A. (2006). "Neighborhood Characteristics and Depression." *Current Directions in Psychological Science*, 15, 188–192.

Cutuli, J. J., Chaplin, T. M., Gillham, J. E., Reivich, K. J., and Seligman, M. E. P. (2006). "Preventing Co-Occurring Depression Symptoms in Adolescents with Conduct Problems: The Penn Resiliency Program." *Annals of the New York Academy of Science*, 1094, 282–286.

Dahlstrom, W., and Williams, R. (1983). "Hostility, CHD Incidence, and Total Mortality: A 25 Year Follow-Up Study of 255 Physicians." *Psychosomatic Medicine*, 45, 59.

Debold, E. (2002, Spring-Summer). "Flow with Soul: An Interview with Mikhail Csikszentmihalyi." *What Is Enlightenment Magazine*. Retrieved Sept. 2007, from www.wie.org/;21/csik52.ap.

Delgado, P. L. (2000). "Depression: The Case for a Monoamine Deficiency." *Journal of Clinical Psychiatry*, 61, 7–11.

Dewsbury, D. A. (1978). *Comparative Animal Behavior*. New York: McGraw-Hill.

Dimidjian, S., et al. (2006). "Randomized Trial of Behavioral Activation, Cognitive Therapy, and Antidepressant Medication in the Acute Treatment of Adults with Major Depression." *Journal of Consulting and Clinical Psychology*, 74, 658–670.

Disbrow, E., Roberts, T., Poeppel, D., and Krubitzer, L. (2001). "Evidence for Interhemispheric Processing of Inputs from the Hands in Human S2 and PV." *Journal of Neurophysiology*, 85, 2236–2244.

Dishman, R. K., Hans-Rudolf, B., Booth, F. W., Cotman, C. W., Edgerton, V. R., Fleshner, M. R., Gandecia, S. C., Gomez-Pinella, F., Greenwood, B. N., Hillman, J. D., van Hoomissen, J. D., Wade, C. E., York, D. A., and Zigmond, M. J. (2006). "Neurobiology of Exercise." *Obesity*, 14, 345–356.

Dobbs, D. (2006). "Antidepressants: Good Drugs or Good Marketing?" In L. Pople, C. Linsmeier, and K. Feyen (eds.), *Scientific American Readings in Clinical Neuroscience* (pp. 88–91). New York: Worth Publishers. (Originally published in *Scientific American* in 2004)

Ducottet, C., Griebel, G., and Belzung, C. (2003). "Effects of the Selective Nonpeptide Corticotropin-Releasing Factor Receptor 1 Antagonist Antalarmin in the Chronic Mild Stress Model of Depression in Mice." *Progress in Neuro-Psychopharmacology & Biological Psychiatry*, 27, 625–631.

Duman, R. S. (2004). "Depression: A Case of Neuronal Life and Death?" *Biological Psychiatry*, 56, 140–145.

Duman, R. S., Malberg, J., and Nakagawa, S. (2001). "Regulation of Adult Neurogenesis by Psychotropic Drugs and Stress." *Pharmacology and Experimental Therapeutics*, 299, 401–407.

Dunbar, R. (1996). *Grooming, Gossip, and the Evolution of Language.* Cambridge, MA: Harvard University Press.

Dweck, C. (2006). *Mindset: The New Psychology of Success.* New York: Random House.

Dykman, J. (2006, Oct. 30). "America by the Numbers: What We Earn." *Time Magazine*, pp. 47–48.

Eaton, S. B., Eaton, S. B. III, Konner, M. J., and Shostak, M. (1996). "An Evolutionary Perspective Enhances Understanding of Human Nutritional Requirements." *Journal of Nutrition*, 126, 1732–1740.

Eaton, S. B., Shostak, M., and Konner, M. (1988). *The Paleolithic Prescription: A Program of Diet and Exercise and a Design for Living.* New York: Harper & Row.

Egeland, J. A., and Hosteller, A. M. (1983). "Amish Study I: Affective Disorders Among the Amish, 1976–1980." *American Journal of Psychiatry*, 140, 56–61.

Elliott, M. (2000). "The Stress Process in Neighborhood Context." *Health & Place*, 6, 287–299.

Everette, A., Fleming, D., Higgins, T., Tu, K., Bardi, M., Kinsley, C. H., and Lambert, K. G. (2007, June). "Paternal Experience Enhances Behavioral and Neurobiological Responsivity Associated with Affiliative and Nurturing Responses." Research presented at the International Behavioral Neuroscience Society, Rio de Janeiro, Brazil.

Falk, J. L. (1958). "The Grooming Behavior of the Chimpanzee as a Reinforcer." *Journal of Experimental Analysis of Behavior,* 1, 83–85.

Faturi, C. G., Leite, J. R., Canton, A. C., and Teiseira-Silva, F. (2007, June). "Anxiolytic Effect of Sweet Orange Aroma in Wistar Rats." Research presented at the International Behavioral Neuroscience Society, Rio de Janeiro, Brazil.

Ferber, S. G. (2004). "The Nature of Touch in Mothers Experiencing Maternity Blues: The Contribution of Parity." *Early Human Development*, 79, 65–75.

Field, T. (2001). *Touch.* Cambridge, MA: Bradford Books.

Field, T. M., Schanbert, S., Scafidi, F., Bower, C., Vega-Lahr, N., Garcia, R., Nystrom, J., and Khun, C. M. (1986). "Tactile/Kinesthetic Stimulation Effects on Preterm Neonates." *Pediatrics,* 77, 654–658.

Fisk, D. M. (2001, Fall). "American Labor in the 20th Century." *Compensation and Working Conditions*, pp. 3–8.

Fleming, D. F., Everette, A. M., Higgins, T. J., Tu, K. M., Bardi, M., Kinsley, C. H., and Lambert, K. G. (2007, June). "Resiliency in Rats: An Investigation of the Effects of Coping Strategies on Neurobiological Responsiveness." Research presented at the International Behavioral Neuroscience Society, Rio de Janeiro, Brazil.

Fordyce, D. E., and Farrar, R. P. (1991). "Physical Activity Effects on Hipppocampal and Parietal Cholinergic Function and Spatial Learning in F344 Rats." *Behavioral Brain Research*, 43, 115–123.

Friedlander, A. H., Kawakami, K. K., Ganzell, S., and Fitten, L. J. (1993). "Dental Management of the Geriatric Patient with Major Depression." *Special Care in Dentistry*, 13, 249–253.

Friedmann, E. (1995). "The Role of Pets in Enhancing Human Well-Being: Physiological Effects." In I. Robinson (ed.), *Waltham Book of Human-Animal Interaction: Benefits and Responsibilities of Pet Ownership*. Oxford, UK: Pergamon.

Fuchs, E. (2005). "Social Stress in Tree Shrews as an Animal Model of Depression: An Example of a Behavioral Model of a CNS Disorder." *CNS Spectrums*, 10, 182–190.

Fuchs, E., Czeh, B., Michaelis, T., de Birurun, G., Watanabe, T., and Frahm, J. (2002). "Synaptic Plasticity and Tianeptine: Structural Regulation." *European Psychiatry*, 17, 311–317.

Fulton, J. F. (1951). *Frontal Lobotomy and Affective Behavior*. New York: W. W. Norton.

Gates, B. (2007, Jan.). "A Robot in Every Home." *Scientific American*, 296, 58–65.

Gellene, D. (2006, May 24). "Teens Who Use Cell Phones Most Found to Be Sadder and Less Assured; Study Defined Heavy Use as Over 90 Calls or Text Messages a Day." *San Francisco Chronicle*. Retrieved Oct. 29, 2007, from www.sfgate/com/cgi-bin/article.cdi?file-/c/a/2006/05/24/mingvk1234.dtl.

Geverink, N. A., Parmentier, H. K., de Vries Reilingh, G., Schouten, W. G. P., Gort, G., and Wiegant, V. M. (2004). "Effect of Response to Backtest and Housing Condition on Cell-Mediated and Humoral Immunity in Adult Pigs." *Physiology and Behavior*, 80, 541–546.

Geverink, N. A., Schouten, W. G. P., Gort, G., and Wiegant, V. M. (2002). "Individual Differences in Behavioral and Physiological Responses to Restraint Stress in Pigs." *Physiology and Behavior*, 77, 451–457.

Gillham, J. E., Reivich, K. J., Jaycox, L. J., and Seligman, M. E. P. (1995). "Prevention of Depressive Symptoms in Schoolchildren." *Psychological Science, 6*, 343–351.

Ginsburg, K. R. (2007). "The Importance of Play in Promoting Healthy Child Development and Maintaining Strong Parent-Child Bonds." *American Academy of Pediatrics*, 119, 182–191.

Glasper, E. R., and DeVries, A. C. (2005). "Social Structure Influences Effects of Pair Housing on Wound Healing." *Brain, Behavior, and Immunity*, 19, 61–68.

Graham, J. L., and Lam, N. M. (2003). "The Chinese Negotiation." *Harvard Business Review,* 81, 82–91.

Greenfield, P. M. (1991). "Language, Tools and Brain: The Ontogeny and Phylogeny of Hierarchically Organized Sequential Behavior." *Behavioral and Brain Sciences*, 14, 531–551.

Grewen, K. M., Girdler, S. S., Amico, J., and Light, K. C. (2005). "Effects of Partner Support on Resting Oxytocin, Cortisol, Norepinephrine, and Blood Pressure Before and After Warm Partner Contact." *Psychosomatic Medicine*, 67, 531–538.

Grippo, A. J., Wu, K. D., Hassan, I., and Carter, C. S. (2007). "Social Isolation in Prairie Voles Induces Behaviors Relevant to Negative Affect: Toward the Development of a Rodent Model Focused on Co-Occurring Depression and Anxiety." *Depression and Anxiety.* Retrieved Oct. 31, 2007, from www.ncbi.nim.nig.gov/sites/entrez?Db=pubmed&cmd=showDetailview&TMT.

Groenewegen, H. J., Wright, C. I., Beijer, A. V. J., and Voorn, P. (1999). "Convergence and Segregation of Ventral Striatal Inputs and Outputs." In J. F. McGinty (ed.), "Advancing from the Ventral Striatum to the Extended Amygdale: Implications for Neuropsychatry and Drug Abuse." *Annals of the New York Academy of Sciences,* 877, 49–63.

Gurley, K. R. (married name Lambert, K. G.), Peacock, L. J., and Hill, D. W. (1987). "The Effect of a Training Program and Induced Cognitive Stress on Heart Rate, Blood Pressure, and Skin Conductance Level." *Journal of Sports Medicine and Physical Fitness,* 27 (3), 318–326.

Healy, D. (2004). *Let Them Eat Prozac.* New York: New York University Press.

Heim, C., Newport, D. J., Bonsall, R., Miller, A. H., and Nemeroff, C. B. (2001). "Altered Pituitary-Adrenal Axis Responses to Provocative Challenge Tests in Adult Survivors of Childhood Abuse." *American Journal of Psychiatry,* 158, 575–581.

Henn, F. A., and Vollmayr, B. (2004). "Neurogenesis and Depression: Etiology or Epiphenomenon?" *Biological Psychiatry,* 56, 146–150.

Hessing, M. J. C., Hagelso, A. M., van Beek, J. A. M., Wiepkema, P. R., Schouten, W. G. P., and Krukow, R. (1993). "Individual Behavioral Characteristics in Pigs." *Applied Animal Behavior Science,* 37, 285–295.

Higgins, T., Everette, A., Fleming, D., Christon, L., Kinsley, C. H., and Lambert, K. G. (2007, June). "Maternal Experience Enhances Neurobiological and Behavioral Responses in an Attention Set-Shifting Paradigm." Research presented at the International Behavioral Neuroscience Society, Rio de Janeiro, Brazil.

Hollon, S. D., and Shelton, R. C. (2001). "Treatment Guidelines for Major Depressive Disorder." *Behavior Therapy,* 32, 235–258.

Hollon, S. D., Thase, M. E., and Markowitz, J. C. (2002). "Treatment and Prevention of Depression." *Psychological Science in the Public Interest,* 3, 39–72.

Hothersall, D. (1995). *History of Psychology.* 3rd ed. New York: McGraw-Hill.

Ihimaera, W. (2006). *The Amazing Adventures of Razzi.* Birkenhead, Auckland, New Zealand: Reed Books.

Iliffe, S., Kharicha, K., Harari D., Swift, C., Gillmann, G., and Stuck, A. E. (2007). "Health Risk Appraisal in Older People 2: The Implications for Clinicians and Commissioners of Social Isolation Risk in Older People." *British Journal of General Practitioners,* 57, 277–282.

Jacobs, B. L. (1994, Sept.-Oct.). "Serotonin, Motor Activity and Depression-Related Disorders." *American Scientist,* pp. 456–463.

Jacobs, B. L., and Fornal, C. A. (1999). "Activity of Serotonergic Neurons in Behaving Animals." *Neuropsychopharmacology*, 21, 9S–15S.

Jacobs, B. L., and Fornal, C. A. (2000). "A General Hypothesis." *American College of Neuropsycholopharmacology.* Retrieved Nov. 1, 2007, from http://www.acnp.org/g4/GN401000044/CH044.html.

Jacobs, B. L., Praag, H., and Gage, F. H. (2000). "Adult Brain Neurogenesis and Psychiatry: A Novel Theory of Depression." *Molecular Psychiatry*, 5, 262–269.

Jacobs, B. L., Praag, H., and Gage, F. H. (2000). "Depression and the Birth and Death of Brain Cells." *American Scientist*, 88, 340–345.

Jacobs, B. L., Wilkinson, L. O., and Fornal, C. A. (1990). "The Role of Brain Serotonin. A Neurophysiologic Perspective." *Neuropsychopharmacology*, 3, 473–478.

Jacobs., R., and Schmidt, R. E. (1999). "Foundations in Immunology." In M. Schedlowski and U. Tewes (eds.), *Psychoneuroimmunology: An Interdisciplinary Introduction*. New York: Kluwer Academic/Plenum.

Jacobson, N. S., Dobson, K. S., Truax, P. A., Addis, M. E., Koerner, K., Gollan, J. K., Gortner, E., and Prince, S. E. (1996). "A Component Analysis of Cognitive-Behavioral Treatment for Depression." *Journal of Consulting and Clinical Psychology*, 64, 295–304.

Joffe, J. M., Rawson, R. A., and Mulick, J. A. (1973). "Control of Their Environment Reduces Emotionality in Rats." *Science*, 180, 1383–1384.

Johnson, S. (1998). *Who Moved My Cheese? An Amazing Way to Deal with Change in Your Work and in Your Life*. New York: Putnam.

Kadison, R., and DiGeronimo, T. F. (2004). *College of the Overwhelmed: The Campus Mental Health Crisis and What to Do About It*. San Francisco: Jossey-Bass.

Kalivas, P. W., Churchill, L., and Romanides, A. (1999). "Involvement of the Pallidal-Thalamocortical Circuit in Adaptive Behavior." In J. F. McGinty (ed.), "Advancing from the Ventral Striatum to the Extended Amygdala: Implications for Neuropsychiatry and Drug Abuse." *Annals of the New York Academy of Sciences*, 877, 64–90.

Kelley, A. E. (1999). "Functional Specificity of Ventral Striatal Compartments in Appetitive Behaviors." In J. F. McGinty (ed.), "Advancing from the Ventral Striatum to the Extended Amygdala: Implications for Neuropsychiatry and Drug Abuse." *Annals of the New York Academy of Sciences*, 877, 71–90.

Kelly, S. D., Kravitz, C., and Hopkins, M. (2004). "Neural Correlates of Bimodal Speech and Gesture Comprehension." *Brain and Language*, 89, 253–260.

Kessler, R. C., et al. (2003). "The Epidemiology of Major Depression Disorder: Results from the National Comorbidity Survey Replication (NCS-R)." *Journal of the American Medical Association*, 280, 3095–3105.

Kiecolt-Glaser, J. K., Garner, W., Speicher, C., Penn, G. M., Holliday, J., and Glaser, R. (1984). "Psychosocial Modifiers of Immunocompetence in Medical Students." *Psychosomatic Medicine*, 46, 7–14.

Kiecolt-Glaser, J. K., Loving, T. J., Stowall, R., Malarkay, W. B., Lemeshow, S., Dickinson, S. L., and Glaser, R. (2005). "Hostile Marital Interactions, Proinflammatory Cytokine Production and Wound Healing." *Archives of General Psychiatry*, 62, 1377–1384.

Kilpatrick, L. A., Zald, D. H., Pardo, J. V., and Cahill, L. F. (2006). "Sex-Related Differences in Amygdala Functional Connectivity During Resting Conditions." *NeuroImage*, 30, 452–461.

Kingsolver, B., with Hopp, S. L., and Kingsolver, C. (2007). *Animal, Vegetable, Miracle: A Year of Food Life*. New York: HarperCollins.

Kinsley, C. H., and Lambert, K. G. (2006). "The Maternal Brain." *Scientific American*, 294, 72–79.

Kinzie, S. (2006, Dec. 6). "Incoming President Draws Praise." *Washington Post*. Retrieved May 15, 2007, from www.washingtonpost.com/wpdyn/content/-article/2006/12/05/AR2006120501311.html.

Kirsch, I., Moore, T. J., Scoboria, A., and Nicholls, S. S. (2002). "The Emperor's New Drugs: An Analysis of Antidepressant Medication Data Submitted to the U.S. Food and Drug Administration." *Prevention and Treatment*, 5, Article 23, posted July 15, 2002.

Kirsch, I., Scoboria, A., and Moore, T. J. (2002). "Antidepressants and Placebos: Secrets, Revelations, and Unanswered Questions." *Prevention and Treatment*, 5, Article 33, posted July 15, 2002. Retrieved Dec. 10, 2003, from http://journals.apa.org/prevention/.

Klerman, G., Lavori, P., Rice, J., Reich, T., Endicott, N., Andreasen, N., Keller, M., and Hirschfeld, R. (1995). "Birth Cohort Trends in Rates of Major Depressive Disorder Among Relatives of Patients with Affective Disorder." *Archives of General Psychiatry*, 42, 689–693.

Knutson, B., Adams, C. M., Fong, G. W., and Hommer, D. (2001). "Anticipation of Increasing Monetary Reward Selectively Recruits Nucleus Accumbens." *Journal of Neuroscience*, 21, 1–5.

Kollatz, H. (2005, Mar.). "Designed for Living: Five Furniture Makers—Their Art and Craft." *Richmond Magazine*, pp. H14–H19.

Koolhaas, J. M., Korte, S. M., De Boer, S. F., Van Der Vegt, B. J., Van Reenen, C. G., Hopster, H., De Jong, I. C., Ruis, M. A. W., and Blokuis, H. J. (1999). "Coping Styles in Animals: Current Status in Behavior and Stress Physiology." *Neuroscience and Biobehavioral Reviews*, 23, 925–935.

Korte, S. M., Koolhaas, J. M., Wingfield, J. C., and McEwen, B. S. (2005). "The Darwinian Concept of Stress: Benefits of Allostasis and Costs of Allostatic Load and the Trade-Offs in Health and Disease." *Neuroscience and Biobehavioral Reviews*, 29, 3–38.

Kozorouitskiy, Y., Hughes, M., Lee, K., and Gould, E. (2006). "Fatherhood Affects Dendritic Spines and Vasopressin V1a Receptors in the Primate Prefrontal Cortex." *Nature Neuroscience*, 9, 1094–1095.

Kuhn, S. L., Stiner, M. C., Reese, D. S., and Gulec, E. (2001). "Ornaments of the Earliest Upper Paleolithic: New Insights from the Levant." *Proceedings of the National Academy of Sciences*, 98, 76416.

Lacasse, J. R. (2005). "Consumer Advertising of Psychiatric Medications Biases the Public Against Nonpharmacological Treatment." *Ethical Human Psychology and Psychiatry,* 7, 175–179.

Lacasse, J. R., and Leo, J. (2005). "Serotonin and Depression: A Disconnect Between the Advertisements and the Scientific Literature." *PloS Medicine,* 2 (12): e32. Retrieved Jan. 20, 2006, from doi:10.1371/journal.pmed.0020329.

Lam, K., Rupniak, N. M. J., and Iverson, S. D. (1991). "Use of a Grooming and Foraging Substrate to Reduce Cage Stereotypies in Macaques." *Journal of Medical Primatology,* 20, 104–109.

Lambert, K. G. (2003). "The Life and Career of Paul MacLean: A Journey Toward Neurobiological and Social Harmony." *Physiology and Behavior,* 79, 343–349.

Lambert, K. G. (2006). "Rising Rates of Depression in Today's Society: Consideration of the Roles of Effort-Based Rewards and Enhanced Resilience in Day-to-Day Functioning." *Neuroscience and Biobehavioral Reviews,* 30, 497–510.

Lambert, K. G., Buckelew, S. K., Staffiso-Sandoz, G., Gaffga, S., Carpenter, W., Fisher, J., and Kinsley, C. H. (1998). "Activity-Stress Induces Atrophy of Apical Dendrites of Hippocampal Pyramidal Neurons in Male Rats." *Physiology and Behavior,* 65, 39–43.

Lambert, K. G., Fleming, D. F., Tu, K., Farrell, M., Bardi, M., and Kinsley, C. H. (2007). "Diminished Depressive-like Symptoms and Accompanying Neurobiological Modifications in Flexible Coping Rats." Presentation at the annual meeting of Society for Neuroscience, San Diego.

Lambert, K. G., and Kinsley, C. H. (2005). *Clinical Neuroscience: Neurobiological Foundations of Mental Health.* New York: Worth Publishers.

Lambert, K. G., Tu, K., Everette, A., Love, G., McNamara, I., Bardi, M., and Kinsley, C. H. (2006). "Explorations of Coping Strategies, Learned Persistence, and Resilience in Long-Evans Rats: Innate Versus Acquired Characteristics." In B. M. Lester, A. Masten, and B. McEwen (eds.), *Resilience in Children: Annals of the New York Academy of Sciences,* 1094, 319–324.

Lanius, R. A., Williamson, P. C., Densmore, M., Boksman, K., Madhulika, A. G., Neufeld, R. W., et al. (2001). "Neural Correlates of Traumatic Memories in Posttraumatic Stress Disorder: A Functional MRI Investigation." *American Journal of Psychiatry,* 158, 1920–1922.

Lee, C. (2005, Mar. 30). "A Pastime of Grandma and the Golden Girls Evolves into a Hip Hobby." *New York Times Online.* Retrieved Aug. 15, 2007, from www.nytimes.com/2005/03/30/opinion/30wed3.html.

Lehrer, J. (2006). "The Reinvention of the Self: A Mind-Altering Idea Reveals How Life Affects the Brain." *SEED Online.* Retrieved Oct. 30, 2007, from seedmagazine.com/news/2006/02/the_reinvention_of_the_self.php–39k.

Lehrner, J., Eckersberger, C., Walla, P., Potsch, G., and Deecke, L. (2000). "Ambient Odor of Orange in a Dental Office Reduces Anxiety and Improves Mood in Female Patients." *Physiology and Behavior,* 71, 83–86.

Lemonick, M., and Dorfman, A. (2006, Mar. 13). "Who Were the First Americans?" *Time Magazine*, pp. 45–52.

Lenhard, E. (2006). *Chicks with Sticks: Knit Two Together*. New York: Dutton.

Lennon, M. C. (1994). "Women, Work, and Well-Being: The Importance of Work Conditions." *Journal of Health and Social Behavior*, 35, 235–247.

Leventhal, A. M., and Martell, C. R. (2006). "The Myth of Depression as a Disease." Westport, CT: Praeger.

Lewinsohn, P. M., Biglan, A., and Zeiss, A. M. (1976). "Behavioral Treatment of Depression." In P. O. Davidson (ed.), *The Behavioral Management of Anxiety, Depression, and Pain*. New York: Brunner/Mazel.

Lewis, M. (2004). "Coach Fitz's Management Theory." *New York Times Online*. Retrieved Mar. 15, 2007, from www.nytimes.com/2004/03/28/magazine-/28COAC.html?ex=1396414800&en=47.

Lillard, P. P. (1972). *Montessori: A Modern Approach*. New York: Schocken Books.

Lorberbaum, J. P., Newman, J. D., Horwitz, A. R., Dubno, J. R., Lydiard, R. B., Hamner, M. B., Hogning, D. E., and George, M. S. (2002). "A Potential Role for the Thalamocingulate Circuitry in Human Maternal Behavior." *Biological Psychiatry*, 15, 431–445.

Lorenz, K. A. (1937). "The Companion in the Bird's World." *Auk*, 54, 245–273.

Love, G., Torrey, N., McNamara, I., Morgan, M., Banks, M., Hester, N. W., Glasper, E. R., DeVries, A. C., Kinsley, C. H., and Lambert, K. G. (2005). "Maternal Experience Produces Long-Lasting Behavioral Modifications in the Rat." *Behavioral Neuroscience*, 119, 1084–1096.

Lydall-Watson, M. (1963). "A Critical Re-examination of Food 'Washing' Behavior in the Raccoon." *Proceedings of the Zoological Society of London*, 141, 371–393.

MacClintock, D. (2002). *A Natural History of Raccoons*. Caldwell, NJ: Blackburn Press.

Macdonald, A. L. (1988). *No Idle Hands: The Social History of American Knitting*. New York: Ballantine Books.

MacLean, P. D. (1964, Feb. 3). "Man and His Animal Brains." *Modern Medicine*, 95–106.

MacLean, P. D. (1985). "Brain Evolution Relating to Family, Play, and the Separation Call." *Archives of General Psychiatry*, 42, 405–417.

MacLean, P. D. (1996). "Paul D. MacLean." In L. Squire (ed.), *The History of Neuroscience in Autobiography* (Vol. 2; pp. 245–275). New York: Academic Press.

MacLean, P. D. (1996). "Women: A More Balanced Brain." *Zygon*, 31, 421–439.

Maddock, R. J., Garrett, A. S., and Buonocore, M. H. (2003). "Posterior Cingulate Cortex Activation by Emotional Words fMRI Evidence from a Valence Decision Task." *Human Brain Mapping*, 18, 30–41.

Magarinos, A. M., Deslandes, A., and McEwen, B. S. (1999). "Effects of Antidepressants and Benzodiazepine Treatments on the Dendritic Structure of CA3 Pyramidal Neurons After Chronic Stress." *European Journal of Pharmacology*, 371, 113–122.

Mahendra, N., Hopper, T., Bayles, K. A., Azuma, T., Cleary, S., Esther, K., and Boyle, M. (2006). "Evidence-Based Practice Recommendations for Working with Individuals with Dementia: Montessori-Based Interventions." *Journal of Medical Speech-Language Pathology*, 14, xv–xxv.

Markowitz, J. C., and Weissman, M. M. (2004). "Interpersonal Psychotherapy: Principles and Applications." *World Psychiatry*, 3, 136–139.

Martell, C. R., Addis, M. E., and Jacobson, N. S. (2001). *Depression in Context*. New York: W. W. Norton.

Martini, A. (2003, Fall). "Hats, or How I Lost My Blues." Retrieved July 15, 2007, from *Knitty Online*. www.knitty.com/ISSUEFall03?FEAT/oncemore.html.

Martini, A. (2006). *Hillbilly Gothic: A Memoir of Madness and Motherhood*. New York: Free Press.

Masten, A. S. (2001). "Ordinary Magic: Resilience Processes in Development." *American Psychologist*, 56, 227–238.

Matsudo, V., Matsudo, S., Andrade, D., Araujo, T., Andrade, E., de Oliveira, L. C., and Braggion, G. (2002). "Promotion of Physical Activity in a Developing Country: The Agita Sao Paulo Experience." *Public Health Nutrition*, 253–261.

Mattson, B. J., and Morrell, J. I. (2005). "Preference for Cocaine- Versus Pup-Associated Cures Differentially Activates Neurons Expressing Either Fos or Cocaine- and Amphetamine-Regulated Transcript in Lactating, Maternal Rodents." *Neuroscience*, 135, 315–328.

Mattson, B. J., Williams, S., Rosenblatt, J. S., and Morrell, J. I. (2001). "Comparison of Two Positive Reinforcing Stimuli: Pups and Cocaine Throughout the Postpartum Period." *Behavioral Neuroscience*, 115, 683–694.

McCann, L., and Holmes, D. (1984). "Influence of Aerobic Exercise on Depression." *Journal of Personality and Social Psychology*, 46, 1142–1147.

McCoy, A. N., and Platt, M. L. (2005). "Risk-Sensitive Neurons in Macaque Posterior Cingulate Cortex." *Nature Neuroscience*, 8, 1220–1227.

McEwen, B. S. (2000). "Allostasis and Allostatic Load." *Encyclopedia of Stress*, 1, 145–150.

McNally, R. J., Bryant, R. A., and Ehlers, A. (2003). "Does Early Psychological Intervention Promote Recovery from Posttraumatic Stress?" *Psychological Science in the Public Interest*, 4, 45–79.

McNeill, D. (2005). *Gesture and Thought*. Chicago: University of Chicago Press.

Meaney, M. J., Aitken, D. H., Bodnoff, S. R., Iny, L. J., Tatarewicz, J. E., and Sapolsky, R. M. (1985). "Early, Postnatal Handling Alters Glucocorticoid Receptor Concentrations in Selected Brain Regions." *Behavioral Neuroscience*, 99, 760–765.

Menard, J. L., Champagne, D. L., and Meaney, M. J. (2004). "Variations of Maternal Care Differentially Influence 'Fear' Reactivity and Regional Patterns of cFos Immunoreactivity in Response to the Shock-Probe Burying Test." *Neuroscience*, 129, 297–308.

Mineur, Y. S., Prasol, D. J., Belzung, C., and Crusio, W. E. (2003). "Agonistic Behavior and Unpredictable Chronic Mild Stress in Mice." *Behavior Genetics*, 33, 513–519.

Moberg, K. U. (2003). *The Oxytocin Factor*. Cambridge, MA: Perseus Books.

Monson, N. (2005). *Craft to Heal*. Tucson, AZ: Hats Off Books.

Montessori, M. (1965). *Dr. Montessori's Own Handbook*. New York: Schocken Books.

Moussavi, S., Chatterji, S., Verdes, E., Tandon, A., Patel, V., and Ustun, B. (2007). "Depression, Chronic Diseases, and Decrements in Health: Results from the World Health Surveys." *Lancet*, 370, 851–858.

Moyers on Addiction. "An Interview with George Koob." Public Affairs Television. (1998). *The Hijacked Brain*. The Moyers Collection. Princeton, NJ: Films for the Humanities and Sciences.

Murray, C. J. L., and Lopez, A. D. (1997). "Global Mortality Disability and the Contribution of Risk Factors: Global Burden of Disease Study." *Lancet*, 349, 1436–1442.

Naughton, K. (2006). "The Great Wal-Mart of China." *Newsweek Online*. Retrieved July 20, 2007, from www.msnbc.msn.com/id/15366026/site/newsweek/.

Nazroo, J. Y. (2005). "Exploring Gender Differences in Depression." *Psychological Times Online*. Retrieved Aug. 5, 2007, from www.psychiatrictimes.com/p010343.html.

Neese, R. M., and Williams, G. C. (1994). *Why We Get Sick*. New York: Vintage Books.

Neigh, G. N., Arnold, H. M., Rabenstein, R. L., Sarter, M., and Bruno, J. P. (2004). "Neuronal Activity in the Nucleus Accumbens Is Necessary for Performance-Related Increases in Cortical Acetylcholine Release." *Neuroscience*, 123, 635–645.

Neill, D. B., and Justice, J. B. (1981). "An Hypothesis for a Behavioral Function of Dopaminergic Transmission in Nucleus Accumbens." In R. B. Chronister and J. F. Defrance (eds.), *The Neurobiology of the Nucleus Accumbens* (pp. 343–350). New Brunswick, Canada: Hue Institute.

Neimeyer, R. A. (2000). "Searching for the Meaning of Meaning: Grief Therapy and the Process of Reconstruction." *Death Studies*, 24, 541–558.

Nielsen, F. D., Videbech, P., Hedegaard, M., Dalby Salvig, J., and Secher, N. J. (2000). "Postpartum Depression: Identification of Women at Risk." *British Journal of Obstetrics and Gynaecology*, 107, 1210–1217.

Nolen-Hoeksema, S. (2001). "Gender Differences in Depression." *Current Directions in Psychological Science*, 5, 173–176.

Nolen-Hoeksema, S., Larson, K. J., and Grayson, C. (1999). "Explaining the Gender Difference in Depressive Symptoms." *Journal of Personality and Social Psychology*, 77, 1061–1072.

Ochsner, K. N., Bunge, S. A., Gross, J. J., and Gabrieli, J. D. E. (2002). "Rethinking Feelings: An fMRI Study of the Cognitive Regulation of Emotion." *Journal of Cognitive Neuroscience*, 12, 1215–1229.

Odendaal, J. S. J. (2000). "Animal-Assisted Therapy—Magic or Medicine?" *Journal of Psychosomatic Research*, 49, 275–280.

Onion. (2003, May 14). "Pfizer Launches 'Zoloft for Everything' Ad Campaign." Retrieved Jan. 8, 2004, from www.healthyskepticism.org/reports/2003/0514.htm.

Panksepp, J. (1998). "Rough-and-Tumble Play: The Brain Sources of Joy." In J. Panksepp (ed.), *Affective Neuroscience: The Foundations of Human and Animal Emotions*. New York: Oxford University Press.

Parker, G., Gladstone, G., and Chee, K. T. (2001). "Depression in the Planet's Largest Ethnic Group: The Chinese." *American Journal of Psychiatry*, 158, 857–864.

Parker, K. J., Buckmaster, C. L., Sundlass, K., Schatzberg, A., and Lyons, D. M. (2006). "Maternal Mediation, Stress Inoculation, and the Development of Neuroendocrine Stress Resistance in Primates." *Proceedings of the National Academy of Sciences*, 103, 3000–3005.

Parker, S. W., Nelson, C. A., and the Bucharest Early Intervention Project Core Group. (2005). "The Impact of Early Institutional Rearing on the Ability to Discriminate Facial Expressions of Emotion: An Event-Related Potential Study." *Child Development*, 76, 54–72.

Paul, C., Ayis, S., and Ebrahim, S. (2006). "Psychological Distress, Loneliness, and Disability in Old Age." *Psychology, Health and Medicine*, 11, 221–232.

Pereira, A. C., Huddleston, D. E., Brickman, A. M., Sosunov, A. A., Hen, R., McKhann, G. M., Sloan, R., Gage, F. H., Brown, T. R., and Scott, S. A. (2007). "An *in vivo* Correlate of Exercise-Induced Neurogenesis in the Adult Dentate Gyrus." *Proceedings of the National Academy of Sciences*, 104, 5368–5643.

Pleis, J. R., and Lethbridge-Cejku, M. (2006). "Summary Health Statistics for U.S. adults: National Health Interview Survey, 2005." Retrieved July 15, 2007, from National Center for Health Statistics, 10, 232. www.cdc.gob/nchs/data/series/sr_10/sr10_232.pdf.

Plotsky, P. M., Thrivikraman, K. V., Nemeroff, C. B., Caldji, C., Sharma, S., and Meaney, M. J. (2005). "Long-Term Consequences of Neonatal Rearing on Central Corticotrophin-Releasing Factor Systems in Adult Male Rat Offspring." *Neuropsychopharmacology*, 30, 2192–2204.

Rathunde, K., and Csikszentmihalyi, M. (2005). "Middle School Students' Motivation and Quality of Experience: A Comparison of Montessori and Traditional School Environments." *American Journal of Education*, 111, 341–371.

Reinberg, S. (2007). "Depression May Be World's Most Disabling Disease." Washington, DC: U.S. Department of Health and Human Services. Retrieved May 20, 2007, from Healthfinder.gov. www.healthfinder.gov/news/newsstory.asp?docID=608045.

Richardson, N. R., and Gratton, A. (1998). "Changes in Medial Prefrontal Cortical Dopamine Levels Associated with Response-Contingent Food Reward: An Electrochemical Study in Rats." *Journal of Neuroscience*, 18, 9130–9138.

Richelsen, E. (2001). "Pharamacology of Antidepressants." *Mayo Clinic Proceedings*, 76, 511–527.

Rilling, J. K., Gutman, D. A., Zeh, T. R., Pagoni, G., Berns, G. S., and Kilts, C. D. (2002). "A Neural Basis for Social Cooperation." *Neuron*, 35, 395–405.

Robins, L., Helzer, M., Weissman, H., Orvaschel, E., Gruenberg, J., Burke, J., and Regier, D. (1984). "Lifetime Prevalence of Specific Psychiatric Disorders in Three Sites." *Archives of General Psychiatry*, 41, 949–958.

Rosenman, R., Brand, R., Jenkins, C., Friedman, M., Straus, R., and Wurm, M. (1975). "Contrary Heart Disease in the Western Collaborative Group Study: Final Follow-Up Experience of 8 1/2 years. *Journal of the American Medical Association*, 233, 872.

Russell, J. C., Twons, D. R., Anderson, S. H., and Clout, M. N. (2005). "Intercepting the First Rat Ashore." *Nature*, 437, 1107.

Rygula, R., Abumaria, N., Flugge, G., Fuchs, E., Ruther, E., and Havemann-Reinecke, U. (2005). "Anhedonia and Motivational Deficits in Rats: Impact of Chronic Social Stress." *Behavioural Brain Research*, 162, 127–134.

Salamone, J. D., Cousins, M. S., and Bucher, S. (1994). "Anhedonia or Anergia? Effects of Haloperidol and Nucleus Accumbens Dopamine Depletion on Instrumental Response Selection in a T-Maze Cost/Benefit Procedure." *Behavior and Brain Research*, 65, 221–229.

Sanchez, M. S., Barontini, M., Armando, I., and Celis, M. E. (2001). "Correlation of Increased Grooming Behavior and Motor Activity with Alterations in Nigrostriatal and Mesolimbic Catecholamines after Alpha-melanotropin and Neuropeptide Glutamine-Isoleucine Injection in the Rat Ventral Tegmental Area." *Cellular and Molecular Neurobiology*, 21, 523–533.

Santarelli, L., Saxe, M., Gross, C., Surget, A., Battaglia, F., Dulawa, S., Weisstaub, N., Lee, J., Duman, R., Arancio, O., Belzung, C., and Hen, R. (2003). "Requirement of Hippocampal Neurogenesis for the Behavioral Effects of Antidepressants." *Science*, 301, 805–809.

Sapolsky, R. M. (1998). *Why Zebras Don't Get Ulcers*. New York: Freeman.

Sapolsky, R. M. (2000). "Glucocorticoids and Hippocampal Atrophy in Neuropsychiatric Disorders." *Archives of General Psychiatry*, 57, 925–935.

Sapolsky, R. M. (2001). "Depression, Antidepressants, and the Shrinking Hippocampus." *Proceedings of the National Academy of Sciences*, 98, 12320–12322.

Sapolsky, R. M. (2004). "Is Impaired Neurogenesis Relevant to the Affective Symptoms of Depression?" *Biological Psychiatry*, 56, 137–139.

Schildkraut, J. J. (1965). "The Catecholamine Hypothesis of Affective Disorders: A Review of Supporting Evidence." *American Journal of Psychiatry*, 122, 509–522.

Schmidt-Hieber, C., Jonas, P., and Bischofberger, J. (2004). "Enhanced Synaptic Plasticity in Newly Generated Granule Cells of the Adult Hippocampus." *Nature*, 429, 184–187.

Schouten, W. P. G., and Wiegant, V. M. (1997). "Individual Responses to Acute and Chronic Stress in Pigs." *Acta Physiologica Scandinavica*, 640, 188–191.

Schwartz, J. M. (1996). *Brain Lock*. New York: HarperCollins.

Seligman, M. E. P. (1988). "Boomer Blues: With Too Great Expectations, the Baby Boomers Are Sliding into Individualistic Melancholy." *Psychology Today*, 22, 50–55.

Seligman, M. E. P. (1990). *Learned Optimism*. New York: Pocket Books.

Seligman, M. E. P. (1996). *The Optimistic Child*. New York: Harper.

Seligman, M. E. P. (2002). *Authentic Happiness*. New York: Free Press.

Seligman, M. E. P., and Maier, S. F. (1967). "Failure to Escape Traumatic Shock." *Journal of Experimental Psychology*, 74, 1–9.

Seligman, M. E. P., and Weiss, J. M. (1980). "Coping Behavior: Learned Behavior: Learned Helplessness, Physiological Change and Learned Inactivity." [Interchange between M. E. P Seligman and J. M. Weiss]. *Behavioral Research Therapies*, 18, 459–512.

Selye, H. (1936). "A Syndrome Produced by Diverse Nocuous Agents." *Nature*, 138, 32.

Selye, H. (1976). *The Stress of Life*. New York: McGraw-Hill.

Sharot, T., Riccardi, A. M., Raio, C. M., and Phelps, E. A. (2007). "Neural Mechanisms Mediating Optimism Bias." *Nature*, 450, 102–105.

Sheline, Y. I. (2000). "3D MRI Studies of Neuroanatomic Changes in Unipolar Major Depression: The Role of Stress and Medical Comorbidity." *Biological Psychiatry*, 48, 791–800.

Sheline, Y. I., Wang, P., Gado, M., Csernansky J., and Vannier, M. (1996). "Hippocampal Atrophy in Recurrent Major Depression." *Proceedings of the National Academy of Sciences*, 93, 3908–3913.

Shellenbarger, S. "Colleges Ward Off Overinvolved Parents." *Wall Street Journal Online*. Retrieved June 5, 2007, from www.careerjournal.com/columnists/workfamily.20050729-workfamily.html.

Sheppard, R. Z. (1980, Apr. 21). "Words from a Sponsor." *Time Online*. Retrieved Feb. 15, 2007, from www.time.com/time/magazine/article/0,9171,924036,00.html?promoid=googlep.

Sherratt, A. (1997). "Climatic Cycles and Behavioral Revolutions: The Emergence of Modern Humans and the Beginning of Farming." *Antiquity*, 71, 271–287.

Shores, M. (producer). (1996). *The Amazing Story of Kudzu: Love It, or Hate It— It Grows on You*. Tuscaloosa: University of Alabama Center for Public TV and Radio.

Shorter, E. (1997). *A History of Psychiatry*. New York: John Wiley.

Silverthorn, N. A., and Gekoski, W. L. (1995). "Social Desirability Effects on Measures of Adjustment to University, Independence from Parents, and Self-Efficacy." *Journal of Clinical Psychology*, 51, 244–251.

Silvestri, A. J., and Joffe, J. M. (2004). "You'd Have to Be Sick Not to Be Crazy." *Journal of Primary Intervention*, 24, 497–511.

Slater, L. (2003, Feb. 23). "Repress Yourself." Retrieved Aug. 15, 2007, from *New York Times Online*. www.josmc.org/pipermail/mednews/2003-February/000313.html.

Smith, E. O. (2002). *When Culture and Biology Collide: Why We Are Stressed, Depressed, and Self-Obsessed*. Piscataway, NJ: Rutgers University Press.

Solomon, A. (2001). *The Noonday Demon: An Atlas of Depression*. New York: Scribner.

Spoolder, H. A. M., Burbidge, J. A., Lawrence, A. G., Simmins, P. H., and Edwards, S. A. (1996). "Individual Behavioral Differences in Pigs: Intra- and Inter-Test Consistency." *Applied Animal Behavior Science*, 49, 185–198.

Standley, J. M. (1998). "The Effect of Music and Multimodal Stimulation on Responses of Premature Infants in Neonatal Intensive Care." *Pediatric Nursing*, 24, 532–538.

Stanford News Release. (8/29/94). "Recovery from Grief Requires More Than Grieving, Psychologist Finds." Retrieved Aug. 29, 2007, from news-service.stanford.edu/pr/94/940829Arc4145.html.

Stein, J. (2006). "My So-Called Second Life." *Time Online*. Retrieved July 15, 2007, from www.time.com/time/magazne/article/o,9171570708,00.html.

Sternberg, R. J., and Subotnik, R. F. (eds.). (2006). *Optimizing Student Success in School with the Other Three Rs*. Greenwich, CT: Information Age Publishing.

Sternberg, R. S. (2003). "The Other Three Rs: Part Three, Resilience." *Monitor on Psychology*. Retrieved Mar. 15, 2007, from www.apap.org/monitor/may03/pc.html.

Stewart, D., and de R. Winser, D. M. (1942). "Incidence of Perforated Peptic Ulcer: Effect of Heavy Air-Raids." *Lancet*, 2, 259–261.

Stranahan, A. M., Khalil, D., and Gould, E. (2006). "Social Isolation Delays the Positive Effects of Running on Adult Neurogenesis." *Nature Neuroscience*, 9, 526–533.

Strickland, P. L., Deakin, J. F. W., Percival, C., Dixon, J., Gater, R. A., and Goldberg, D. P. (2002). "Bio-Social Origins of Depression in the Community." *British Journal of Psychiatry*, 180, 168–173.

Stroebe, W., Schut, H., and Stroebe, S. S. (2005). "Grief Work, Disclosure, and Counseling: Do They Help Bereaved?" *Clinical Psychology Review*, 4, 395–414.

Taira, K., and Rolls, E. T. (1996). "Receiving Grooming as a Reinforcer for the Monkey." *Physiology and Behavior*, 59, 1189–1192.

Taylor, C. S. R., and Gross, C. G. (2003). "Twitches Versus Movements: A Story of Motor Cortex." *History of Neuroscience*, 9, 332–342.

Taylor, M. J., Freemantle, N., Geddes, J. R., and Bhagwagar, Z. (2006). "Early Onset of Selective Serotonin Reuptake Inhibitor Antidepressant Action." *Archives of General Psychiatry*, 63, 1217–1223.

The Internet Movie Database. (1989). Memorable quotes for *Steel Magnolias*. Retrieved Oct. 20, 2007, from www.imdb.com/title/H009834/quotes.

The Mind's Big Bang. (2001, Sept. 24–27). Episode 6 in PBS Series *Evolution*. Boston: WGBH Educational Foundation and Clear Blue Sky Producers.

The Post Colonial Web, University Scholars Program, National University of Singapore: *Women in Nigeria Today.* Retrieved Apr. 10, 2005, from www.scholars.nus.edu.sg/landow/post/Nigeria/ contwomen.htm.

The Source Book for Teaching Science. Retrieved Apr. 30, 2006, from www.csun.edu/science/health/docs/tv&health.html.

Tinbergen, A. (1974). "Autobiography." In W. Odelberg (ed.), *Les Prix Nobel*. Stockholm, Sweden: Nobel Foundation.

Tinbergen, N. (1952). "The Curious Behavior of Sticklebacks." *Scientific American*, 187, 22–26.

Tomes, N. (1994). *The Art of Asylum Keeping*. Philadelphia: University of Pennsylvania Press.

Tremblay, L. K., Naranjo, C. A., Graham, S. J., Herrmann, N., Mayberg, H. S., Hevenor, S., and Busto, U. E. (2005). "Functional Neuroanatomical Substrates of Altered Reward Processing in Major Depressive Disorder Revealed by a Dopaminergic Probe." *Archives of General Psychiatry*, 62, 1228–1236.

Tricomi, E. M., Delgado, M. R., and Fiez, J. A. (2004). "Modulation of Caudate Activity by Action Contingency." *Neuron*, 41, 281–292.

Tsiouris, J. A. (2005). "Metabolic Depression in Hibernation and Major Depression: An Explanatory Theory and an Animal Model of Depression." *Medical Hypotheses*, 65, 829–840.

Ubali, W. A., Rocha, M. J., and Coimbra, N. C. (2007, June). "Antipanic-like Effect of Chronic Treatment with Fluoxetine on Fear-Induced Responses Elicited by Preys in Confrontation with Rattlesnakes." Research presented at the annual meeting of the International Behavioral Neuroscience Society, Rio de Janeiro, Brazil.

Un, H. (2004). "Current Trends for the Management and Treatment of Depression." *American Journal of Managed Care*, 10, S171–S172.

U.S. Public Health Service. *Mental Health: A Report of the Surgeon General.* Retrieved Apr. 20, 2005, from www.surgeongeneral.gov/library/mental health/home.html.

Valenstein, E. S. (1998). *Blaming the Brain*. New York: Free Press.

Vedantam, S. (2004, Dec. 3). "Antidepressant Use by U.S. Adults Soars." *Washington Post*, p. A15. Retrieved Sept. 15, 2007, from www.washingtonpost.com/wp-dyn/articles/A29751–2004Dec2.html.

Vedantam, S. (2006, Mar. 23). "Drugs Cure Depression in Half of Patients." *Washington Post*, p. A01. Retrieved Aug. 10, 2007, from www.washingtonpost.com/wp-dyn/content/article/2006/03/22/AR2006032202450.html.

Vestergaard, K. S., Skadhauge, E., and Lawson, L. G. (1997). "The Stress of Not Being Able to Perform Dustbathing in Laying Hens." *Physiology and Behavior*, 62, 413–419.

Wachsmuth, I. (2006, Oct.–Nov.). "Gestures Offer Insight." *Scientific American Mind*, pp. 20–25.

Walton, M. E., Bannerman, D. M., and Rushworth, M. F. S. (2002). "The Role of the Rat Medial Frontal Cortex in Effort-Based Decision Making." *Journal of Neuroscience*, 22, 10996–11003.

Watanabe, Y., Gould, E., and McEwen, B. S. (1992). "Stress Induces Atrophy of Apical Dendrites of Hippocampal CA3 Pyramidal Neurons." *Brain Research*, 588, 341–345.

Watterson, B. (1995). *The Calvin and Hobbes 10th Anniversary Book*. Kansas City, MO: Universal Press Syndicate Company.

Waugh, C. E., Wager, T. D., Fredrickson, B. L., Noll, D. C., and Taylor, S. F. (2006, Jan.). "Rolling with the Punches: An fMRI Investigation of Emotional Resilience When Anticipating and Responding to Possible Negative Events." Research presented at Society for Personality and Social Psychology, Palm Springs, FL.

Weze, C., Leathard, H. L., Grange, J., Tiplady, P., and Stevens, G. (2005). "Evaluation of Healing by Gentle Touch." *Public Health*, 119, 3–10.

Whitaker, R. (2002). *Mad in America*. Cambridge, MA: Perseus Books.

Whybrow, P., and Bahr, R. (1988). *The Hibernation Response*. New York: Arbor House.

Wilder, L. I. (1953). *Little House on the Prairie*. New York: HarperTrophy.

Wolfe, S. (2003, Sept. 19). "Sweetening the Pill." *Public Citizen Health Letter*, pp. 1–10.

Woolley, C. S., Gould, E., and McEwen, B. S. (1990). "Exposure to Excess Glucocorticoids Alters Dendritic Morphology of Adult Hippocampal Pyramidal Neurons." *Brain Research*, 531, 225–231.

World Health Organization. (2005, Apr. 5). *Depression*. Retrieved Nov. 15, 2006, from www.who.int/topics/depression/en.

Wynn, T., and Coolidge, F. L. (2003). "The Role of Working Memory in the Evolution of Managed Foraging." *Before Farming: The Archaeology and Anthropology of Managed Foraging*, 2, 1–16.

Young, A. H. (2004). "Cortisol in Mood Disorders." *Stress*, 7, 205–208.

Young, E. A., and Breslau, N. (2004). "Saliva Cortisol in Posttraumatic Stress Disorder: A Community Epidemiologic Study." *Biological Psychiatry*, 56, 205–209.

Young, L. J., and Wang, Z. (2004). "The Neurobiology of Pair-Bonding." *Nature Neuroscience*, 7, 1048–1054.

Zeveloff, S. I. (2002). *Raccoons: A Natural History*. Washington, DC: Smithsonian Institution Press.

Zink, C. F., Pagnoni, G., Martin-Skurski, M. E., Chappelow, J. C., and Berns, G. S. (2004). "Human Striatal Responses to Monetary Reward Depend on Saliency." *Neuron*, 42, 509–517.

Index

281